God through Binoculars:
A Hitchhiker at a Monastery

"A witty, provocative, and thoroughly engaging memoir about the difficulties of faith, the complexities of love, and the consolations often found in nature. Whether she's writing about hyenas or jihad, hitchhiking or the perils of political correctness, Goska is always interesting. I loved this book!"

— Daiva Markelis, author, *White Field, Black Sheep: A Lithuanian-American Life*

"As unsparing as it is tender, this book is a high-octane lyric meditation by a larger-than-life soul. Amid a multitude of coincidences, controversies, and calamities, the reader is invited to laugh, grieve, ponder, take exception, and especially, take heart."

— Claire Bateman, author, *Locals: A Collection of Prose Poems*; grant recipient, National Endowment for the Arts

"The great books about spiritual journeys never give you easy answers. They don't say 'Do these ten things and you will find peace or faith or salvation.' Goska knows this truth. She has lived this truth. As you read her beautifully written, witty, and inspiring book, you will find yourself not only following her journey, you will find yourself living your own journey."

— John Guzlowski, author and Montaigne Medal recipient, *Echoes of Tattered Tongues: Memory Unfolded*

"A moving, inspiring, heartfelt expression of love, pain, and healing, skillfully written with equal amounts of grace and compassion."

— Larry Dossey, physician and author, *One Mind*

"I read *God through Binoculars* the way I read everything that I enjoy or that interests me: at increasingly breakneck speed. I finished it this morning and plan to begin again, reading more slowly and thoroughly for the subtler bits. The two writers this book reminded me of most were Thomas Merton and Henri Nouwen. They also have an edginess and a sense of putting themselves out there without giving a damn what others think."

—Julie Davis, author, *Happy Catholic:*
Glimpses of God in Everyday Life

"Goska reminds every birder and nature lover that they are connected spiritually to the birds they see and the experiences they have outdoors. Our souls and hearts are refreshed and renewed by allowing ourselves to understand in some small way that we are connected to something in nature that is ancient and forever."

—Don Torino, naturalist, Wild Birds Unlimited;
president, Bergen County Audubon Society

"Impossible to put down. Goska is a true original, a gifted writer and an even more gifted spiritual explorer. Like her previous book, *Save, Send, Delete,* this one displays a remarkable range of philosophical and religious knowledge, accompanied by profound insights that will stay with a reader long after they are encountered. Goska has packed more experience into each one of her years on this earth than most of us will in a lifetime. I urge you to give a look at this irresistible journey of faith in search of answers."

—David Horowitz, author, *Radical*
Son: A Generational Odyssey

"Goska is one of the very few writers whose words I'm impelled to read, words that pull me forward the way being roped to a runaway horse might."

—Charles Adès Fishman, winner, 2012
New Millennium Award for Poetry

"An effortlessly wise voyage, not only into the human soul but also into some fundamentals of the Western tradition. Goska is a formidable writer who combines sensitivity and kindness with extraordinary toughness, and her vigorous prose reflects this unusual combination. Her prose grabs you and does not let you go."

— DARIO FERNÁNDEZ-MORERA, author, *The Myth of the Andalusian Paradise*; associate professor of Spanish and Portuguese and comparative literature, Northwestern University

"Danusha Goska is a walker, an observer, a thinker. This pilgrimage-in-a-book reminds me of Paolo Coelho in its thrust and scope. But Coelho merely walked the camino; Goska walks the byways of the world, from rural Virginia to the wilderness of Asia. Always questioning, always seeking, Goska shows us the profound in every living being, from hyenas to humans. If you are willing to accompany her on this journey, you will be changed yourself."

— BRIAN O'BROIN, author, *Thógamar le Gaeilge Iad*, professor of linguistics and medieval literature, William Paterson University

"Goska is a true wordsmith, a writer you enjoy reading for the prose as well as the imagination and education. Moving from thought to thought and scene to scene in no obvious order, you later realize the grand plan underneath it all, the coherent worldview that shapes how she appraises her experiences. And unlike secular writers of similar works, she is able not only to be romantic about life's rich variety, but to ground it in the good God of revelation. That combination of orthodox faith, humorous observations of eccentric people and moments, and practical philosophy is rare in contemporary writing."

— REV. EVAN MCCLANAHAN, producer and host, *Sin Boldly Podcast*

"An inspiring and inspired read by one who has long since heard the music."

— KEVIN DI CAMILLO, author, *Now Chiefly Poetical*; columnist, *National Catholic Register*

"*God through Binoculars* is . . . complicated, just like the natural world Goska so compellingly describes; just like the spiritual insights she gleans from her well-traveled life. She is a committed monotheist who believes in evolution, but expresses annoyance with Darwinist absolutes. She is awed by Mother Nature, but recognizes the random cruelties that play out within the wilderness. Through her binoculars, she observes a world constantly in flux, shaped and reshaped by variables that somehow work together in unbelievable complexity. Because of that complexity, she is skeptical about any 'straight-line' redemption of life's disappointments by an all-loving God. Yet she believes that God is indeed all-loving, that her own burdens might not be lifted, but can be transmuted into blessings. If she can believe that, maybe even the greatest skeptics among us can too."

— MELANIE FORDE, author, *Hillwilla* and *On the Hillwilla Road*

"I always get the sense through Goska's writings that God is all about us, that is, with us. In her writing of the simple things in life, you will find deeper meanings, feelings, and emotional connections that will widen your perspective on events, love, and loss. We are pulled out of ourselves long enough to see a fuller life of observational gravity that can be applied to our own experiences. Read this book. Learn another way to see beyond just looking."

— EDWARD "RUSTY" WALKER, artist; author, *Transparent Watercolor*

"Amazing. Ordinary situations brought to life. Observant, with a real wit. A pleasure to read!"

— BRIAN KORAL, blog reader

"Goska is brilliant with words, painting highly evocative pictures. She's unafraid to explore emotional, spiritual, and philosophical frontiers. She's been all over the world, learning about cultures from the inside. This book brings these gifts and experiences to bear on a personal journey to a place few readers know."

— KAREN A. WYLE, author, *Twin Bred*

"A masterpiece. I couldn't put it down. Goska has an incisive mind, an insatiable curiosity, and a captivating writing style. As a veterinarian, I particularly appreciated her colorful and informative writing about the animals she has encountered in her adventurous life."

— MORTON A. GOLDBERG, veterinarian;
volunteer, Project Gutenberg

"C. S. Lewis wrote in his great novel, *Perelandra,* that though 'there seemed to be, and indeed were, a thousand roads by which a man could walk through the world, there was not a single one which did not lead sooner or later either to the Beatific or the Miserific Vision.' Goska is a pilgrim walking the roads of this world and trying her best to follow the Spirit as he leads her at each fork in the road toward that 'one Face above all worlds which merely to see is irrevocable joy.'"

— MARK P. SHEA, author, *By What Authority? An Evangelical Discovers Catholic Tradition*

"Goska takes the reader on a remarkable journey, first encountering the personal and political corruption of academia in the soul-crushing age of political correctness, and then finding escape and finally restoration of spirit. This is no harangue or political manifesto, but rather a compelling tale of exploration and growth from a natural storyteller who just happens to illuminate the intellectual and moral issues of our age."

—THOMAS LIFSON, founder, publisher, and editor, *American Thinker*; former assistant professor, Harvard Business School

"All that Goska has done here is to give us a simple, straightforward account of a brief episode in her life. And yet she has captured something about the mystery of life and human interaction that is at once deep, moving, and universal."

— BRUCE BAWER, author, *Stealing Jesus: How Fundamentalism Betrays Christianity*

"You catch a monkey, they say, with trinkets in a wide-bottomed, narrow-necked vase. The monkey inserts his paw, and opens it up to capture his treasure. When he tries to withdraw his fist, he can either hold on to the trinkets or let them go and free himself.

"Jesus invited, 'Leave everything you have, and follow me!' That might seem fairly easy for a pilgrim who can't afford her own car. But even the poor must surrender.

"Goska's monastery journey is a meditation on the deliberate opening of hands. With the slow freeing of each finger, another trinket is jettisoned and a new perspective is revealed. Nature provides her window to the divine: indigenous fruit, a hawk's soar, and being arrested by an unlikely savior. This hero's journey ends where she began, but as a new person, with a new vision.

"Goska is a bold spirit who has fine-tuned her soul to encounter grace in unlikely places. In the spirit of Flannery O'Connor, as well as the Beats, she is wonderfully refreshing. Her sensitivity to God's possibilities is awe-inspiring. Step beyond predictability and embrace one heck of a ride!"

— Deacon Kevin McCormack, co-host, WABC radio, *Religion on the Line*; principal, Xaverian High School; adjunct instructor of theology, Molloy College

"*God through Binoculars* is a mesmerizing book. The primary narrative concerns the author's visit to a monastery, but this is interspersed with reflections on the habits of hyenas, the spiritual defects of Meso-American art (Goska seems to like the hyenas better), the Holocaust, and a host of other subjects. The satirical account of her visit to the monastery makes the book worth reading all by itself. Fierce, hard-won, deep-rooted piety breathes through the snark. In an age of cutesy, feel-good memoirs with easy answers, this is the real thing: a book that brings you in touch with the restless, passionate intelligence of its author and forces you to think in a fresh way about every one of the many subjects it addresses."

— EDWIN WOODRUFF TAIT, writer, farmer, and consulting editor, *Christian History* magazine.

"Goska dares to ask the universally elusive questions: will any deity or doctrine fully suffice in this life? Is the duel beauty and brutality of nature and human interaction enough to fill our spiritual reservoirs? In examining the mysterious trifecta of God, the natural world, and human industry, Goska illustrates how a truly benevolent God would want us to experience the brutality of life along with the transcendence of beauty. Time and again her words illuminate the agony *and* the ecstasy of this life that ultimately inspire us towards love, awe, and wonder. Goska's intellectual inquisition proves that the very acts of motion and inquiry are a kind of devotion all their own."

— TINA SCHUMANN, editor, *Two-Countries: U.S. Daughters and Sons of Immigrant Parents*

"Goska finds goodness and moments of beauty and synchronicity amidst a world of hurt and oppression. Kindness and serendipity give her, and give the reader as well, hope for the future and a sense of religious wonder and faith. Birds are her passion, and her avian encounters — some downright magical — occur at just the right moments in her experience, offering tantalizing evidence of greater forces at work than can be explained by pure science or reason. Goska's book is provocative, in-your-face, and uncompromising, all the trademarks of the author herself. It is bracing to read strongly-held opinions backed up by facts and evidence instead of feel-good but unsubstantiated politically correct writing. "

— MARC J. CHELEMER, New Jersey birder

GOD
through
BINOCULARS

GOD THROUGH BINOCULARS

A Hitchhiker at a Monastery

Danusha Goska

Shanti Arts Publishing

Brunswick, Maine

God through Binoculars: A Hitchhiker at a Monastery

Published by Shanti Arts Publishing

Cover and interior design by Shanti Arts Designs

Shanti Arts LLC
Brunswick, Maine
www.shantiarts.com

Printed in the United States of America

First Edition

ISBN: 978-1-947067-61-5 (softcover)
ISBN: 978-1-947067-62-2 (digital)

LCCN: 2018961899

I dedicate this humble work to Deputy Victor Sutherland of the Clarke County, Virginia, Sheriff's Office, and to all others like Vic who heed Jesus's words in the parable of the Good Samaritan.

I dedicate this work, also, to Brother Stephen, born William Joseph Maguire, Jr., who served as beloved Guest Master at Holy Cross Abbey in Berryville, Virginia, for twenty years, and to all monks and nuns. You have my love, gratitude, respect, and prayers.

CONTENTS

PREFACE

In 2005, I was facing many challenges. I am Catholic. I decided to take my problems to God and ask for guidance. I wanted to be someplace silent so I could hear any reply God might provide. I made a week-long retreat to the Holy Cross Abbey in Berryville, Virginia.

After my return to New Jersey, I typed up an account of my strange experiences at the abbey. I sent this account to friends. I then put it away.

In 2015, ten years after the retreat, I posted some paragraphs from my account on my blog. Karen A. Wyle, author of the *Twin-Bred* series and other novels, encouraged me to publish the monastery account.

These pages are humble. I'm often crabby. Travel writing seems predisposed to crabbiness. See, for example, Bill Bryson's *A Walk in the Woods: Rediscovering America on the Appalachian Trail*, Robyn Davidson's *Tracks: A Woman's Solo Trek across 1700 Miles of Australian Outback,* and Paul Theroux's *The Great Railway Bazaar: By Train through Asia.*

In this book, I say critical things about the monastery, about the monks, and about the Catholic Church. The friends to whom I sent the manuscript know I am a devout Catholic. That I report finding dead bugs on the windowsill of a church would be understood by my friends as part of a detailed invoice of my road encounters. They would know it was not meant as a global dismissal. The monks in this account are human. I am glad of that. If they were all saints, it would be a bit freaky, and it would not provide guidance to those of us who are also not saints. I depict myself as human, as well, warts and all.

I voice my reservations about the perpetually cloistered life. If I were pope, and I am glad I am not, I would work to make the life of a monk or a nun a temporary, one- or two-year term of service option for all Catholics. I certainly believe that temporary cloistering, either internal or external, is a necessary skill for everyone seeking a balanced life.

I am profoundly grateful to the Holy Cross Abbey, its monks and staff, for hosting me at almost no charge. I am mindful of the profound gifts of monasteries and convents to world civilization. Catholic monks and nuns gave the world much of what it knows of universities, hospitals, and agriculture. One recent, accessible source of information on this heritage is Rodney Stark's 2006 book, *The Victory of Reason: How Christianity Led to Freedom, Capitalism, and Western Success*.

Robert Ellsberg captures the gift of monasteries in his biography of St. Benedict from his 1998 book, *All Saints: Daily Reflections on Saints, Prophets, and Witnesses for Our Time*:

For centuries, the Benedictine monasteries presented the challenge of an alternative world governed by the spirit of Christ. At a time of extreme social hierarchy, they presented an ideal of equality. At a time when manual labor was derided, they affirmed the spiritual value of work. During a time of cultural disintegration, they maintained islands of learning and civilization. At a time when violence was commonplace, they lived by the motto of peace. The Benedictine monasteries represented a vision of health, wholeness, and ecology in a world badly out of kilter. To the extent that that world remains our world, the vision of St. Benedict retains its relevance and attraction.

I invite anyone who stumbles across *God through Binoculars* to read also at least one other work. It is a brief, online celebration of the life of Brother Stephen, a.k.a. William Joseph Maguire, Jr., who was the Guest Master at Holy Cross Abbey for twenty years. The essay in his honor, along with the salutes and testimonials from past retreatants, present an aspect of monastery life that I, as someone who visited for one week only, never could. The salute to Brother Stephen is here: <https://www.virginiatrappists.org/2014/05/br-stephen-maguire10-octonber-1929-27-may-2014/>

◆

I mention real people in these pages. In some cases, I have changed minor details in order to protect people's privacy. I sometimes use pseudonyms rather than real names; I place quotation marks around pseudonyms the first time they are used. I did not change the timing, import, or substance of events. I did contact several people I write about in these pages to inform them that they appear in this work.

◆

I thank readers who read my work and see and speak its worth, and those who comment on my work in ways that contribute to it. I will not attempt to name my readers because I fear I will forget someone, but you can bet that names cascade through my head at this moment with attendant warmth, fond memories, and gratitude. Our bond is comparable to the bonds of blood or love. You have placed a safety net beneath me that otherwise would not exist; you have embraced me warmly; you have given me reason to go on. Thank you.

Karen A. Wyle generously read these pages before publication. Karen alerted me to errors in the text, and I am very grateful to her for that. Every writer wishes she had eyes as careful and a heart as warm as Karen's to rely on. Thank you, Karen!

I am also grateful to reader Dr. Morton A. Goldberg, who brought his expert proofreading skills to his generous contribution of time and talent. I also thank Lyle S. Henretty for proofreading and for many encouraging comments.

Otto Karl Gross, author of the provocative essay "Ripples of Sin," carefully read material I was having trouble with and helped greatly. *Danke sehr mein Freund.*

Liron Rubin read and commented from Israel. *Toda raba!*

I was touched beyond words when David Horowitz, though he was facing challenges himself, took time to read this book and to encourage me in my efforts at publication. Your words pushed me over the top of the fence. Thank you.

CHAPTER ONE

THE RAINBOW, OR WHY I BELIEVE

I t was a cold, weekday morning in November 2004 in Paterson, New Jersey. I was living in a two-hundred-year-old silk mill. My apartment had a ceiling of bare, massive wooden beams; it rose to twenty-five feet above my head. I had just stepped out of the shower.

"You have to go outside right now," my little voice said. Exactly those words. Emphatic. No explanation. No debate.

I'd never heard that message from my little voice before. I've never heard it again since. "You have to go outside right now."

I'm obsessive compulsive. I have to be. I am also cognitively impaired. I am dyslexic and I suffer from attention deficit. I live alone. If I confuse "on" and "off" and "left" and "right" on my electric stovetop, no one will rescue me from the ensuing fire. Paterson is built of bricks and wood. The glass-and-steel architectural era sped right past Paterson. I've watched fires burn here for weeks at a time. Three men have been murdered directly in front of my building in the past five years — two shot, one stabbed. Police questioned me. I could not contribute to their investigation. I slept soundly as a man breathed his last breaths thirty feet away.

So, yes, I am obsessive compulsive. I check off daily rituals in a routine before leaving the apartment: hair brushed, nails filed, bag packed, NOAA webpage consulted for its forecast, outfit honed to meet the weather, apartment scanned — is there anything I need to turn on or off? Prayer to Saint Joseph to protect my home from robbers and fire while I am away. Prayer to Saint Christopher to bless my feet as I travel. The little voice insisted I ignore this routine and exit the apartment immediately. To make matters worse, I had just washed my hair. It was still wet.

I obey my little voice. When I hitchhiked coast to coast and back again, when my little voice said, "Don't get in that car; this other car is safe," I listened. I was once a Peace Corps volunteer in an isolated outpost in Nepal, five days walk from the nearest road, without electricity, radio, or telephone. When my little voice told me that my brother Mike, eight thousand miles away, was dying, I listened. I left that place, trekked to the nearest airport, flew to Kathmandu, and was greeted by a doctor who believed she had the difficult task of informing me that one of my family members was dying. I told her I already knew. When, after I got out of the shower that morning in November 2004, the little voice said "You have to go outside right now," I listened.

Force hand: put comb down. Hurry up feet, no time for socks, slip on flip-flops. Drag long coat over pajamas. Twist knob on door. Open door. Walk out. Close door. Lock.

My hair a wet tangle, with no further instructions from the little voice, I wandered toward the seventy-seven-foot-high Great Falls, just a five-minute walk from my apartment.

Holeee Cow.

The biggest and most perfect rainbow I've ever seen stretched over the waterfall. It sprouted in West Paterson and poured its seven hues into Hinchliffe Stadium, historic home of the Negro Leagues. An artist would never paint this rainbow; it was too perfect, too gigantic.

It hadn't been raining; the rainbow was formed by the rising sun shining through the morning mist. I walk past the Falls regularly. I'd never seen that effect before, and I have not seen it since.

I used to wallow in beauty in Nepal; it was served up on heaping platters. Backpack on my back, trekking alone on foot, I'd round a bend in a footpath and there, splayed out across the horizon, would be Himalayan peak after Himalayan peak, pink in dawn, gold in the alpenglow of dusk, a lime-white and ochre village nestling in a crook of the mountain. One of the most beautiful girls I'd ever hoped to see would remove her brass water jug from her hip and rest it against the wall of a terraced rice paddy that was the deep green shade of steamed broccoli. The girl would re-wrap, with casual expertise, her red sari, stand straight, place her hands palm to palm, and greet me, "Namaste, Miss."

In Paterson, my neighbors have decided it is socially acceptable to throw garbage on the street, to urinate, beg, peddle their own flesh, and inject heroin on the street. When I see what a mess humanity can make in this age of non-biodegradable apocalypses, I find reconciliation with never having had kids. But this day, Paterson was beautiful.

Passaic Valley Water Commission workmen laid down their tools and stared, as did pedestrians. The rainbow sliced right through our urban defenses as if it were a blade and we were cans. We on the sidewalk spilled out to each other, white to black to Hispanic to Muslim. *Wow*, we said. *Wow. Hot damn. Mashallah. Ay dios mio.* We smiled like babies. We smiled as if we were looking at babies.

The little voice. The rainbow. The moments that make me believe.

CHAPTER TWO

My Backstory, Or Why I Doubt

I also doubt. The very God I am supposed to love has beaten me to nothing more than a chalk outline on the sidewalk. "How long, Oh Lord, how long?" the ancient Jews asked in Psalm 13, in Revelation 6, and in Habakkuk 1.

I was an abused kid. My people were peasant immigrants from Eastern Europe. They were at the receiving end of epic amounts of injustice. We Bohunks have not done a good job of telling our story in America. Just imagine the very worst Dickensian nightmare you can, and add "ski" to the end of everyone's last name. I could divulge to you the transatlantic details of my parents' biographies: the lynching; the black lung; the mine bosses calling out "Get me a Hunky, I need a donkey"; the scavenging for food in a garbage dump; the feds smashing my grandma's moonshining still, her one source of income to feed her kids; the constant, grinding humiliations and betrayals from my mother's own siblings; the betrayals at the hands of the red-white-and-blue, the streets-paved-with-gold, and the Statue of Liberty, who hustled my people out of steerage, checked them for lice and TB, and handed them a mop and a pickax. But please just take my word for it. If you heard my parents' biographies, you would not judge them any more than I do, any more. You would merely weep and seek God, or the worker's revolution, or some other transcendent light, and resolve to be a better person.

That's the macrocosm, the vast, superhuman forces: history, genes, human nature. The microcosm is my scarred body. The story is too long to tell here. But it's not just length that silences me. If I told you every way they hurt me, you would sneer at my love and judge it counterfeit and folly. If I told you everything they suffered, your pity would blind you to the pain they caused. If I told you of the joy, that joy would erase everything else, like the tropical solstice sun that eats every shadow.

When I asked my Polish-American father why we came to America, he replied, "Because the czars burned our books." Reading was his favorite pastime. His mother never learned to read. My Slovak grandmother, also a peasant, was so brilliant she could look at a newspaper in Hungarian, the language of the oppressors who tore down Slovak schools, and she could read it out loud in Slovak, a totally unrelated language. My mother was one of the best writers I've ever read. She cleaned houses and worked in factories. I stored up every scrap of her writing I could and placed it, for safekeeping, in the vault of a stable friend's apartment closet while I was on the road. He managed to get himself robbed, and now my mother's writing is all gone, except for stray fragments that echo in my ear like the songs sung in a lost Eden. My father was a manual laborer, from coal miner as a child to golf course caddy as an old man. I was the youngest of six, the last of nine pregnancies, the smallest, the fattest, the ugliest, the weakest, and the stupidest. Everyone beat me, except my oldest brother. He merely threatened to sell me into slavery.

There was a particularly traumatic assault my senior year in college. I threw on some clothes — what I was wearing had been torn off of me and I was naked — and ran out of the house. I was homeless for a while. I ate from dumpsters. I still got straight

A grades. None of my throngs of siblings or cousins or aunts or uncles asked where I had gone after I fell off the face of the earth. None made any attempt to contact me, to ask, "Are you okay?" I approached my sister Antoinette in a public place and asked if she could bring some of my clothing to one of my couch-surfing crash sites. She said, "Fuck you. Go to Hell." She made no eye contact with me and rushed past. She had hit me before, and insulted me — "fat pig" was the standard — but she had never before not looked me in the eye when talking to me. That new violation was the worst. My brother Mike got married that year. I received no invitation. His youngest sister's absence left no empty place in Mike & Maureen's wedding party. When you are an abused kid, everyone in power in your life looks away. When the abused kid disappears, no missing person's report is filed. People have been looking away for so long, airbrushing you out of their consciousness, that they never realize you were no longer actually there.

I joined the Peace Corps and spent my twenties traveling in Africa, Asia, Europe, and North America. I smuggled in Burma, hitchhiked in France, made love on a white Thai beach under a full moon with a man who was both genuinely good and Greek-god gorgeous. I ran from Russian tanks, African kidnappers, and ate haggis in Scotland on Burns Night. I hung with the kind of people who, if you asked them, "What are you doing tomorrow?" might respond, "Antarctica." And they were serious. I stayed up till dawn swapping Himalayan tall tales with Sir Edmund Hillary, the first man to climb Everest. Lech Walesa, the Solidarity leader who helped bring down the Soviet Empire, told me that looking in my eyes inspired him. I lacked guidance. I felt myself to be worthless.

I met Arno in Poland in 1987. We were both taking summer courses on Polish-Jewish relations at Jagiellonian University, which was founded in 1364. Copernicus, who redrew the map of the universe; Sobieski, who defeated the Turks at Vienna, thus halting a thousand years of advancing jihad; Malinowski, who redefined anthropology; and Pope John Paul II are among the university's notable alums.

Arno's father had been a prisoner in the Plaszow Concentration Camp, the one depicted in the 1993 movie *Schindler's List*. Arno's father abused him. Arno and I both had parents who had been wounded by life because of sweeping historical forces, and we both had in turn been wounded by our parents. Long past midnight, Arno and I strolled over medieval cobblestones, under Romanesque towers, through epic history, and we, negligible little blips of time, little microcosms of pain, tried to make our own brief episodes matter in the unending Polish panorama, the Jewish chronicle of genocidal defeats and heroic last stands. Our fingers struggled to thread the needle; mending, joining, stabbing, we tried to animate our tiny characters in the vast tapestry. Arno understood me in ways no one else ever had.

Arno and I fought. And we talked and we danced and we drank and we recited poetry in Polish from memory. Once I left Poland, I wanted to forget Arno. I wanted to forget Arno when I was sitting across the table from him.

I returned to Berkeley, California. I didn't realize this when I moved to Berkeley, but I soon found out: there were Twelve Step meetings every day of the week for ACOAA—Adult Children of Abusive or Alcoholic Parents. Those meetings were jam-packed with people who wanted to help because they realized that by helping others, they were helping themselves in the truest way possible. Those meetings remain my most profound experience of organized religion.

My first month back from Poland, after I had packed memories of Arno in mothballs and relegated them to my past, I had a series of strange encounters. One day I returned home from work to find a woman sitting on the couch. She explained she was my housemate's guest. We made small talk, and within minutes, I discovered that one of her parents had been in a Nazi concentration camp. Wow. Just like Arno's dad. A week later I was at an ACOAA meeting. The man sitting next to me, *à propos de rien*, almost immediately disclosed that his father was a Holocaust survivor. Wow. Just like Arno's dad. A week later I was at another

ACOAA meeting. I arrived late, I left early, and I said nothing. As I was walking away, a man chased me out onto the sidewalk. He said, "Excuse me, I know this will seem like an odd question, but are you the child of a Holocaust survivor?"

Three weeks of weird coincidences. I sat down at the kitchen table and began writing a letter to Arno. I had no idea what I was going to say. All I remember was that I said I recognized I had done things that had hurt him, and that I was sorry. I consciously chose not to mention he had done things to hurt me. I felt my writing this letter was my spiritual task, not his. If a bunch of Bohunk women from New Jersey started popping up in his life and reminding him of me to the point where he felt he had to apologize to me to exorcise them, great. If not, so be it.

It was early fall by this point, and I lived in the paved-over Berkeley flatlands. As I wrote the letter to Arno, a hermit thrush, wings fluttering, leading with its breast, beat its body against the window. Birds do this during the mating season, thinking that their reflection is a rival. This wasn't mating season, and a woodland bird like a hermit thrush had no business in an urban setting. As soon as I finished writing the letter, the bird flew off, not to be seen again.

Arno phoned late at night. It was one of those conversations that makes you wish, years later, that you had recorded it. Arno talked about violation and forgiveness, honoring the past without becoming enslaved to its ghosts, living a vital life in the here and now while remaining mindful of history's demand for compassion, preparing the way for a better future, and Polish-Jewish relations in the post-Holocaust era. He was brilliant. Deep. Witty. Glittering. No teacher, no talking head on TV, no diplomat at the UN had ever been more compelling to me.

I felt the urge to — *do* something.

For me, going to graduate school was as inconceivable as rocketing off to colonize Mars. I hadn't even known that graduate school existed until a few years before I went. I was a cognitively challenged kid. Slow to learn to read and write. Always oblivious to what was obvious to everyone else, and yet always aware of things that no one else paid any attention to. I often can't recognize people's faces or remember their names, but I always buy the perfect present because I pay attention to who they are.

I didn't realize until I took the GRE and scored in the 98th percentile that I am not mentally retarded.

◆

In autumn 1991, before the fall semester began, I had not yet met the chair of my department at the University of California at Berkeley, Alan Dundes. I was standing in Black Oak Books on Shattuck Avenue. Two young men, handsome, elegant, and, I assumed, a gay couple, picked up a book from a table near me.

"This is that guy whose talk we went to, isn't it?"

"Yes. Dundes."

"He was . . . something!"

"Wasn't he though."

"So . . . dirty. In a good way. Hysterically funny. And so very fat, and yet, also, somehow, so . . . "

I hung on their every word.

"I know what you mean. Sexy."

"Yes!"

Sexy? After "dirty," "funny," and "fat"?

Alan Dundes was the only other person I've ever met who was as intimidating as my mother. He was a one-man battlefront. He yelled at me. Constantly. He even yelled when apologizing. "I couldn't give you the fellowship. It had to go to a minority. You understand."

But he made arrangements for me. I was to be the live-in domestic servant of the mother-in-law of one of Dundes' fellow scholars. Her name was Mrs. Pattershall. She was a ninety-year-old WASP from Maine. She would cover my housing and allot me a generous sixty dollars a month to buy enough food for both of us. An added bonus: I would lose weight.

Mrs. Pattershall had the kind of place my brother would've broken into — when he was into that — never to steal, just to destroy. It was his spiritual and political commentary. I faced less risk and resistance on entry than he; I was handed a key by the building manager who had received a call from Mrs. Pattershall in Maine, who had received a call from Alan Dundes. People did what Alan Dundes told them to do. I deposited my backpack on a Persian carpet in a dusty ill-lit room. "She wants you to clean the place before she gets back; it's been closed all summer." My brother and I diverged in the routes we took into Their homes, but our missions were parallel: reaching Them with our story

I pulled back heavy drapes to her view, the requisite Berkeley view: hills falling to flatlands dipping to bay, Golden Gate Bridge, the distant Pacific. Late morning light flooded maroon and navy, doilies, crystal, displayed teacups too small to be useful. It was the kind of place my mother used to clean. And grandma. The chain wasn't broken yet. I promised to break it.

It was a beautiful day, and I wanted to write something. I kept trying to clean quickly, but well. I noted the progression of sun across Persian carpets as I vacuumed them. After seven hours, a disconsolate melon light rimmed the gray and distant bay. The days were getting shorter. The smell of Clorox ate away what I wanted to write. I was on all fours on the bathroom floor when I caught a glimpse of myself in the mirror: stained sweat pants and sweat shirt, hair in a *szmata*, my face red and dull. I had been accepted by Alan Dundes, a world-class scholar, as a graduate student at a university with more Nobel Laureates on its current faculty than Harvard, I was told. Yet this was me, still: the Bohunk cleaning woman. At that moment, I forgave my mother for so many things.

I showered off the Clorox and attended a reception for new graduate students. It took every ounce of self-control I had to keep from taking up the tablecloth by its four corners, slinging it sac-like over my back, and carrying off the food: strawberries, raspberries, Camembert, wine, very fine crackers. I am always amazed at how much better expensive crackers taste than cheap ones. What so special could they do with flour, salt, and lard? I don't know; they did it. I wanted to call my mother and say, "You were wrong. Some of rich people's food really does taste better, even with an appetite."

I wasn't talking to anyone. It was too hard. Sometimes high school kids succumb to sincere sentiment and write terrible poems, and their teachers, trying to be honest but kind, say, "Do you ever use this word in real life?" Those are the words everyone used in academia, that everyone was using at this reception. The words you don't use in real life.

Prof. Dundes zeroed in on me, certain and grim as an executioner. "Don't just eat. Talk to people. Schmooze!" he ordered. He grabbed a passing, skinny lad with very long hair and pale, pocked skin. "Him. He's just about to get his PhD."

I put down one of my two wineglasses.

"So. You're about to get your PhD."

"Yes, yes, I am."

"What did you study?"

I immediately chastised myself. No one ever said, "What do you study?" They said either, "What are you working on?" or "What are you interested in?" I suspected that saying "working on" allowed graduate students to feel like macho proletariat, manually producing some handcrafted, artisanal artifact at the end of another day of regurgitated theory. "Interested in" was a reminder that it was all a game, that to survive departmental politics, one should never have a clear position that could be revealed with a precise verb like: "supporting," "refuting," or "wasting my time with."

"What are you interested in working on?" I asked, fumbling.

"I've been working with Aztec mythology."

"Tell me about Aztec mythology."

"They have a cannibal God."

"Oh," I said, genuinely interested, seeing a chance for the fruits of academia to illuminate current real world problems. "Do you see any connection between ritual cannibalism and Jeffrey Dahmer?"

He bowed his head, considered manfully. I could sense his inner wrestlings. "Now, remind me," he said, finally. "What's his thesis again?"

"Jeffrey Dahmer is a serial killer who ate his victims. He was just arrested. It's been in all the news lately."

The PhD. candidate laughed with relief. "Ah, yes. Levi-Strauss had something interesting to say about that . . . "

I kept asking myself, "What am I doing here?" Everyone I'd ever loved had ground into me: "They" — and everybody knew who "They" were — "They are phony, all show, the game is rigged, it's like a drug, it's worse than that, better you should be an alcoholic, on heroin, 'cause whadaya do with an addict, you feed 'em, you house 'em, and we can do that. What can we do with someone who gives in to this drug, the American Dream? They make promises and those promises are all lies for people like us, our effort is the very blood on which they feed, the game is rigged, because they would never, ever, let one of us win; just try — you've made your first and last mistake."

I remembered what my mother once said about grandma to an American daughter-in-law. "What was she like?"

I left the dishes in the kitchen and scurried toward the parlor, drying my hands on my apron. I leaned on the threshold, listening. Which story would my mother tell? Everyone told stories of grandma. I needed them. Those stories were her flesh, her deed, and shadow to me. She died before I was born.

Mommy looked up at the ceiling. I tried to anticipate the plot, the version. I hoped it would be a story I could add some flourishes to. I didn't have the originals, but I listened hard and remembered details from one version I could add to another. My mother spoke to her American daughter-in-law, a girl whose parents and grandparents, all the way back to its invention, spoke English. How would my mother pass the story on to her? To the womb that would bring into the world Grandma's great-grand-children? My mother sighed. "If she'd a been born in America, she wouldda been fantastic."

33

No. No!

My grandmother, who gave birth to my mother in the river Nitra during a hot day of sugar beet harvest? My grandmother, who sliced a tumor out of my grandfather with just her homegrown poppy for anesthesia so he got to live and die from happier things, like fat and old age? My grandmother, who through prayer alone pulled Uncle Joe back to life when a fever had him; he survived, deaf, and through guile she bribed the guards at Ellis Island when they said, "Take him back. He's not whole"? My grandmother, who buried her firstborn, Mary, taken in the Influenza Pandemic of 1918? Who harbored wetback Slovaks, and when the Feds came in the front door to arrest them, she had the escape route ready — out the back window? Who wore French designer dresses she sewed herself after making copies from storefronts? Who spoke, read, and wrote three languages, though she'd never gone to school? Who was asked to sing at every wedding and funeral? Who had until her death the muscles to wrestle a cow to the ground and a gut so flat and hard you could roller-skate on it? That woman was not fantastic?

"Yeah, she wouldda been fantastic if she'd a been born in America."

I wanted to do the American thing, the thing that would be fantastic. For my grandmother.

I rapidly realized I'd have to sink or swim in grad school when it came to my dyslexia and ADHD. I cooked up a do-it-yourself cure: caffeine, sugar, headphones, repetitive sounds, a timer, iron discipline, plus one surprise ingredient: people. Throughout grad school I had a diet cola in one hand, peanut M&Ms in the other, and I was listening, through headphones, to trains, ocean waves, chanting, or Philip Glass. One hour. I forced myself to read or write or even just collapse for one hour — and only one hour — at a time. The people part surprised me. I worked best not in complete isolation, but when surrounded by people to whom I was more or less invisible. I'd don my headphones and report to Stephens Lounge on campus. I found I could perform as I never had before. I also found that when I was in Olympic mode, I had almost no experiences with the little voice. During vacations, when I broke training, the little voice, with all its sixth-sense awarenesses and synchronicities, would return.

Prof. Dundes' thesis was pretty easy to follow, once you got the key components. Anything longer than wide — a lipstick, say, or a magic wand, flagpole, shotgun or carrot — was obviously a phallic symbol. Things in pairs — earrings, eyes, twins — were breasts. All fluids were semen, unless of course they were urine or breast milk. Verbs were usually euphemisms for sexual intercourse: to see, to know, to take off, to lift off, to vibrate, to juggle, to yodel, to split rails, to drive really fast. He had no problem using the medical vocabulary, but wouldn't if a suggestive wiggle of his eyebrows, crude gesture with his sausage-fingered hand, or dramatically timed pregnant pause would convey the same data. Watching a fat old man in a tight bad suit thrust his hips forward like Elvis at a key moment in the discussion of a cherished folk tale can be either grotesque or hilarious and life-affirming, depending on how open you are to the experience. Dundes' X-rated lectures were never just about shock value. He knew his field, and he backed up every argument with massive research. It's a cliché: "He was so big, it was amazing to see the grace with which he danced." As with the big man dancing, I was awestruck by the grace and symmetry Dundes brought to the epic amount of information in his head.

He told a dumb Polak joke in class. The students laughed. I reported to his office and sternly lectured him. He let me lecture him. He devoted the next class to a sermon on the equal worth of all humans, no matter their race, creed, or national origin. The students applauded.

We had a much worse fight over his interpretation of "The Maiden with No Hands." It's a folktale about a girl whose father propositions her. She is distraught and cuts off her own hands. In some versions, the father cuts off the girl's hands. Dundes insisted that this amputation expressed the girl's Freudian Electra Complex, that is, her repressed sexual desire for her father. Though no such desire is mentioned in the tale, Dundes theorized that the girl cut off her hands because she had masturbated while thinking about her father.

I wish I could turn back the clock and replay this debate. I wish I could present my point of view to him in a calm and rational way. Instead, I raised my voice, he raised his voice, we both ended up lobster-faced, and onlookers became concerned and gossiped about us.

"Are you nuts? You're imagining things that are not in the tale. Look at it at face value. She has no hands. What happens when you have no hands? You are helpless. You can't do anything. That's what this tale is expressing: the girl's utter powerlessness. She's a child in an adult world, a girl in a man's world, a peasant in a monarchy. She's been betrayed by her own father, the very man who is supposed to protect her. The first of the Ten Commandments not devoted to God orders us to 'Honor your father.' She can't drop a dime on her old man. She can't even enjoy the release of talking it out. Why can't you see any of that?"

"You seem to think that parents habitually abuse their children."

"Not all. But some. Enough. There are parents in real life who do very bad things to their children, and it's not because the children ask for it, or want it, or deserve it."

He insisted that I was exaggerating and that my exaggerations blinded me to the truth of the tale.

It's a funny thing. Dundes himself said we had entered the age of the victim. UC Berkeley was one of the ultra-liberal universities that ushered in our era of political correctness, of heightened sensitivity to various victim narratives. We were all tiptoeing on eggshells lest we offend this or that victim group. And Dundes told me he had to give the fellowship to a "minority," a girl with a Harvard BA whose father had driven her, cross-country, to UC Berkeley. All that sensitivity. And none for abused kids.

I was still having the nightmares in Berkeley. One night I dreamt I was on all fours, mired in the mud and excrement of a pigsty. My mother stood on a surrounding stone wall. "That's right! You always were shit and you're shit now! You'll never get out of there 'cause you'll have to get past me, first!" I was eating Comet cleanser, trying to cleanse myself, but I just began to bleed, internally. I tried to rise, but the mud just kept sucking me down.

As in childhood, when something triggered many nightmares back-to-back, my hands would melt into ferocious bouts of eczema, eczema that stopped dead at my wrists and never touched any other part of my body. My brother Greg used to call me "Rash Rot." When my hands were covered with scales and spontaneous open wounds, flaking, and bleeding, I was close to helpless. Shirt buttons were an obstacle course. Typing was excruciating; smearing blood and pus made the keys slippery and sticky. The slow work of extracting the right number of bills and coins in a supermarket checkout line risked clerks' and customers' impatience, pity, or disgust. This was a helplessness that neither Dundes nor anyone else could see.

If you theorized, "The eczema is your body's response to the child abuse; your hands weep perpetually because your eyes can cry no more," I'd have to correct you. The eczema wasn't the result of child abuse; I'm tough and I survived the beatings just fine. The eczema was caused by love. I loved my parents, and every now and then they would struggle to love me. Love is the thorn. Love is the sleepless night. Fighting is not unbearable. It's actually fun. Like a lot of abused kids, I used to beat up other kids. It was a rush. This is unbearable: the boundary violation between love and hate and right and wrong. People who do wrong are trying to do the right thing. The most frequently repeated message in Twelve Step meetings, the thing we needed to hear over and over and over and over just to live out our daily lives was not "Poor you"; such words were rarely said. The thing we needed to hear over and over was "You can't save someone who doesn't want to be saved." My parents' demons would never allow my love to reach them.

When peace of mind returned, the eczema disappeared. I didn't seek that peace among human beings. "You have to believe it to see it," declared the bumper stickers on Berkeley hippies' cars. People believe what they have themselves experienced. After I left Africa, I never talked about Africa. Who would understand? In fact, no one asked. No one I'm related to, no friends ever asked about any of it. If you live an unusual life, you will always be lonelier than those who lead conventional lives. People want to talk about what affects them. People don't hear what they have not experienced. People read to embrace their own beliefs expressed and confirmed. They reject writing that contradicts them. Nothing is more dangerous than saying something or writing something that disagrees with power. The facts were right there in front of Dundes, my mentor and one of the smartest men in the world. He couldn't see them. Thus, I sought peace where I had always sought it.

◆

I found an unprepossessing, unmarked, and very steep trail that snaked up behind the white, rambling Claremont Hotel, which miraculously survived the 1991 firestorm. Switchbacks wound through fragrant eucalyptus. Pale-backed leaves licked at the breeze. Skin-smooth bark, mapped with white and gray and green splotches, turned the trail into a Rorschach test, or the soothing map of an imaginary island planet. These alien trees burn very well; wise homeowners in the hills had slate-tiled roofs. Eucalyptus was imported by Australians during the Gold Rush. Illegal immigrants, these trees did not assimilate ecologically. Birds and bugs found neither dinner nor home in them, and hiking through them, I heard no birdsong or bee buzz, only the eerie creak of their limbs rubbing, lonely, only against one another. Halfway up, the trail dropped steeply from both sides, and was lined with yellow-flowered scotch broom, purple vetch and lupine, blood-red and gray-felt Indian paint brush and prickly milk thistle, the plant that promised an antidote to mushroom poisoning. This thistle's "milk" is a white stain dribbling sloppily down its stiff, spiked, green leaves.

Once I reached the pines and the banana slugs — bright yellow and, at almost ten inches long, the world's second-largest terrestrial slug — I could hear a peacock in the canyon below; further on the hyenas. The banana slugs were about their humble but necessary work of ever-so-slowly eating up dead plant material and the occasional animal poo. In turn, the slugs excrete fertile soil. Hyenas fill their evolutionary niche with a bit more speed and drama. The hyenas would open with a lion's roar and climax with a mule's whiney rasp; the sound carries three miles. The hyenas would roar most in the morning when the fog was thickest, adding to the eeriness of it all. They would also answer a chainsaw. Their sound was so abrasive, so blistered, horrible and wild, I knew that being eaten by a hyena would be far worse than being eaten by anything else except maybe from the inside by a parasite. I would tell myself this as I sweated up steep and shadeless stretches of trail. "They're loose! Hurry! The hyenas are coming!"

Spotted hyenas were penned for study by university researchers. Stephen Glickman and Laurence Frank co-founded Berkeley's hyena colony in 1985. Hyenas aroused interest because the females have pseudo-testicles and pseudo-penises. Spotted hyenas are the only mammals lacking any external vaginal opening; they are thus, biologists claim, impossible to rape. The hyenas' pseudo-penises are in fact enlarged clitorises. Through these, hyenas copulate and give birth; they say it's like sucking a golf ball through a straw. The pseudo-penis ruptures; ouch! Sixty percent of hyena cubs of new mothers suffocate. Then twenty-five percent of cubs are killed by their own siblings. While siblicide is not uncommon among insects and birds, hyenas are the only mammals to practice it with such frequency. Also unique among mammals, hyenas are born with open eyes and protruding incisor and canine teeth. Berkeley's researchers witnessed one newborn twin attack its sibling while it was still in the amniotic sac. "Most neonates root around for their mother's teat. Hyena newborns root around for the back of their sibling's neck," said Glickman. With a few shakes, that pesky kid sister is reduced to a limp and lifeless practice dummy, just another obstacle the victor vaults to attain high status. The hyena who kills his or her own sibling shows greater size and dominance later in life. Status is inherited and even the great-granddaughters of dominant hyenas are themselves likely to be dominant.

Wait. There's more. Hyena clans are always matriarchal. All males are lower status than all females. There is, however, one grace female hyenas show the males they dominate: daughters show less aggression toward their own fathers. Matriarchal clans, you might think, would be great places for daughters. Not so. Frank noticed that more female hyena cubs were murdered by their siblings than male cubs. Frank's theory: while low-ranking mothers try to ensure that both of their cubs survive, high-ranking mothers prefer sons. Given the realities of sex, a female will parent fewer children over her lifespan than a male. Females have to devote time to pregnancy and cub rearing. Males just have to spend a few minutes copulating. That being the case, a son offers his mother greater chances that her genes will survive in more grandchildren.

These extreme facts do not surprise me. I have heard the hideous call of the hyena, and I assumed as much: fake penises, suffocated babies, and siblicide. If someone told me that hyenas smoke, litter, and cheat on their taxes, I'd believe that too.

We want, of course, to make hyenas as little about ourselves as possible. We can't. Berkeley's hyena research was not funded by the Bronx Zoo or the Wilderness Society. It was funded by the National Institute of Mental Health. One of the researchers was a professor of obstetrics and gynecology, seeking answers to polycystic ovarian syndrome in women. Another researcher was studying the development of human language. Immunologists wanted to plumb the mystery of how hyenas survive anthrax and rabies. Some wanted to know if their high testosterone levels triggered hyenas' — or humans' — aggression.

"Man is wolf to man," goes the old Latin proverb. The Romans were too hopeful. Man is hyena to man. My peasant neighbors in Nepal were some of the best people I ever hope to know. Hospitable, resourceful, beautiful. In the peasant families I knew at all well, the youngest daughter, if there was one, was severely malnourished. Healthy Nepalis have jet black hair. Her hair would be thin, wispy, and the telltale color of straw. She'd be barefoot, even if her older brothers had shoes, and dressed in the shabbiest clothing. The males eat first. Then the higher status females. Youngest daughters took scraps. They would see no doctor or traditional healer when they got sick. They were the least likely to survive.

These aren't statistics to me; they're little girls. I brought lentils to Sharada to feed her youngest daughter, Sushma. Sharada put the lentils on the shelf. If she cooked them at all, she gave them to me or to her son. Peace Corps staff lectured us not to impose our "imperialist" values on "host country nationals." Their values came from the Vedas, bursting with hymns praising sons, but none praising daughters. "Bounteous Indra, endow this bride with great sons and fortune. Give her ten sons, and make the husband the eleventh," goes an ancient marriage blessing from the over three-thousand-year-old Rig Veda. This marriage blessing is still repeated today. "The son is one's own self; the daughter is a source of trouble," states the Mahabharata. Punjabis recited this magical rhyme when committing female infanticide: "Eat molasses; spin thread; we don't want you, but a brother, instead." Hyena mothers look the other way when the oldest kills the youngest. Human mothers all too often do the killing themselves.

Early Christianity condemned the female infanticide that had been sanctioned by Romulus' Roman legal code: "Rear every male child and the firstborn of the females." But Christians have not always been so nice to little girls. Read "Hansel and Gretel." Read "Cinderella." The fairy tale hero is often a youngest son or stepdaughter who is mocked and discounted and must hit the road and enter the world with nothing but his or her own wits. Primogeniture guaranteed that the oldest son inherited everything. Not a few disinherited youngest children populated the New World. Outsiders, the dispossessed, the dreamers were our founders. It's not surprising that they would be the ones to insist that all men are created equal.

◆

Various tribes enter the wilderness. There are the Hemingway Tribe, the Walt Disney Tribe, the Biblical Seeker Tribe, the Henry David Thoreaus, the Ansel Adams, the Roger Tory Petersons, Athletes, Hermits, Lunatics, Fugitives, Criminals, and Women in High Heeled Shoes. This last group enters the wilderness only because new boyfriends or old girlfriends — women like me — drag them.

My brothers, like Hemingway, entered the woods to put food on the table, money in the bank, notches in the belt, and stories in the repertoire. My brothers brought home deer and fish for dinner, and they trapped squirrels and muskrats for fur. Greg once brought home a copperhead just because he could. Daddy had had enough killing on the frontlines in World War II. He brought home sacks of mushrooms. He always ate them first, waited a day, and then let us eat them.

When I was a kid, I wouldn't eat Phil's venison till they tricked me and told me it was "hamburger," something I'd already eaten without thought for its origins. Only after I swallowed it did they say "Ha, ha, ha. You just ate Bambi." I was crushed. To me, a deer was a recognizable creature. Beef was something in a Styrofoam tray in a supermarket. Later I grew up and realized that cows are creatures too. I didn't eat more venison. I ate less beef. Still later I grew my own backyard garden and matured some more. I developed a craving for venison as fierce as any hyena's. As a gardener, I wasn't seeking satiation, I was seeking revenge. The concept of a "crime of passion" once gave cuckolds a free pass for murdering a cheating spouse. Gardeners should be legally allowed, not just to shoot, but to prosecute deer.

I often go to the woods without the one weapon I allow myself: a knife. I rarely go to the woods without my binoculars, and I just about never go without pen and paper. That makes me a member of the Roger Tory Peterson Tribe. Peterson was a child of poor immigrants in western New York state. His own father had been sent to work in textile mills at age ten. Peterson's father expected his son to get a job, not spend every free minute in the woods. Peterson resented his dad but later came to understand "the odds that this man struggled against." He was teased in school as "Professor Nuts," and the family's Lutheran minister said that love of nature "makes for unbelievers." This put Peterson off religion. He found transcendence elsewhere. Peterson had a childhood encounter with a yellow-shafted flicker, a common woodpecker with rather drab camouflage, until it flies — then its wings' golden linings flicker forth like rays of captive sunlight in the dusky forest. This moment, Peterson said using religious language, was "like a resurrection. I came to believe birds are the most vivid reflection of life." Peterson all but invented bird watching with his series of field guides. His 1934 *Guide to the Birds* sold out in one week.

I love Roger Tory Peterson as if he were my best friend, though of course we never met. Perhaps no artist has influenced his fellow humans so significantly in how they relate to nature. Even so, if Peterson had had infinite time and tools, and had produced the single finest, most aesthetically pleasing, most scientifically accurate illustrations of any given bird, its development in the egg, its transit from nestling to adult, its habits, habitat, and innards, something would still be missing. A bird is something, a bird is saying something, that neither art nor science alone can ever fully reach.

Thus, I'm also a member of the Biblical Seeker Tribe and the Thoreau Tribe, the folks who go to the woods to live out their full humanity in a way that is not possible in civilization. My pen and paper record Peterson-style nature notes, and spiritual reflections, as well. I religiously do not bring a camera. I do not want to crowd my obsessions. I am merely an awed fan of the Ansel Adams Tribe.

I have sometimes wondered if my membership in the Thoreau Tribe competes with my membership in the Biblical Seeker Tribe. At those times, the words on the Biblical page seem a pale shadow of the numinous I encounter in nature. But I prod myself to consider: perhaps my comprehension of those words on the Bible page is what needs to expand. When I bring what I experience in nature to the page, the page blossoms.

Suddenly I meet, anew, the Jesus who aches to gather his chicks under his wings as does a maternal and protective bird. I know a God who is mindful of each sparrow's fall, each lily's petals, and who tells his luckier children to care for the least of his creations: "The righteous care for the needs of their animals."

"For six years you are to sow your fields and harvest the crops, but during the seventh year let the land lie unplowed and unused. Then the poor among your people may get food from it, and the wild animals may eat what is left." I hear language that communicates through the earth: "Some seed fell along the path, and the birds came and ate it up. Some fell on rocky places, where it did not have much soil. It sprang up quickly, because the soil was shallow. But when the sun came up, the plants were scorched, and they withered because they had no root. Other seed fell among thorns, which grew up and choked the plants." And communication through the sky: "When evening comes, you say, 'The weather will be fair, for the sky is red'; and in the morning, 'Today it will be stormy, for the sky is red and overcast.'" Moses encountered God not in a temple, but in "the far side of the wilderness." Jesus, like me, went to the wilderness; in seeking the divine "he was with the wild animals." God wants to save all of creation, not just us humans. "We know that the whole creation has been groaning as in the pains of childbirth right up to the present time." When I bring what I feel in nature to the Bible page, I recognize nature not as my god but as my sibling.

There are some wild creatures I like as if they were friends, for example chipmunks and chickadees. I've fed them, and they've eaten from my hands. I rarely kill sow bugs, even when I find them in my apartment. They defend themselves by rolling up into little balls, and I find that cute. To me, "cute" and "kill" are in separate boxes. That's true for my brother Greg, as well. He told me he found it hard to kill a deer if they'd made eye contact.

I don't kill spiders. I hate household insects; the enemy of my enemy is my friend. But I'm not a full-fledged member of the Disney Tribe. Once at a party in the Redwood wilds of northern

California, a man encouraged me to pet his wolf. I did. That wolf wanted to eat me. I could see it in its eyes. I don't think it makes much sense to keep a wolf as a pet. To me, loving nature doesn't mean I want to cuddle with every living thing. I want to appreciate every living thing. I'm horrified by hyenas. But I appreciate them.

"The Gemara states that the male hyena turns into a female," writes "Zoo Rabbi" Natan Slifkin. Because of their pseudo-penises, hyenas are condemned as gender outlaws in the folklore of many nations. Rabbi Slifkin cites a Talmudic cure for rabies that involves writing one's name on the skin of a male hyena. Of course, this cure won't work, but it is interesting that the ancients saw a link between hyenas and rabies survival, a link that modern science has only recently discovered. Though striped hyenas live in Israel, hyenas are mentioned only briefly in the Bible. "Ruined houses will be full of hyenas" is the prophet Isaiah's guarantee that everything will go bust in Babylon. There will be fire and brimstone, yes. Infants will be "dashed to pieces" as their parents look on, yes. Women will be "ravished," yes, but none of these horrors will signal the lowest depths. Babylon will hit rock bottom when undesirables move into the old neighborhood. Hyenas "shall howl in Babylon's castles." Jeremiah warns, "My heritage is a prey for hyenas." Sirach asks, "Can there be peace between the hyena and the dog? Or between the rich and the poor?" This is not a line that causes you to anticipate universal brotherhood.

Hyenas are mentioned in Hinduism's Rig Veda, possibly the world's oldest still-used religious text. After an erotic passage involving "heavenly nymphs who laid aside their raiment," the Veda counsels, "With women there can be no lasting friendship: hearts of hyenas are the hearts of women." Hyenas and I have something in common. The Rig Veda has been hating on us both for a damn long time. The Koran mostly mentions animals in relation to man; animals are not a main theme of the book, reports the *Encyclopaedia of the Qur'ān*. The Koran does not mention hyenas, but hadiths do. According to one hadith, Muslims have permission to eat hyena meat because "Arabs like it and find it delicious."

The Vinaya Pitaka, an ancient Buddhist monastic code, specifically proscribes monks from eating hyena, "even in times of scarcity," along with nine other animals, including humans. The 1642 "Decree on the Protection of Animals and the Environment" exempted hyenas from protection; Tibetan Buddhists could, in good conscience, harm them.

The Biblical Book of Job famously tells the so-sad-it's-almost-funny story of a nice guy, Job, who is afflicted by God. Into this catalog of pustules, economic ruination, and God-as-hitman, the author slipped the Bible's most exuberant celebration of the natural world. I don't think that juxtaposition is mere coincidence. God, the singer of this lengthy song, displays love that is both awesome and mighty as well as tender and intimate. Verses devoted to mountain goats and lions, the aurochs and the wild ass are both touching and show the attention to nature for which Henry David Thoreau and John Muir, the kind of folks credited with "inventing" nature writing, strove. God even expresses parental care for the leviathan, whose "snorting throws out flashes of light," whose "eyes are like the rays of dawn." "Smoke pours from its nostrils as from a boiling pot over burning reeds," as the Book of Job says. "Its undersides are jagged potsherds, leaving a trail in the mud like a threshing sledge." God also loves the behemoth, a creature so stalwart, so cocksure that even "though the Jordan River should surge against its mouth" it is not afraid. Neither the leviathan nor the behemoth is to be found in modern field guides; the best guess is that the leviathan is a crocodile and the behemoth is a hippopotamus.

No one, not even God in the Book of Job, can summon up enough love to write hyena poetry. The Bible promises redemption for wolves, leopards, and lions. When Messiah comes, the wolf will room with the lamb, the leopard and the goat will lie down, and the lion and the calf will graze together. There is no such promise for the hyena.

C. S. Lewis made a lion the Christ-figure in his Narnia books. I don't know if Lewis ever wrote about hyenas, but if he did, I'll bet he had no use for them. Hyena societies are matriarchal. Lewis wrote, "in the hive and in the anthill, we see fully realized the two things that some of us most dread for our own species: the dominance of the female and the dominance of the collective." No, Lewis, who elevated the lion to Christ status, would probably not like hyenas at all.

Hyenas are the low-rent, second-string villains of *The Lion King*, the all-time third highest-grossing film of Walt Disney Animation Studios. Disney animators spent two days in Berkeley observing the hyena colony. Researcher Laurence Frank begged the Disney animators to depict the hyenas positively. Frank insisted that his wards are "real lap-lovers" with "a deep, warm, nurturing, complex personality" and "bottomless brown eyes." He described a favorite hyena, Tuffie. "I would go into the cage with her, and she would still make little baby noises and hurl herself at me in great joy and cuddle on the floor. Just an extraordinary lifelong relationship." Researcher George Bentley said that Berkeley's hyenas are "comical, charismatic, social, and very intelligent animals. They're fantastic to watch and incredibly intriguing." Typical Berkeley bleeding hearts. Their efforts at hyena PR fell flat. The "vicious" and "malicious" Disney hyena queen is named "Shenzi," meaning "savage," "pagan," "half-breed," "uncouth," or "barbarous" in Swahili. Disney animators drew Shenzi with simulated eye shadow and lipstick because hyena clans are always matriarchal. It's clearly the lion *king* versus the hyena *queen*.

Europe's cave hyenas, depicted in Paleolithic cave art, went extinct 12,000 years ago as European grasslands gave way to woodlands that favored wolves. There were, of course, no hyenas in medieval Europe. This did not stop medieval Europeans from fearing hyenas. The twelfth-century *Aberdeen Bestiary* depicted such manly creatures as lions, horses, and rams without their organs visible, but the hyena, that female who dared to have a pseudo-penis, is depicted with a striking anatomical accuracy that all but pokes the viewer in the eye. Her private parts dangle downward as she munches on a human corpse. In another medieval image, a hyena appears to be kissing its human victim. One medieval hyena's mouth is pressed against a dead woman's privates in what looks like an act of bestial, necrophiliac cunnilingus; all your anxieties about sex, death, orality, gluttony, morality, and the violation of bodily integrity, not in a teen slasher flick, but in one medieval package. The hyena's gender transgressions and penchant for necrophagy inspired a thirteenth-century bestiary from Salisbury to compare hyenas to Jews. Jewish men, given all that time they spent indoors reading books, were perceived as not adequately manly. There was a medieval belief that Jewish men menstruated. Jews and hyenas transgressed gender boundaries. Also, Jews practiced business in economically primitive feudal societies. Jewish mercantilism was sometimes praised and often sought, but those evil conjoined quadruplets — fear, hate, envy, and ignorance — spawned the stereotype of Jews "feeding on" non-Jews. This comparison says nothing negative about Jews or hyenas but much negative about the person making the comparison.

The International Union for Conservation of Nature warns that hyenas' negative reputation puts them at risk for extinction, both in the wild and in captivity. Fewer than seven percent of American zoos feature hyenas. Why are hyenas so universally hated? Because we humans are shallow.

We don't like hyenas because they violate our sense of order. I'm not the only obsessive-compulsive on the planet. We all want things to be neat and tidy, and to reflect our own concept of the rational. Needing to think things through, confronting thoughts we had not thought before, terrifies people. The Book of Leviticus hands down a series of rules that seem arbitrary. Anthropologist Mary Douglas detected an underlying pattern: don't mix categories. Don't mix meat and milk. Don't mix linen and wool. If you are a man, don't lie with a man as with a woman. Don't violate people's expectations. If you smear borders, you just might accidentally cross the railroad tracks from the sacred and step into the profane.

Hyenas do that. Female hyenas have false penises. Females run the clans. Hyenas have snouts and non-retractable claws like dogs, but they are phylogenetically closer to cats. Even hyenas' most famous characteristic, their voice, annoys us. Hyenas communicate orally — they have to — they are social animals that hunt together at night. Each clan member recognizes each hyena's unique voice. Their vocal communication reaches a level of sophistication comparable to that of primates. These creepy animals are like us in another way: hyenas "lie." Low-ranking members fake alarm calls — "Here comes a lion!" — to scatter their fellow clan members and gain access to dining on a kill from which they'd been excluded. Pliny the Elder wrote that hyenas have such command of speech that they can lure people outside by calling their names. Then, of course, the hyena tears the gullible human to bits.

Humans, whose greed may yet make life impossible for every other creature, attribute greed to hyenas. The hyena's greed is manifest in its appetite. We humans want to be elegantly slim and self-controlled and gracious enough calmly to allow our guest the final treat on the tray. Instead, we indulge in that second ice cream cone and hope no one is looking. So we humans tell folktales about hyenas being so orally greedy that they consume their own bodies. Hemingway told just one such tale in *The Green Hills of Africa*. Hemingway writes well enough to taint the hyena forever in the mind of his reader. Ironically, it was Hemingway, not the hyena, who traveled thousands of miles for no other reason than to kill innocent life just for the fun of it.

We humans wish we could rise above our own flesh. We wish our substance could be our own dreams about ourselves. We think we are too good to defecate, to lust, to fall, to sicken, to age, to die. This anxiety gave birth to the Gnostic movement, whose members strove to attain to a higher dimension than mere physical humanity. Islam, too, has roots in this need to arrange the world into mutually exclusive, black-or-white categories. God is over there; we humans are over here, utterly different. Islam has a huge problem with the incarnation. "God does not have a son!" Islam has been loudly insisting for 1400 years. The Dome of the Rock, built in 691 AD, is one of the oldest extant Muslim structures. Abd al-Malik raised it as a defiant rival to the Christian Church of the Holy Sepulcher, nearby in Jerusalem. The Dome of the Rock shouts, repeatedly, in Kufic script: God does not have a son!

Jesus defied our anxiety about our physicality by becoming God-in-the-flesh. Jesus ate meat. Jesus drank wine. Jesus almost certainly farted. We don't always listen to Jesus so we project our own self-hatred onto critters like hyenas. We don't reject a God-made-flesh because we have trouble loving God. We reject a God-made-flesh because we have trouble loving ourselves.

Chimera: a monster that is more than one thing. The Jersey Devil is a chimera: part crane, part bat, part goat. Baphomet, the Devil card in tarot, is a chimera: part goat, part bat, part man, part chicken. I am a chimera. I clean houses. I read and write. This upsets people.

Yes, hyenas kill. Stephen Glickman wrote that hyenas may eat more pounds of flesh than any other land carnivore. Hyenas weigh roughly what humans do but they can eat forty pounds of food at one sitting. No one has to clean up after hyenas dine; they swallow everything, including bone, so much so that "their feces look like chalk," Frank said. Hyenas discretely wait till later to regurgitate inconveniently swallowed horns and hooves. The oldest known human hair, approximately 200,000 years old, was found in hyena coprolites, fossilized droppings. Hyenas eat us.

Hyenas do what lions and tigers do. They reduce wide-eyed cutie-pies like gazelles and baby buffalo to shreds of dinner stuck between their teeth. Hyenas seize bones that perform savannah ballet and demote them into snow stain in their scat. In fact, hyenas and lions dine at the same kill, hating and damning each other with each morsel. Hyenas and lions: an ancient feud that dysfunctional families at Christmas and Thanksgiving can never hope to equal. Here's the thing, though. Lions have those regal manes, their sun-like, sun-colored corollas. Tigers are sexy, inscrutable Orientals. And lions and tigers are proportional. Nothing on their body is distastefully exaggerated. Symmetry is a universal criterion for beauty.

Hyenas weigh between ninety and one-hundred-fifty pounds. Lions can weigh over five hundred pounds. Lions' bite force is close to six-hundred-fifty pounds per square inch. When a human eats, he exerts a bite force of about one-hundred-fifty pounds per square inch. Hyenas are a fraction of the weight of lions and tigers, but their bite force is over a thousand pounds per square inch. Spotted hyenas are scientifically classified as "bone-crushers." Hyenas weigh as much as we do and they can bite through giraffe femurs. What they lack in size they make up for in overtly ambitious anatomy. Hyenas are shaped like an obtuse scalene triangle pointed directly at your softest parts. They are all neck, shoulders, jaws, and beyond those Halloween-mask teeth, an obscenely pink, soft gape. That shade of pink in nature should be reserved for kinder vessels, like dahlias or conch shells or women.

Given their smooth, tawny hides, it's hard to look at a lion's shapely hips and not be reminded of well-developed athletes and swimsuit models. No one is intimidated by the hind quarters of a hyena. From the rear, a hyena looks more like something that gets eaten — or bullied — rather than the machine that does the eating. Hyenas lurch-lope forward, like predatory teeter-totters, the weight of the teeth in the front end forever weighing down the skimpy hinder quarters. Their anatomy is destiny: hunger lightning-struck into savagery. The curse of Eden in a heavy, toothy head. Even if you'd never heard of a hyena, and you saw one approaching, you'd know exactly why. There could be nothing else on the agenda. You'd probably be scared stiff, and folklore attributes to hyenas the magical ability to freeze humans in place. Lions and tigers are patrician. In spite of frequent news accounts of bear attacks on humans, "bear" is slang for a husky, hairy, huggable guy. Even grizzly bear anatomy is roly-poly and symmetrical enough to be a model for children's toys. "Teddy bear" is a default term for any stuffed animal. Give a kid an anatomically accurate hyena stuffie — if you can find one — and observe the child's reaction. On second thought, don't. You could be investigated. Hyenas are working-class killers. They could probably identify with my old pal from Jersey who liked to say, "When the WASPs do it, it's called 'free enterprise.' When we do it, it's called 'organized crime.'"

C. S. Lewis knew he didn't like some of God's creation simply because of its lack of charisma. Lewis was terrified of insects. A friend explained to him, "The trouble about insects is that they are all like French locomotives — they have all the works on the outside." Lewis said he was disturbed by insects' "angular limbs, their jerky movements, their dry, metallic noises," like "machines that have come to life or life degenerating into mechanism."

Me too. I loved Berkeley's feral peacocks and parrots. Their calls transported me right back to magical, mystical Nepal. Their beauty intoxicated me. Berkeleyites complained about peacock droppings and parrot noise. I thought they were nuts. Droppings and noise, to me, were a minuscule price to pay for peerless beauty, moving green flashes in the sky, and the peacock's catwalk strut. The hyenas? As I hiked in the hills and heard their howls, I was never so grateful for a chain link fence topped by barbed wire.

We believers insist that "The heavens declare the glory of God; the skies proclaim the work of his hands." We believe because we see God reflected in nature. That belief exposes us. We can't run. We can't hide. God is reflected in hyenas. Hyenas make love of God challenging. They make love of nature challenging too. The Book of Wisdom offers an even greater challenge. "For you love all things that are and loathe nothing that you have made; for what you hated, you would not have fashioned." God loves . . . hyenas???

I love nature. I don't want to cuddle nature. Hyenas make my jaw drop with fear, horror, and awe. I appreciate them. When Messiah comes the second time, what will become of hyenas? Will they chill out with lambs? If that happened, would they still be hyenas? Of course they would not. Our sainthood criteria would redefine heavenly hyenas out of existence. Hyenas want to deliver mewling innocents to a grisly death, roll in mud, and sniff each other's genitals. That's a good day for them.

One step toward hyena redemption — a redemption in which we humans must partake — is to recognize the most elemental motive for human-hyena hatred. This motive is most obvious to Africans, who share turf with hyenas, and most remote to those of us who acquire meat at the supermarket. Hyenas and we are sidling toward the exact same buffet, snaking through the same velvet rope line. We lust after the same real estate so we can eat the same critters.

Science offers the cold redemption of mathematics. *Chasmaporthetes ossifragus* was the "bone breaker who saw the Grand Canyon open up." That sounds like a movie version of a Native American name, but this is actually the meaning of the scientific name coined by paleontologist Oliver Perry Hay. The jaw fragments of an unknown species were found in 1901 at Val Verde Copper Mines in Anita, Arizona. These fragments made their way to Hay. Hay sat in a cluttered, dusty, dimly lit museum office. Looming over Hay: the skeleton of a huge fossil turtle, standing upright, surrounded by its shell, with all the drama of Dracula unfurling his cape. Hay lived with the remnants of the dead, their footprints in ancient mud, their five-million-year-old claw marks dug into the bones of their extinct prey, fossilized struggle, fossilized screams, fossilized satiation. Hay carefully classified every feature, except, perhaps, these remains' elusive, inescapable, otherworldly ghosts. He obsessively focused, through his thick, wire-rimmed glasses, on the hills and valleys of the mysterious Val Verde fossil's molars. The dental patterns told him this was not, as its discoverers thought, the jaw of a big cat, but rather North America's only known hyena. His imagination brought these previously unknown creatures to vivid life; rather than animating them snarling over a kill, he pictured them watching the creation of the Grand Canyon. Many scientific names are equally poetic. My favorite is *Aix sponsa*, "waterfowl in wedding raiment," the scientific name for the spectacularly colorful wood duck.

As tough as hyenas are, North America hosts the descendants of the creatures that outcompeted them: gray wolves. *Chasmaporthetes'* last American fossils date from a million years ago. Competition with wolves probably helped drive the American hyena to extinction, just as similar lupine competition may have contributed to the disappearance of Europe's cave hyena.

In his heartbreakingly beautiful book, *A Sand County Almanac*, Aldo Leopold tracked how he came to peace with wolves, pack hunters who fill the hyenas' niche in North America. At first, afflicted with "trigger-itch," Leopold assessed wolves merely as "a challenge of fang against bullet." He had thought that since "fewer wolves meant more deer, that no wolves would mean hunters' paradise." Leopold did his part to eradicate wolves. He gleefully massacred a mother and all her pups. And he witnessed not just the macro death of ecosystems destroyed by too much grazing, but also the micro death of individual deer, each one "dead of its own too-much." He learned that "only the mountain has lived long enough to listen objectively to the howl of a wolf . . . A thing is right when it tends to preserve the integrity, stability, and beauty of the biotic community. It is wrong when it tends otherwise." This is a carnivore redemption that any member of the Peterson Tribe would bless. Too many Biblical Seekers' hair would burst into flames. "Blasphemy! Paganism! God, not nature, determines what is right and wrong!" What these folks forget is that God told us that our shepherding of the earth is one of his ethical demands of us. When we fail at this charge, as Leopold wrote, "we have dustbowls, and rivers washing the future into the sea." We can't escape: hyenas are us.

Leopold's mathematical redemption is accurate, but not sufficient; for me, like Peterson's ideal bird portrait, it lacks something essential. Rabbi Slifkin, who, like me, is a member of the Biblical Seeker Tribe, struggled to redeem hyenas using God's words. He was horrified by a YouTube video of several Arab men near Hebron stoning one lone, wild hyena to death. If they had done this to a lion, Slifkin insisted, there would be international protest! Slifkin found inspiration in the *Perek Shirah*, an Ancient Jewish text in which all of creation, from stars to dogs, sings God's praises. In rabbinical literature, Slifkin came across this promise: even the hyena "has its hour." "To have its hour" is an unusual phrase, he said, found only in one other place "in all of Mishna, Talmud, and Midrash": "do not be scornful of anything, for there is no person who does not have his hour, and there is nothing that does not have its place."

I'll leave the last redemption to a member of the Thoreau Tribe: James L. Dickey's poem, "The Heaven of Animals." Dickey allows predators their essence: their hunger, their sharp claws, their need for speed, and he does his poet's best to grant them transcendence as well.

For some of these,
[Heaven] could not be the place
It is, without blood.

That we humans want to share heaven with animals, maybe even hyenas, is proof enough for me that we are not mere Darwinian meat puppets, but rather creatures of a loving creator God who is more than the agony of this world, but also its ecstasy.

Once I'd hiked above the voice of the hyenas haunting the hills above Berkeley, I would see deer, coyotes, foxes — both gray and red — and their dinner — lots of rabbits — and, once, a rattlesnake, its rattle rapidly menacing, its body perfectly still, and its quivering, forked, violet tongue darting. Red-tailed hawks were so common I didn't raise my head when their shadows draped over me. Turkey vultures flapped low if I lay down still. At dusk great horned owls, silent, winged torpedoes, prowled the skies. On top of Grizzly Peak, I would face west and pause and try to appreciate what my sweat had earned me: the rich man's view, the one at Mrs. Pattershall's elbow as she watched TV. Scrubby hills like a roller coaster hitting the flats, the poor part of town, the bay, the bridge, the ocean, San Francisco. I would open my arms wide. "I am ready. Do to me what you did to Kerouac and Tony Bennet. Make me love you." Always oddly unmoved by this panorama, I would begin the climb down rounded hills, all brown. A Californian attempted to correct me: "Our hills are not brown! They're gold." No, they're brown, brown, dead dry grass. There was green in the vertical gorges tracked by rain run-off, but when I bushwhacked, I found these green gullies were neither milk nor honey but poison oak.

I'd never gotten poison ivy, so I felt safe bushwhacking through a thicket of poison oak. I developed a small rash. The itch, especially when I was taking a hot shower, was one of the most intense sensations I'd ever had, as sharp as hunger or sex. When it reached a certain pitch that I couldn't resist any longer, I'd scratch, and a predictable relief would flood me with an orgasm that was not centered in my genitalia but that filled every cell with a sweet, urgent climax and a blissful denouement. I would moan and groan and throw back my head and immediately feel a chilly trickle of blood and puss and realize I had lumps of raw flesh under my fingernails. The sudden pain was scathing. I always felt so Biblically chastised at those moments.

I liked the feeling that climbing up 1,700 steep feet of trail gave me: what I felt as a kid. There is so much life; it is all alive, pulsing, moving all the time, urgent, needing, colorful, enough to feed me and challenge me forever, to sing and make anything, everything bearable. I experienced myself as merely a unique package of, expression for, an outline of resistance to the life all around me. My heartaches were mere plot twists, knots in a perpetual cord; personal oblivion and reincarnation made blissful sense. And then I would think, no, this can't be. I haven't felt this for so long. I thought life was over. I thought this warm pressure against me, this urge forward just from the passing rush of it, was a childhood fantasy, a cliché; don't we all know better? We don't. Life keeps happening.

But then I would have to go down, down South Park Drive — often closed to vehicular traffic because the ember-colored, orange-bellied newts had to cross the road to mate — down to Mrs. Pattershall's apartment. "Are you in for the night, dear? Could you please . . . "

Shanti Shanti Shanti: "the Peace which passeth understanding."

The hike gave me that. I soon found a startling peace someplace else, where I least expected it.

◆

Prof. Dundes had introduced me to an essay about a Hungarian peasant storyteller named Lajos Ami. Ami told of a place where the sky is so close to the ground that swallows, elsewhere carefree masters of air, must kneel. He told of a black place the sun's rays never penetrate. He told of a place so cold planes cannot fly. He told of air so thick no one can see through it; air so thick no human could cut through it to escape to a better world. He told of a tree, the Sky-High Tree, that tried, as its name foreordained, to reach the sky. The tree couldn't pierce the sky, though. It "curved thirteen times under the firmament because it should have grown more." But it could not. The so-called "Sky-High Tree" was forever bent, humbled, thwarted, mocked by its own name. Prof. Dundes explained, "Lajos Ami believes man's place is severely limited by time and place and class structure . . . one cannot break through boundaries."

All my life I had felt something was missing. I experienced terrible pain from that lack, though I had no idea what that missing thing was because I had never yet encountered it. I suffered phantom pain, not ever having known the limb that had been amputated.

There was a place I used to go to study at UCB — Stephens Lounge. I would sit there for hours, as others did, just reading and writing, in complete silence, except for the sounds of coffee percolating, Pepperidge Farm cookie bags opening, or coins clunking in the donation can. When overtaxed I'd simply drift off to sleep, and then wake up and rub my eyes, go to the ladies' room and splash cold water on my face, and then go back and start reading or writing again. One day in Stephen's Lounge I realized that the phantom pain I had experienced all my life was miraculously gone, the emptiness replaced by contentment. Suddenly I recognized what I had been yearning for: the disciplined life of the mind. Before this, yes, I had climbed to Everest Base Camp. I had made love on a beach with a good and gorgeous man. But it was only then, in Stephens Lounge, that I found and filled that need. My Sky-High Tree had stretched. I did it for myself and my peasant ancestors, and for those to whom I hoped to pass on the knowledge I was gaining.

But. Money.

One day Mrs. Pattershall was staring at my feet. I had no idea why. "Don't be ridiculous," she finally said.

"What?"

"Really, dear."

"What is it?"

"Your socks! Get some new ones."

I looked down at my feet. My socks were spider webs. I really hadn't noticed.

Mrs. Pattershall was covering food and housing, but I had to cover tuition. I had no sock money. I panicked.

But then, I began to see something I'd never noticed before. The streets are full of socks. Maybe someone died and everything but his socks decomposed. Maybe socks are especially resistant to the adhesive force of clothespins and spring off and wander on the wind to rest in the streets. Maybe someone had the bare-assed naked sex urge, right there. I don't know. All I know is that I began to see socks that had been invisible to me before, just sitting there, flattened by cars, balled up behind a bush, but essentially, sock like.

And I found the Free Clinic, a hold-out from the sixties, where righteous middle-class kids who want to get into medical school, but need something extra on their resume, volunteer to provide band-aids to street people. There was a "free box," where people dropped off odds and ends for the poor.

I was picking through the free box along with a black man who reeked so badly of sweat and alcohol I thought he should be incarcerated on aesthetic grounds alone, and a skinny blonde who kept repeating, "I'm gonna kill you, Janet," though there was no potential Janet present. The men wondered off and a patrician from the hills came in to drop a brown paper bag into the box. I dove on it. The men returned. "Guess I got here too late, huh?" the black guy said.

"Nope, there's plenty." I dumped the bag out so we'd all have access to its contents.

I couldn't contain myself. "Socks!" I screamed, rapturous, ready to testify. These socks had been worn once, or not at all; virgin white with high, piled fibers. I wondered what kind of person would wear socks once and then donate them to the Free Clinic. I grabbed a handful to my chest. The black man smiled. "Any more?"

"Plenty!" I gave him a big smile back. The blonde was too obsessed with thoughts of Janet to process what was happening. I unrolled a pair, jammed them into his palm. "Socks," I said, like Annie Sullivan to Helen Keller. "S O C K S."

"Oh, yeah, cool."

I was amazed by these socks, and I knew only the smelly man and Janet's potential assassin could share this amazement with me. It was a wonderful communal moment.

I began packing my socks away, quietly. The black guy and the blonde were picking out what they wanted, quietly. The weedy clinic volunteer approached me and said, in his best imitation of an authoritarian voice, "Only one pair of socks per person."

"When's the last time anybody's told you how many socks you're allowed to have?" I asked, as I was leaving with my more than one pair of socks.

Scavenging is assessed as a lowly profession. Another reason people hate hyenas. If I were a respectable lion, I would be killing and dragging home my own socks.

I had socks, but no idea how I'd pay the next year's tuition. One day in late spring, I had to report to an unknown administrator for a reason I've since forgotten. The woman saw my name on my form and said, "Ah, Alan's student. He must think a lot of you. We pulled strings we didn't know existed."

I didn't know what that meant, and since I didn't know what that meant, I was terrified. I reported to the graduate seminar, held in a tiny room with about seven other students. Prof. Dundes fixed me with a Bronte-esque scowl. "Danusha. Please step outside. We need to discuss something."

I practically pooped my pants right then and there. This was it. He was kicking me out. Deporting me. To Devil's Island. Because of that bad thing I did. That bad thing that everyone saw and judged me and made fun of me for doing. Behind my back. Without my realizing it. Probably the entire campus was laughing at me, condemning me, resolving never to name any child "Danusha." I braced myself and stepped into the hallway.

It was just the two of us. Mano a mano. Again, the scowl. But then something else. The glimmer of something around his lips. Play. Was this some kind of a joke?

"Danusha, I've found you full funding for next year." And then he smiled.

I can see him now, standing there, the entire sun on his face, radiating from his smile. And, for a nanosecond that I still, somehow, inhabit, a nanosecond in which I am still suspended as if in amber, I am about to throw my arms around his neck. But I check myself. Because he is the great professor. I simply clap my hands and twirl around. Do I regret not obeying that urge, that I still feel, to embrace Alan Dundes? I do not know, but I know that part of me is still in that moment, ready to throw my arms around the neck of a man who has just, for this moment, loved me as a father loves his child.

◆

I did it. I earned a Berkeley M.A. Berkeley didn't offer the PhD, so I had to go someplace else. I went to Indiana. My first semester in Bloomington, I was put to work for a professor. Antoinette, who had not spoken to me for years, phoned. She said, "Daddy's dying; don't come home. No one wants you here."

I loved my father, no matter the history. No matter the risk, I had to go. I told my new boss, a highly-placed professor. Through my working for her, my tuition was paid, and I also received a salary. My boss told me I could not leave because she was about to host a conference, and she needed me to type up the program. I left. My father died just as my train was pulling in to Penn Station. I attended the funeral. I stole moments of solitude in my childhood home to regain my equilibrium as best I could. During one such moment, one of my siblings' children, a child I had never met or spoken to, opened the door of my childhood bedroom, said, "I don't like you . . . you are weird," and left, whining to her mother. My aunt encouraged my mother to hit me, and my mother did, and everyone watched and did nothing. It was a traditional family gathering.

Actually, I always much preferred traditional family gatherings to day-to-day life at home. My mother was always a much nicer person around her siblings. That she gave them a different version of herself—a lighter, brighter, funnier, kinder, warmer version—fascinated me.

My mother was born in a poor, peasant country where she lived, blissfully, till she was eight years old. "I knew my mother didn't like me," she told me. I don't know if this is why, but she was born after my grandfather left sheep herding to dig American coal. The villagers insisted that my mother was the bastard child of the village priest, who was in love with my grandmother, the smartest woman in the village. Her grandmothers loved my mother, though. They told her she was the prettiest girl in the village, and she led village processions to religious shrines like Saint Anna's church, beyond the rye fields, on the rise of the hill abutting the mountains. I can see her ice-white beauty, the ribbons in her hair and the flowers in her hand. She's not wearing any underwear; she didn't even know what it was till she came to America.

The mines destroyed my grandfather's lungs. He had to quit work. My mother was deputized to leave home and work as a live-in domestic: nanny, cook, and servant for a wealthy New York family of Jewish jewelers. She hated leaving school. "*Kto bude krmit velku kravu?*" "Who's going to feed the big cow?" my grandmother asked her. She developed a stutter and gained weight. I can see such total despair in her final school photo.

My mother didn't just feed "the big cow," that is, herself. She fed her siblings, who were born in America. Her sisters didn't gain weight; they didn't develop stutters; they grew up to be great beauties. All her siblings would grasp the American Dream and enjoy economic comfort that my mother never could.

I don't know all the ins and outs here. My mother did take a risk by marrying my father, a known rapscallion. But I remember one story. One of my mother's siblings went to the Old Country. Our people there gave this person two full Slovak folk costumes. One was for the recipient; one was to be given to my mother for all her help to them over the years. We never saw that folk costume. My mother's sibling gave it to their own children. My mother heard this story later from the villagers. I heard it from her. Was it true? I don't know. I just know that my mother favored her siblings over me. Her siblings were much better off than we were, and the giving seemed to be a one-way street, what she gave them so they could grow up in relative security. Status bleeds through generations. My siblings had somehow communicated to their children, in the total void of my presence, that I was "weird" and not likeable — I needed to be informed of this by a child at my own father's funeral. Hyenas are us.

When I got back to Indiana, after missing four workdays, my boss began to harass me. After a month, I reported the harassment to a dean. This dean and another administrator pressured me to testify against my boss. They told me that my boss was "psychotic," that she "ruined people," that she "almost killed someone," but that no one would take action because everyone was afraid of being labeled "racist" or "sexist" for criticizing an African American female professor. They wanted me to be the one to testify against her because I had "nothing to lose." No scholarship. No pension. Not a member of any group with any organized support. I was the perfect whistleblower. If I didn't stop her, who would? They told me I'd be saving future potential victims. I couldn't say no.

I realize now what a sap I was. I should have just sued the bastards. That thought never entered my mind.

Throughout the spring semester, I walked into hushed, wood-paneled rooms with leather upholstery and expensive window treatments, rooms inhabited by complete strangers in suits and shiny shoes. I detailed ugly events in a manner that became more mechanical with each retelling. Then I left, having no idea what any of this was adding up to. My last such meeting was with Vice Chancellor for Academic Affairs and Dean of Faculties Deborah Freund. She asked me what I wanted the university to do to the professor. I said that I was a Christian and did not want revenge, and the professor was not the problem; she was plainly nuts. The problem was that the university put such a person in a position of power and kept her there long after she revealed exactly who she was.

I began to experience bizarre symptoms I could not describe. One day I could not walk down a hallway with freshly laid tile in a jarring black-and-white pattern. I had to report to a classroom halfway down that hallway, so I kept trying. Finally, I realized that if I closed my eyes and felt my way along the wall, I could walk down the hallway.

What I didn't realize at the time was that my inner ear had burst. The inner ear makes it possible for us to navigate three-dimensional space. Without my realizing it, that ability was gone. I had been using my eyes to compensate for lost vestibular function. The tiles' jarring black-and-white pattern overwhelmed my eyes, and my body shut down.

I would spend the next six years vexed by vomiting and often effectively paralyzed by crushing vertigo unlike anything I had ever experienced. The vertigo caused my eyes involuntarily to dart back and forth. This is called nystagmus. I could barely see, certainly not well enough to read. I could not work. I lost my life savings. I went door to door, begging for help. Most doors were slammed in my face. Indiana State Senator Vi Simpson's legislative aid, Rick Gudal, opened his door to me. I would later ask his coworkers why. They said he was Catholic, and his faith inspired him. This doesn't explain, of course, the many Catholics who didn't open their doors. I received three pro bono, experimental surgeries. Photos of my inner ear appear in a medical journal. The third operation, by Dr. Richard T. Miyamoto at Riley Hospital for Children, made me deaf in one ear but restored my ability to function.

I wrote *Bieganski*, the dissertation about Polish-Jewish relations I'd been planning to write. With every word I typed, I hoped to honor Arno's courage and compassion that had inspired me in that late-night phone call. And I wanted to produce a final product that was every bit as good as anything that Alan Dundes ever wrote. I did both. *Bieganski* hopped from publisher to publisher, from "We love it! It's unique and valuable! We can't wait to get it out there!" to "We're sorry to have to tell you this. This topic is *sensitive*. It is *controversial.*"

The job market for a middle-aged, formerly crippled, new PhD who wrote a controversial dissertation was comparable to the chase scene — actually the entire movie — of *Mad Max Fury Road*. I was one of the extras who got run over again and again.

I applied for hundreds of jobs. Here's one. It took me two hours, one-way, on a bus and a train to arrive at a world apart from Paterson — the campus of a prestigious university. I resigned myself happily to that commute. I planned on listening to classic novels on tape.

I was interviewed by X, a professor who was also a white, American-born, Zen master. He would shortly publish a book explaining how Christian "illusions" and Christianity's "despising" of the world had "destroyed" the Western mind and brought about environmental collapse. Christianity, he would argue, caused Westerners to be obsessed with the simplistic question of right and wrong, and the unhelpful concepts of "past," "present," and "future." There is no right. There is no wrong. There are just different points of view. We must accept that, with typical Buddhist compassion. Tenses should be reserved for verbs. We have only the present moment.

Reviewers, for better or worse, would identify this professor as a potential "messiah" who would prove that "we cannot save the world in the Christian sense" because "saving" implies that something is "wrong," and the illusion of right and wrong is imposed by Christianity. "The world" is not outside of us, but part of us — it's all one. With a paradigm shift informed by Buddhism, we just might "save" "the world" as long as we didn't call it "saving" "the world" and went through the trouble to put scare quotes around "save" and "the world." That makes sense if you don't ask any penetrating questions, or if you are high. Hey, it's all one.

I listened attentively to what Prof. X had to say (preach) during the lengthy job interview (monologue / harangue). He habitually lifted a Styrofoam cup of coffee by placing his entire hand in claw position over the entire mouth of the cup, as if to muffle it. I wanted to say, "I am so with you on your concern for the environment. You might want to consider bringing a ceramic mug to campus and reusing it. Styrofoam breaks down, under normal environmental conditions, only after five hundred years."

I did not say that. Interviewees are supposed to flatter and thank and be enthusiastic and obsequious, and I did and I was. My neck got sore from nodding, my back from leaning forward, my eyebrows from assuming the "I am fascinated" position. I asked Alan Dundes to send a letter of recommendation. He did. Prof. Dundes' over-the-top letter was the cherry on the sundae. I got the job.

Training consisted of Prof. X pontificating to a captive audience of new PhDs desperate for work and eager to please. I sat in the first row. I laughed appreciatively or grimaced sympathetically, where appropriate. I took notes; I asked pertinent questions.

Later we were told to create a freshman composition assignment comparing eating at McDonald's to genocide. Politely — I am a former Catholic schoolgirl — I asked, "What if students don't experience eating at McDonald's as comparable to genocide?"

Prof. X escorted me out of the building. We reached a veranda. "College campuses are liberal places. A right-wing person like you doesn't belong here," he said. "This job is like a marriage. I don't want to be married to you," he said.

Tears flooded my cheeks. I told him that it was a few days

before the beginning of the semester, that I had just completed graduate school and paid off thousands of dollars in student loans, and that I had no cash, that I needed money for groceries, for rent, that I was counting on my first paycheck at this job, that I had turned down other jobs for this job.

And — "right-wing"? I was "right-wing"? Me? My mother used to vote for Gus Hall, the Communist Party candidate for president. My Uncle John was a member of the Communist Party in Czechoslovakia, a real Communist country. I had marched, published, and broadcast for the environment and gay rights and against war and Republicans. I was right-wing?

Prof. X was unmoved.

Prof. Dundes gave me hell. "I warned you, Danusha. Keep your big mouth shut till you get tenure!"

I hustled. I found work as an adjunct professor. Adjunct professors work for less than minimum wage for hours worked, have no job security and no benefits. Adjuncts teach the most basic courses with the highest number of, and the neediest, students. I was sure it was just temporary. Eventually I'd get that full-time, tenure-track teaching job that would allow me to put my years of work and sacrifice to use. For that, I needed letters of recommendation. Not a problem. Several world-class scholars thought well of me. And I needed publications. Again, not a problem.

Alan Dundes was the first teacher I ever had who encouraged me to publish my writing. In fact, he may have been the first teacher I ever had who mentioned to me that I write well. The nuns in Catholic school used to rubber stamp crying angels to my papers. They would hang these on the classroom walls for parent-teacher night. They rubbed my nose in my disability, though they saw it as defiance and Satanic possession, and humiliated my parents in front of other parents. Dundes' compliment was typical, for him, in that it was accompanied by yelling.

"You should publish this," he said, about the first paper I wrote for him. "But first eliminate every place where you sound like a working class Polish girl from New Jersey."

When Prof. Dundes told me I should publish, I felt airborne. When he criticized the fingerprints of my identity in my writing, I felt the sting of a ripped-off bandage. So, I marched right down to a dean's office and filed a discrimination complaint. Actually, no, I did not. That's what too many in today's victim culture do.

Immigrants and dyslexics have this in common: what other people can see is invisible to us. We know this about ourselves, and so we live with a constant, low-level fear: am I, at this moment, without realizing it, doing something completely uncool, and are all the normal people laughing at me behind my back?

Dundes was right. More, he was brave, and he was caring. He educated me, and I think I educated him. I think through knowing me, he discovered that working class white ethnics are a "minority" on elite college campuses. He saw that if I tweaked a few things, I would do better. Too many teachers would be afraid to say what he said to me. The man had balls.

I geared up with my trusty diet cola, peanut M&Ms, headphones, and stopwatch. I went over the paper again and suddenly every sentence that signaled "working class" or "Bohunk" or "girl" was as if written in neon. I went over the paper as if with an X-ACTO knife and sliced out every trace of my identity. He had given me feedback on the granular level. He yelled at me to use more hyphens. He yelled at me to put the period after, not inside, a parenthetical citation. "Golem as Gentile, Golem as Sabra: An Analysis of the Manipulation of Stereotypes of Self and Other in Literary Treatments of a Legendary Jewish Figure" became my first academic publication. While trying to find a publisher for *Bieganski*, I continued to publish short pieces. With publications, letters, and good reviews on my adjunct teaching, I was confident I would eventually find a job.

In spring, I asked Prof. Dundes to say a prayer for my job search. He sent me an email on March 29, 2005, that began, "I am not religious enough to pray seriously." The rest of Prof. Dundes' email moved me deeply. It was elegiac in tone and much more vulnerable than he had ever been with me.

I felt honored that he shared deeply with me his ideas about God and the afterlife. I thought, wow, here is my chance to witness to him about my Christian beliefs. This would require preparation. Dundes had published an article using Freudian symbolism to prove that Jesus was nothing more than a phallic symbol. Funny thing, that was not his most controversial publication; that would be his piece arguing that football is homoerotic. He got death threats over that one. I knew from experience that Dundes would entertain any argument as long as it was backed up with research, so I hit the books. He and I had known each other for fourteen years at that point. Perhaps, after this email exchange, I would venture, for the first time, to address him by his first name, "Alan." I test drove it. "Dear Alan," began an email reply I composed in my head. I got butterflies. My palms and soles sweat. Maybe I wasn't yet ready.

The evening of April 2, 2005, I was eating leftover pizza, pondering my response to his email, and processing my grief over Pope John Paul II's death, when my friend "Nathan" phoned me to critique *The New York Times* obituary of Alan Dundes.

My mentor left this earth on March 30, the day after sending that email to me. He collapsed and died while teaching the graduate seminar he once taught me.

But I had other writers of letters of recommendation on whom I could rely for my job search.

Prof. Tim Wiles jumped off the top story of a parking garage in the center of town. I really lost it at the memorial service when a dean read a letter I had sent him testifying to Prof. Wiles' worth as a professor, a mentor, and a man. Prof. Wiles had prestigious publications, extensive community service, and a thirty-year teaching career. His wife, Mary McGann, would later say that his department chair, his boss, "made it a point to make Tim feel inadequate." Tim's successes "never seemed quite enough."

Every fall, before the job search began, I would go to the office of poet and professor Rachel Wetzsteon, give her envelopes with stamps on them, and beg her to address them and fill them with letters of recommendation for me and mail them out. Rachel had observed my teaching and praised me highly. Asking her for letters, I would feel like the Little Match Girl begging the revelers for crumbs from their feast, and Rachel would compliment me and my writing and my teaching, and make me feel as if I were every bit as worthy as she. She would smile her vast, warm smile, and I would wonder at her abundant hair.

One fall semester, Rachel was enjoying that golden apple enjoyed only by full-time faculty: a sabbatical. She got to take the semester off, and she would still have a job to return to! I contacted Rachel at home. And I begged. "I know this is your sabbatical, and I am so ashamed to ask . . . "

"Sure," she said. "I'll gladly serve as a reference for you."

"How are you, Rachel?" I asked, hesitantly. Who was I to ask an academic queen, a poetry star, how she was? But I asked. "How are you?"

"Going through a rough patch."

Rachel had been so kind to me. I wanted to be kind to her. I felt like the mouse in Aesop's fable. Can a mouse offer a lion . . . anything?

"What is it, Rachel? You can tell me."

"A bad breakup."

"Rachel!" I insisted. "You have been kind to me. Let me be kind to you. I can take the bus into the city, and you can cry on my shoulder." I can travel from Paterson, the city where adjunct professors live, to Manhattan, where tenured professors live, and comfort you. I can. "I can read your Tarot cards!"

"Maybe," she said. "But not today." And she again said she'd be sure to get the letters of recommendation out. And she did. And the letters were great.

Shortly thereafter, I attended a meeting on campus for adjunct professors. I was handed an agenda. Three quarters of the way down the colorful page — the paper was goldenrod-colored — I read, "The memorial service for Rachel Wetzsteon."

My conscious awareness immediately began to play hide-and-seek with the meaning of the words. "Memorial service." When

Danusha Goska

do people hold memorial services? For what reason? Well, when someone dies. Okay, but at what other times? Can't think of any. Maybe Rachel won another award for her poetry? No, that would be an "awards ceremony." What might "memorial service" mean in this context? It can't mean anything else but what it means.

She hadn't been sick. She was aggressively alive. Her springy-haired, vast-smiled aura wrestled the air in the room to the ground, and she became the name in lights, the main character of any space she occupied. It could have been an accident. It wasn't an accident. What did I do? Why didn't I save her? I knew she was sad. I did not do enough.

I began to cry with much more volume and intensity than I knew was appropriate. People looked at me. They could not understand the intensity of my emotion. I could not understand their coldness.

The New York Times reported that, single at forty-two, Rachel was depressed over the breakup of a relationship. She had gassed herself on Christmas Eve.

I volunteered to speak at the memorial. My offer was declined. Tenured professors spoke. One eulogist actually said, "This is such a tragedy, such a waste. The committee voted unanimously to grant her tenure."

After all the full-time professors were done, and people were beginning to rustle their programs and look at the clock and wring squeaks from chairs by repositioning their butt cheeks, Rachel's students were allowed to speak.

"You thought you were finished," one wet-faced student said. "I disagree."

Another, fumbling, shy, young, "I wanted to be like you when I grow up. Now I can't."

The students' frank pain; their unavoidable exuberance, even at a wake; their embrace and their celebration of the campus as a place where they could color outside lines and re-imagine life and meet others doing the same — they made the memorial service.

The professors' obsession with curriculum vitae bullet points as that which makes a life worth living made me squirm. The love

I felt for the students and the alienation I felt from the professors said much about why I hadn't yet gotten a full-time college teaching job, and why I kept trying.

Prof. Dundes, Wiles, and Wetzsteon — I added the names to my daily rosary. I pray the Sorrowful Mysteries on Tuesdays and Fridays. The fifth sorrowful mystery commemorates Mary witnessing the dead body of her son, Jesus, on the cross. We Catholics pray for "The Great Gift of Final Perseverance" — *magnum usque in finem perseverantiae donum* — the gift of sticking it out to the bitter end. When I pray this mystery, I pray for Prof. Wiles, I pray for Rachel.

In addition to changing my prayer life, these deaths caused me to think three thoughts I blushed to think.

My first taboo thought: Suicide? Really? Suicide made all too much sense for us lowly adjuncts. On the campus where I was now an adjunct, one of my fellow adjuncts killed himself. The department secretary who sent out the mass email death notice added this postscript: "Prof. 'Smith' handed in all his end-of-semester grades before the registrar's deadline and before taking his own life." I admired him for that so much. One last time he demonstrated how hardworking and reliable he was, no prima donna, not like the tenured profs, too many of whom do work if they feel like it, when they feel like it.

Wiles and Rachel? These were *successful* academics. Prof. Wiles was the director of the Polish Studies Center. Rachel was the poetry editor of *The New Republic*. She'd been published by *The New Yorker!* Tim Wiles was married to a lovely woman who felt "lacerated and tortured" by his choice. "I keep seeing him fall, in that space between the garage and the row of houses," she would write. Rachel left a loving mother, Sonja.

Yes, yes, yes. The old "Richard Cory" story. In Edwin Arlington Robinson's poem, Richard Cory is "clean favored," "imperially slim," and "richer than a king." Everyone in town wishes that he were Richard Cory. "One calm summer night," Cory "went home and put a bullet through his head." Yeah.

Give me a break. Sadness? I'll see your sadness and raise you my own. Imagine feeling Richard Cory's sadness, and on top of that, existential sadness, having just sacrificed years of your life to rise above every setback and earn that PhD and then discovering that you will never be able to get a full-time job that offers health insurance and retirement. Imagine how much regret, shame, humiliation, and terror you can pack into any given hour of any given day. Then talk to me about sadness. We adjuncts joke among ourselves that "Suicide is our retirement plan."

Do you think I'm revealing my lack of compassion? No, I'm exposing the boundaries of my comprehension. Do you think it's petty to say you can't kill yourself if you've been published by *The New Yorker*, but it's okay to kill yourself if you are a struggling adjunct? I bet you feel the same way. If a fifty-something bachelor received a terminal diagnosis and killed himself, I bet you'd feel differently about that than if a single mom in her twenties with three young children killed herself. And I bet that God has a similar checklist he refers to when he assesses sins.

My second thought that I knew I should not think: who will write letters of recommendation for me now? Those letters of recommendation that are vital to a successful job search? Alan Dundes believed in my mind. Tim Wiles believed in my work on Polish-Jewish relations. Rachel Wetzsteon believed in me as a teacher and as a writer. Rabbi Laurence Skopitz, a healthy, happy man in his fifties, had been more of a spiritual guide to me than any priest, more of a "girlfriend" to me than any woman, and more of a support to my work on Polish-Jewish relations than any Polish Catholic. He died of a rare illness whose name I never could bring myself to learn. There was no one who could replace any of them.

The third taboo thought: I began to wonder if whatever was wrong with my life were not contagious, or if some vigilante deity were not stalking and slaying anyone who might see my worth and step forward to help me.

I networked. At a conference, I met an Ivy League scholar and former member of the SDS, or Students for a Democratic Society.

He was one degree of separation away from a MacArthur Genius Grant winner. He gave me one of his books for free and told me he'd like to see my work. He was sympathetic, he said, to the plight of a working-class girl like me in the Ivory Tower. Comrade!

During our lengthy back and forth, that began in person and continued through email, he first insisted that my writing about Polish Americans was a dumb thing to do because Polish Americans don't really exist anymore as a distinctive ethnic group. They had all assimilated. Then he went on to say that Polish Americans do exist, but they are all comfortably ensconced in the white middle class. There was no longer any prejudice against Poles. No more "dumb Polak" jokes. Toward the end of our conversation, he said that Polish Americans were pathetic, self-deluded racists, and anti-Semites. Like all those other formerly blue-collar white ethnic scum, the Poles, Irish, Italians, and Greeks, and all those white trash in the South, who betray their own best interests, expose their gross ingratitude to the vanguard that had fraternally invited them to the Revolution, and vote Republican.

How many times was I told "You are the wrong ethnicity," or "We need to hire an Asian." How many times was I asked in phone interviews, "What color are you? Your first name sounds black." Enough time went by that people did start saying, "You are too old."

"I am sorry to have to tell you that you were not chosen to go forward to the next stage of the selection process. There were a large number of superb candidates that we were unable to include on the interview list. Many factors that had nothing to do with the intellectual quality of your dossier contributed to our decisions. Those of us who do have full-time college teaching positions are acutely aware of the difficulties faced by adjunct professors and of the cruel realities of the very competitive academic job market."

"You were not selected . . . "

"We wish you the best of luck . . . "

"Another candidate was chosen . . . "

Day after day.

Week after week.

Envelope after envelope.

Email after email.

Year after year.

Don't talk to me about dreams deferred. I could school Langston Hughes.

Next year I will be able to buy a car, and go places, and meet people, and make friends . . .

Next year I will be able to afford to go to the dentist . . .

Next year I'll be able to afford health insurance, and I can finally get this lump checked out . . .

Next year . . .

That never comes.

If I were doing it wrong, I could, in true working class, Bohunk fashion, roll up my sleeves, apply my nose to that grindstone, and improve. And then enjoy the rewards that come from being a good teacher, a good writer, an okay person.

It hurt to read my students' end-of-semester feedback:

"I will never forget how our class was able to speak about issues I am not able to speak about with my family or my friends. We achieved a close bond that I have never before felt. This class has given me the power to believe that no matter what, I can make something of myself. Prof. Goska, I would like to thank you for opening my eyes to the potential within myself I didn't know existed."

"The professor was incredible! She is honest, sincere, and not afraid."

"Dr. Goska fosters a feeling of respect and dignity. Discussions get intense, but never heated."

"She is very caring. I feel very comfortable talking to her. She encourages students to do well. It is very clear that she cares about all her students! Excellent professor!"

"Prof. is very knowledgeable and keeps class interesting with cliff hangers."

"This class, quite honestly, is amazing. Every day I am challenged and forced to rethink my ideals and whether they fit in with my morals. I've never gotten so much out of a class before."

"This is by far the best class I had in college. I look forward to coming, and that is a testament to you and how you teach."

"I don't think there was ever a boring day. You did a wonderful job and couldn't have helped me anymore than you already have."

Not every student offered such positive evaluations. Just enough to break my heart. That year, as an adjunct, I made $6,119. I was told days before the semester began what classes I would be teaching. I would be chewing dinner: rice and beans, pasta and beans, or potatoes and beans. I would hit something hard and realize it was part of a tooth.

My mother always used to call her mother "Mama." She would repeat her words of wisdom. "Mama used to say . . . " My peasant grandmother, my mother told me, valued knowledge and envied those with formal educations. "Mama used to say, 'When you carry it on your back, it is heavy. When you carry it in your head, it is light.'"

Grandma, sometimes the things you carry in your head are very, very heavy.

I began to lose hope. I began to plan my exit. As a Catholic, I knew suicide was a sin. I needed to book some serious facetime with God.

I decided on a retreat. I asked about potential venues on an electronic discussion site. A helpful guide posted the following:

I think Holy Cross in Berryville, Virginia, would suit your needs. It is a Trappist monastery. The guesthouse holds fifteen in single rooms. Silence reigns and a monk reads during meals. The retreat is completely self-directed. The only thing they ask is that you come to meals on time or tell them in advance that you aren't going to eat. One is invited to the Divine Office, beginning with Vigils at 3:30 A.M. and ending with Compline at 7:30 P.M. There are acres of walking through the fields to the Shenandoah River.

I emailed Holy Cross Abbey. I asked if I could come even though I didn't have money. I provided tax forms. I also mentioned that my mother used to clean the church to put her six kids through Catholic school, and volunteer at the carnival, and count collection donations, and that she gave so much that there is a plaque naming our family, and a plaque in the church in her natal village in Slovakia, as well. I, too, have donated labor to the church. I said that I would be happy to offer an eight-hour day every day I was there, cleaning, cooking, landscaping, tending animals, or whatever else they would have me do.

They said I could come.

CHAPTER THREE

WASHINGTON, DC

Nathan, my best friend from UC Berkeley, was living in Washington, DC. I could bus from Paterson to New York City and then take a low-cost Chinatown bus from Manhattan to Washington. Chinatown buses occasionally burst into flames, spin out of control, or have their tops sheared off by overpasses, but you cannot beat their prices. Or so I thought. I actually found a cheaper Greyhound ticket. I paid twenty dollars for the two-hundred-and-twenty-six-mile trip. There were no buses from DC to Berryville. I would have to hitchhike that leg — about sixty-five miles.

I had to go when the monastery had an opening and when Nathan would be able to put me up for the nights before and after my retreat. Between these two considerations, my retreat had to occur between June 13th and June 17th. A sudden, little voice message, utterly from left field: Would Bruno be there? Bruno from Eastern Europe and from Africa? No, he would not, but someone there would somehow remind me of Bruno.

I made two lists: things to pack and things to do. To do

before leaving: return or renew library materials, put mail on hold, move items likely to spoil from fridge to freezer, eat up food that does not freeze well, close windows and pull shades down halfway. Pray to St. Joseph to protect the apartment while I'll be away.

Items to pack: one pair of undies in addition to pair being worn, ditto socks, a denim dress and a pair of shorts, a bra, a chunk of ginger for motion sickness, a handful of peppermint and fruit-flavored Life Savers, the stack of brand new Christian books that Bruderhof had given me as payment for speaking for them — I'd donate these books to the monastery — a raincoat, DEET, fanny pack, binoculars, field guide, Ibuprofen, Vaseline, toothbrush, fingernail file, rosary, wallet, pens and blank paper to write on, Walkman, maps.

I designed wrapping paper for the gifts I'd be bringing Nathan. I selected that fabulous passage from Thoreau's *Walden*.

> This is a delicious evening, when the whole body is one sense, and imbibes delight through every pore. I go and come with a strange liberty in Nature, a part of herself. As I walk along the stony shore of the pond in my shirt-sleeves, though it is cool as well as cloudy and windy, and I see nothing special to attract me, all the elements are unusually congenial to me. The bullfrogs trump to usher in the night, and the note of the whip-poor-will is borne on the rippling wind from over the water.

I cut and pasted that passage multiple times into a Word document so that it covered the entire page. Then, to each repetition of the paragraph, I applied a different, attractive font: Gothic, art deco, handwriting, stencil, etc. To me the finished page looked very pretty and showed the care I feel for Nathan. He is a Thoreau fan.

My backpack was heavy because of all the books I was bringing as donations. The Columbia Sportswear Company backpack I was using was badly designed. It was the only daypack with a waistband that I could find at Campmor, an outdoor gear hub in Paramus, so I bought it, to my regret.

The bus smelled of cinnamon Christmas-tree-shaped air freshener and the fumes from the onboard restroom. I played the alphabet game with myself, finding sights along the highway that began with each letter of the alphabet, in turn. People who can read on public transportation are so alien I can't even envy them. It would feel like envying jellyfish for being transparent.

♦

Antoinette could read on a bus. She could read big fat paperbacks, cover to cover, as if the world around her were merely the accoutrements of her private castle. I do envy her her smarts. With my ADHD I read one paragraph, and my focus, like a hot air balloon, just floats away. She knew that about me. She would see it on my face and try to pull me back into consensus reality.

My sister Antoinette and I are like the Corsican brothers. I am a spiritual conjoined twin; we share a storehouse of memories bound with infinite, invisible, unbreakable cord. We speak our own language that belongs to us alone. Older than I, she left home first. In those first wrenching months of sleeping alone in bed, I would think something specific on a given date at a given time; then I would receive a letter from her, and there it would be: she and I had been thinking the same thing on the same day. This happened so many times we stopped telling stories about it. Nothing can change this: for years, Antoinette and I slept in the same bed, prayed at the same Mass, bathed, together, in the same tub with our brother Greg, and loved the same dogs: Tramp, Artie, and Benjie. She wore clothing and passed it down to me. She read books — *Gone with the Wind, Little Women, The Story of the Trapp Family Singers, The Stranger* by Albert Camus — and then I read them. We watched dozens of movies together.

The autumn sun set on us as we, like cedar waxwings, birds that bond through sharing fruit, worked over the apple trees at

Skylands Botanical Garden. The autumn twilight enveloped us as we ferried apples home in paper sacks, washed them, and dug out their worms. Under our Slovak mother's tutelage, over a white cotton tablecloth abloom with blowsy red roses and green leaves, we used the backs of our hands to pull at strudel dough from its underside till it was so thin we could see our knuckles. "Stretch it till you can read a newspaper through it," our mother, a passionate reader, adjured us. (To really satisfy our mother, I think, we would have had to read that newspaper, out loud, in Hungarian.) Together Antoinette and I smelled our apple strudel enchant an autumn kitchen.

Antoinette never became a birdwatcher, but I did, sitting in her car as she drove. She was driving us back along Country Road 511, which skirts the Wanaque Reservoir, a site so scenic that to describe it we refer to a location outside of New Jersey: the English Lake District. We were coming back from Skylands; we rounded a bend; up in the sky, holy cow. I saw something I had never before seen. Dozens of dark, massive creatures hung low overhead like scraps of flapping Jurassic laundry. Antoinette didn't seem to see them. I could not take my eyes off them. Before I could focus on anything else in my life, I had to find out what they were. I did. They were turkey vultures, and I've been a birdwatcher ever since.

I was fourteen, too young to drive. Antoinette drove me to Great Swamp, someplace she would probably would never have gone if she hadn't had a little sister who was a birdwatcher. She was proud when Phil DelVecchio, who wrote the "Nature and Science" column for the *Paterson Evening News*, mentioned my sighting of a rarity, a Lawrence's warbler, on the banks of the Wanaque River. I can remember the excitement in her voice when she read his column aloud. Antoinette and I hiked together. A lot.

"That's far. That's *way* far. You cannot walk there from here." Antoinette and I say that to each other, and we know exactly what it means. We warm, and we laugh, and a spark leaps between us, and in spite of everything, we are connected.

Antoinette and I walk out into the world, not sure where

we are going, not sure how we will get back. We rely on asking directions and following the spoor of our own ballsy drive. Years ago, in Stokes State Forest, we were walking through woods and night was falling. We asked someone, "How do you get to such and such by foot?" And the person looked at us as if we were peasants in Transylvania asking directions to the count's castle at sunset. "That's far. That's way far. You cannot walk there from here," the person insisted, with a rising sense of alarm. We had to, first, convince this couch potato that we damn well could walk that far, and then we had to get directions before making our way. We did. And we did. And we did.

◆

A fit, young, and well-dressed white guy on the Greyhound bus insisted that it was humanly impossible to walk from Union Station, where the bus would get in, to Nathan's apartment.

"That's far. It's just too far. You can't walk from the bus station to DuPont Circle," he insisted, as if reporting a medical fact. The human body is just not designed to cover that distance, any more than it is designed to fly or to digest lumber.

"How many miles do you think it is?" I asked.

"It's gotta be at least ten miles!" he insisted.

It's two and a half miles. Does anyone under age forty walk anywhere, anymore, ever? Are they still capable of walking?

A soft-spoken, conservatively dressed black lady overheard our conversation. "I'll make you a map," she offered. She sketched a route for me to walk and promised to direct me once we got to the station. She did.

I walked past a lot of trashed housing projects. Over their sagging, ramshackle roofs gleamed the marble tops of architectural celebrities: the Capital dome, the Washington Monument. From the perspective of the neighborhood I was walking through, these sights looked like a Potemkin Village. Once I got to wealthy-looking areas of downtown — glass, steel, skyscrapers — I was amazed by the numerous black men sleeping, begging, or just sitting passively on benches. I wondered when America will become the America we want America to be.

Nathan lives in DC's DuPont Circle neighborhood. Oddly enough, I am from a DuPont neighborhood. In January 1917, a DuPont gunpowder plant exploded in what would become Wanaque, New Jersey, my hometown. The earthquake-like explosion was felt in four states. As a child, I clambered over and played hide-and-go-seek amidst the forested ruins of this cataclysm. I always knew that there was something a little bit spooky, a little bit mythic about my small hometown, surrounded by holy woods studded with geographic hotspots we kids christened with names like the Devil's Cave, the Back Beach, the Tree that Couldn't Make Up Its Mind, the Logs, the Quarry, and the Old Man's Living Room. Believers claim that the 1917 explosion created the Wanaque Vortex, a portal between dimensions. Other believers say, no, the 1917 DuPont explosion was merely a manifestation of the pre-existing Wanaque Vortex. One internet user, posting under the screen name "xzoomorphicx," claims he encountered "demonic entities, angels, numerous orbs of various colors and sizes, and one Sumerian demi-god" at the Wanaque Vortex. I'm not sure if he was kidding, serious, or reviewing *Ghostbusters*. Talk of the Wanaque Vortex is a fun distraction from the quantifiable legacy of DuPont in my hometown: cancer. DuPont left the state significantly contaminated soils. Several members of my immediate family have had cancer.

Nathan's neighborhood, the DuPont Circle neighborhood of Washington, DC, has nothing in common with the post-industrial landscapes I inhabit in New Jersey. It is overrun with art, restaurants, and fine bookstores, along with meticulously restored Victorian homes and over-spilling herb gardens. It is a neighborhood that productive, blessed, healthy young people plan to go to and wish to live in. The human is rewarded just for existing in Nathan's neighborhood.

A rainbow flag was run through the uprights of the wrought iron fence around an outdoor café. A short and average-looking man walked up and down the block, perhaps attempting to polish his visual appeal by brandishing a couple of whippets on leashes. The whippets stepped hangdog, like the neglected children of a socialite mother.

DuPont Circlers marched past me. They were male and female, all young, all purposeful, all displaying their casually fit bodies in baggy khaki shorts and plum-colored tank tops. They were all carrying a rolled-up *Washington Post*, walking a pedigreed dog, talking into a cell phone, or guiding graphite bicycles by one hand placed with casual authority on the seat.

I found the uniforms dispiriting. With such evident cash and youth and luck, did everyone really have to be wearing the same clothes? The steely gazes. I wanted them to be giddy with joy that they get to live where they get to live. The coldness. In near collisions, I smile at passersby. I caught no smiles here. The grimness in the many outdoor cafés. No hilarity erupted. They were perfectly nice, of course. Eventually I'd be stopping some and asking for directions, and they would be perfectly nice. A bit like Naval cadets, but, hey.

I had been thinking, if I take a few days to escape from Paterson, maybe that will lift my spirits. Uh, uh. It hurt me to walk DuPont Circle, to be so forcefully reminded of what I can't have, of what no work I could possibly produce would allow me — not now, not ever. One thing I wish I could have: I wish I could walk, every day, sidewalks not strewn with garbage. Like those garbage-strewn sidewalks of Paterson. I look at that garbage and think of the Passaic River washing it all down to the Atlantic Ocean, a mere thirty-five miles away. I wrestle with despair. These clean sidewalks of Dupont Circle would allow me to avoid that hourly confrontation. Tiny, very sharp needles of punishment penetrated my flesh. Going from being a misanthrope in Paterson to being a misanthrope in DuPont Circle emphasized for me what a thorough misanthrope I am.

When Nathan and I lived in Berkeley, we lived a street apart. After I left Mrs. Pattershall's, I had that sunny, elfin teacup that opened onto a wooden deck that hosted raccoons and parties. My large windows on two sides looked out on a lush green yard with its own productive apple tree. So close to the bay, fog enveloped the property on cool mornings, but bees buzzed once the sun broke through; I could have been on an English ancestral estate. Nathan's place was bigger. Unlike me he had an oven and a bathtub and room for all those books, but his apartment was on the ground floor. Its only, east-facing, windows were across from a very close aluminum-sided shed and an outdoor, frequently used, metal staircase. Nathan's apartment felt like being under house arrest in a Soviet backwater on the best weather days. Anyone who lived there too long could be excused for concluding that the sun sheds gray light. As grad students, Nathan and I shared the same streets, cafés, bookstores, and demonstrations. He was treated better by the old Chinese woman who worked the by-the-pound electronic scale at the Berkeley Bowl produce market; that felt like the only caste difference between us.

One of my friends once said to me, "Nathan's not what you'd call triple-A gay."

"Why?" I asked, knowing she was wrong, but curious as to her reasoning.

"You," she said. "The two of you. I've seen you two together."

Nathan and I were friends. One night after I had gone to bed, and indeed after I had gone to sleep, Nathan entered my apartment and sat on the mattress on the floor on which I slept. He unburdened his heart about an unhappy relationship. I woke up a little bit but not entirely. I advised him as best I could. He said that my advice was "better than any of my fellow graduate students in the English department."

We were different, but it was okay. Plenty of gay men or Jews have made so many nasty comments to me about my faith that interacting with them is like being spun around in a thorn bush. Not Nathan. He has never made one single Christophobic or anti-Catholic crack to me, and he totally gets my work on fighting stereotyping of Poles. In fact, one Christmas Eve he invited me over. I expected popcorn, if that. He had made an elaborate dinner for us. I remember the baby corncobs and almond slices in the spinach salad. I was so touched that he honored my holiday. Of course, he is so secular that when we went to see the 1991 film *The Quarrel*, I had to explain to Nathan why it was a big deal that one of the Jewish characters had bacon for breakfast on Yom Kippur.

At first, after he finished his PhD, Nathan, like me, applied for many jobs and faced the mounting terror of repeated rejections. Like me, he chafed against the politically correct Thought Police in the Ivory Tower. Like me, he risked drowning in a market flooded with new PhDs chasing too few jobs. But no one was going to accuse a gay scholar with a Yale BA and two advanced degrees of being too right-wing. Nathan, after years of effort, landed a job. By the looks of his neighborhood, it was a highly remunerative job. Walking the streets of DuPont Circle, all I could think was: how can Nathan and I connect? Can we?

Even at our best in Berkeley, even after the night we slept together, there was always some tension. We didn't sleep together for sex. I had phoned New Jersey just to see how my parents were doing. I had not seen them in years. And my mom punched me in the gut, as I knew she would. I went to Nathan's and knocked on the door. It was night. He had already gone to bed. He answered the door bare-chested — whoa, Nathan had been working out! I tried to act "normal." I asked, "Can I borrow some sugar?" and in spite of myself, I burst into tears. Nathan, wordlessly, without a heartbeat's hesitation, wrapped his arms around me. I cried so much he bundled me up and put me to bed and hugged me all night long. I was very confused by his erection and impressed by its size and duration, but neither one of us made mention, or use, of it.

But Nathan was a gated community. After intimacy, he would pull back. I was okay with that; I do the same. After any extended time spent with humans, I was always ready to spring for a daylong solo hike in the Berkeley Hills.

I remembered a poem I had written about Nathan in Berkeley.

Sometimes a cigar is just a cigar; sometimes a penis is actually a metaphor for a cigar. In this poem I used sex as a metaphor. I loved living in Berkeley. I had a lot of friends. We were thrown-away people: gay men, formerly abused kids, book-readers, movie-lovers, and artists who created and exhibited their art only in their own rooms. We were from small towns where such folk are nothing but weird. We became family to each other. But were those bonds real? I remember Berkeley emptying out around the holidays, as even social lepers migrated back to their ancestral spawning grounds. I always felt as if everybody had a somebody somewhere on Thanksgiving and Christmas except for me and Nathan. I wanted to feel that Nathan and I really did belong to each other, that we could have expectations of each other, that we weren't just playing games. Sex was my metaphor for that leap into commitment.

Ground Rules

Knowing you,
but not too well.
Receiving,
but not expecting you.
I perforate that you may bounce
off of me,
or come in,
or be stored for,
the moment when you're ready.

I like to think I read your face
and I've obeyed
the green for stay
the red for fade.
Sometimes this is hard for me;
I hold my breath.

When you move me,

I am amazed.
I left my home long ago
left familial swamps, hills;
never thought to hear them here, or smell them.
But then I am exposed;
I lack legal tender.
I must drain my juice
pump it to
the heart ordained to love you.
This is nothing new for me.

I envy those who have "love"
in their vocabulary.
They get respect.
People assume ritual, whole webs of meaning.

I want to feed you, mark you, make you groan
ram my tongue in your mouth
knead your face till I view
the exact appreciation
I desire.
I want, just once, to have more power
than your red-light, green-light face.

I can't pretend to meaning here;
there's no transcendent ritual.

I was raised by wolves, you know.
I hear some distant howling now.
I've gotta go —
cause this is just too hard for me.

I reached Nathan's DuPont Circle address. A plaque on his
apartment building brags that it was built in 1901. Ha, ha, ha, I
thought. My Paterson silk mill was built in 1817. Nathan and I had

planned to meet at eight, and it was eight, but Nathan wasn't there. If he were cold to me, I'd be really wounded, and I wasn't in the mood to be really wounded. I decided that the best approach would be to be guarded and distant. I was girding myself for contact with Nathan in the same way that I was girding myself for contact with God. I was sitting with my arms wrapped around my stomach.

Nathan, whom I had not seen in eight years, was walking up the steps. His hairline seemed to be where it was the last time I saw him. This impressed me, as he was always griping about losing hair and trying various schemes so as not to, including Chinese herbs, which he complained about in detail to me. He complained as if I would care. His details were very precise. I did care, not about the herbs, but about why on earth this person would report to me such details about whether or not Chinese herbs can prevent baldness in men. Like I'd ever go buy Chinese herbs for *anything*? Not. Like I'd ever need to know about what prevents baldness in men? Ah, the sweet mystery of life.

He looked thin. In Berkeley he used to work out — I encouraged him to do so — and he had had good musculature. I could see now that his cheeks were hollowing. His baby fat was gone. I didn't see the sweet and warm "little boy" Nathan I used to see in Berkeley.

"I'm coming to DC," I had told him. "I'm gonna sleep at your place and pee in your toilet and eat leftovers from your fridge. The laws of friendship entitle me to no less."

He had confessed: his apartment was not in presentable shape, and he was afraid that I'd "say something."

"Grow up!" I had said. "If you are going to associate with me, you are associating with someone who is going to say something!"

"Hi," I said.

"Hi," he said.

And that was it.

I followed him in. He grabbed his mail, went over it, throwing much of it into the trash. I could never go through my mail if a friend I hadn't seen in eight years was standing right next to me with a crushingly heavy backpack tied to her back. We made safe small talk. Safe small talk! As if we were WASPs on the verge of divorce.

In Nathan's apartment, there was barely a trail from room to room. Boxes of books were stacked everywhere. The sink was full of dirty dishes. There were Q-tips in the toilet! A brown stain in the bathtub. He said there was no food in the fridge. He rapidly opened the presents, not commenting on the wrapping paper.

I know I just claimed that I always get the perfect gift, and now I report that Nathan took no note of the gifts I brought him. But he used to like the gifts I gave him in Berkeley. Time had moved on. Both of us had finally left school and moved to cities that have winter.

Then Nathan left. He said he had to attend a dinner.

I stood in his apartment, alone, wondering why we were friends. I looked up, and there on his bookshelf was *Dating for Dummies*, and I thought of that time in Berkeley when he had invited me over after he was mugged. Nathan had refused to comply with the mugger's demands, who then beat Nathan with his pistol. Nathan stained the sidewalk with his blood. Nathan invited me over because he needed someone to look after him. He would eventually pay me one of the best compliments I'd ever receive: "I know how much you love me."

I tried to figure out how to navigate his Collyer-Brothers style apartment. Letters from nationally recognizable financial names lay on almost every flat surface. I wasn't peeking. They were so obvious they were all but peeking at me. I have asked Nathan for financial advice. What should I do, Nathan, what can I do? He always says he doesn't know, so I don't ask any more. If Nathan has so many investments, why can't he advise me? The same is true for Antoinette. She has none of my cognitive impairments. I have yet to figure out how to balance a checkbook; I go to the post office monthly to buy money orders for my rent. Antoinette invests in the stock market. She brags that she makes money. She never has a word of advice.

I found a three-foot by six-foot space under a spiffy glass table and rolled out the blanket Nathan had given me. The sheet, though, of course machine-washed, smelled of Nathan. If someone had handed me that sheet, out of context, in New Jersey, I would have sniffed it once and diagnosed, "Nathan." Funny how people can be distant but Mother Nature leaves her calling cards.

CHAPTER FOUR

Berryville, VA, Monastery

Monday morning I joined beltway commuters jolted to life for their start-of-the-workweek race. I walked across a bridge over the Potomac River into Rosslyn, Virginia. I unfurled my sign: a sliced and flattened brown paper bag reading, "Berryville, VA, Monastery." Behind me was a hedge, in front of me was a busy highway, and just beyond that a Northrop Grumman building. It's the world's fifth-largest defense contractor.

I checked out the sky overhead and said to myself, "That is a peregrine falcon." I'd never before seen a peregrine falcon. Peterson's field guides include black-and-white silhouettes of birds in flight, silhouettes I have committed to memory. Colors are nice but a real birdwatcher doesn't need them. We learn the shoulder slump-slouch of a bluebird versus the upright perching posture of a phoebe, the V-shape of a soaring vulture versus the flat-winged soar of an eagle. The bird I saw looked like the model for a Peterson silhouette of a falcon. I noted the slate-gray wings, angled at the wrist, with swept back tips and long tail. It was larger than the more common falcon species I have seen — kestrel and merlin. Then it was gone. I kept craning my neck, scouring the sky. I never did see it again. At two-hundred miles an hour, they are the world's fastest animals.

Since I never caught sight of it again, I cannot include it on my life list. That's how birding works — it's an honor system. I once saw a swallow-tailed kite fly over the brown and churning Wanaque River after a big summer storm. I saw its every feature: its four-foot wingspan, white and black-edged, pointed and slender as a ballerina's arms, its snow-white breast, and the inky black, deeply cleft tail that it switches and twists to and fro to navigate as it sifts flying insects out of bruise-blue humid skies. As it flew north to south and out of sight, I stood there open-mouthed. Swallow-tailed kites live only in a few southern states. Because I knew this, I feared that the storm had bewitched me. This was too exotic a bird for New Jersey. It should be brushing past Spanish moss and casting its shadow on alligators. I didn't believe it, so I couldn't see it. I didn't include it on my life list. I need to make IDs in a methodical, rational manner.

The ideal bird ID works like this: I've just lowered my binoculars, through which I calmly noted every pertinent feature of a bird. I suspect it is a species whose salient features I have memorized in advance, not consciously, but through compulsive paging through bird books as if they were drawers full of candy. I pull out my Peterson, stuffed somewhere easily reached in my daypack. I go to the page for the species I think I have just seen. I methodically run down the checklist of color, shape, behavior, size, location, season, plumage, and vocalization. When I identify a new bird, I have discovered something. I have concluded something using evidence. When I was a kid, I wanted to be a spy. I get to be a spy in this. Birds are the world's ornaments as well as its essence. Every time I know a new bird, its behavior, migration patterns, needs, and gifts, I know a new patch of earth, and my habitation of this planet expands. I'm pretty sure I saw a swallow-tailed kite after that big storm; birds do move with storm systems. And that may well have been a peregrine over the Potomac. But in neither case was I able to go through the process that rewards me, so neither sighting resulted in a check on my life list.

When I was a fledgling birdwatcher, pesticides like DDT had all but wiped out peregrines east of the Mississippi. If I had sighted a peregrine over a US city in the 1970s, it would surely have been a hallucination spawned by wishful thinking. Rachel Carson roused the public with her 1962 book, *Silent Spring*. Chemical companies, including DuPont, attacked Carson relentlessly. Because she was not married, her accusers said she was "probably a Communist." A chemist with American Cyanamid, which would bequeath New Jersey one of the country's most toxic waste sites, said, "If man were to follow the teachings of Miss Carson, we would return to the Dark Ages, and the insects and diseases and vermin would once again inherit the earth."

Inevitably, Carson has been attacked as an anti-Christian, Neo-Pagan, flake. She wrote that people called her a "high priestess of nature . . . a mystical cult having to do with the laws of the universe which my critics believe themselves immune to."

Carson was a scientist. She wrote a PhD dissertation. She had to leave her PhD program because her father died, she lost his financial support, and she needed to take care of her mother. That didn't stop her. She turned to writing. She published several best-selling science books.

Carson came from an observant Presbyterian family. Her grandfather was a pastor, her mother attended seminary, and she chose a Christian college where church attendance was mandatory for students. Her approach remained informed by Calvinism: through appreciation of nature, guided by scripture, humans could experience and serve God. John Calvin wrote, "Many burning lamps shine for us in the workmanship of the universe to show forth the glory of its author." Compare this to Rachel Carson: "I accept the theory of evolution . . . there is absolutely no conflict between a belief in evolution and a belief in God as the creator . . . and it is a method so marvelously conceived that to study it in detail is to increase — and certainly never to diminish — one's reverence and awe both for the Creator and the process."

Carson was no flake. Research showed that what DDT was doing to birds — disrupting their reproduction — it was also doing to humans. DDT was hitting birds harder and faster, but we were next. Peregrines are us. DDT was banned in the US in 1972.

DDT continued to be used in other countries. Mosquitoes breed much more rapidly than do humans or falcons. One estimate: under ideal conditions, one female mosquito can produce seven million mosquito descendants in three weeks. Mass, rapid breeding guaranteed that mosquitoes would rapidly develop resistance. In much of the world, DDT no longer works against mosquitoes.

The American subspecies of peregrine had been wiped out in the east. Rescuers gathered peregrine stock from as far away as Europe. Human hands were disguised with peregrine puppets so chicks would not come to understand humans as their parents. Falconry, the at least 2,700-year-old partnering of humans with raptors to hunt, provided rescuers with age-old wisdom. From falconry, rescuers learned "hacking," a regimen for acclimatizing hand-raised birds to heights, wilderness, and the hunt. Their human parents put peregrines in a box or cage in a high, wild place and stopped feeding them. The adolescent birds had to put two and two together and realize that to address their hunger, they could no longer wait on a puppet hand. They had to kill. A nesting pair was finally reported in New Jersey in 1980. Peregrines were removed from the endangered species list in 1999. Peregrines now thrive in cities, divebombing pigeons, ducks, and gulls from steeples, skyscrapers, and bridges.

All believers have stumbling blocks that make it hard to surrender completely to faith. You hear a particularly nightmarish story, and you ask, how could a good God allow such suffering? Atheism confronts its own stumbling blocks. My inner atheist cannot get over the nostrils of the peregrine falcon.

All animals require air, but as anyone who has survived a hurricane can tell you, air at high speed kills. The peregrine weighs between one and three pounds. It dives at two hundred miles an hour — faster than a hurricane. That's the speed of an F-3 tornado. How can the peregrine breathe? Air pressure should burst its lungs. The peregrine's nose is equipped with tubercles: baffles that "create a whirled, conch-like passage of air into the anterior nasal cavity . . . to aid proper respiration at high speeds." This design was adopted by engineers of jet aircraft. The kind of guys working over at Northrup Grumman. Inlet cones, similar to peregrine nostril baffles, enable jets to fly without choking the engine.

No one tries to convince you that inlet cones just appeared on jets one day purely by chance. Who lavished such TLC on the peregrine's nostril? Please don't tell me "evolution did it" unless you can provide me with evolution's name, address, and phone number so I can ask follow-up questions: What are your motivations? Intentions? Modus operandi? Hourly rates? How did you juggle all these elements in space and time — the proto-peregrine's speed, its lungs, its nose, its dives, its survival until it could reproduce in enough numbers to keep the successful traits — without being obliterated by its failed traits? How did you suspend each element on some shelf somewhere until you managed, purely by chance, to orchestrate them all into harmony? Until I get answers to these questions, "evolution did it" makes as much sense to me as "Santa Claus brought all these presents."

If the bird I saw were a peregrine, that would be a special blessing, as "peregrine" means "traveler, foreigner, or pilgrim," and as I stood on that road, that's exactly what I was.

Oops. Did I just say that seeing a peregrine falcon at the beginning of a religious retreat would be a "blessing"? Am I, then, as her opponents dubbed Rachel Carson, a Neo-Pagan?

Let's turn back the clock to the early thirteenth century. A hungry brother high in the mountains of Umbria wrestles with the devil. God reaches out to this man "through the ministry of the wild mountain birds." A falcon "awakened him every night a little before the hour of Matins by her cry and the flapping of her wings, and would not leave him till he had risen." If the man was sick and needed extra rest, "this falcon, like a discreet and charitable Christian, would call him somewhat later than was her wont." I went to a school named after this man. Saint Francis is depicted with a bird on his shoulder and a wolf at his feet. Francis is one of the most popular and influential saints. He is known as *"alter Christus"* — another Christ.

Hitchhiking is Russian roulette. Would the bullet find me, this time? I prayed to Saint Christopher, patron saint of travelers, who has never let me down. Many Jaguars and even one Porsche passed. It's always instructive to see faces that in other contexts might be "tolerant," "open," "compassionate" or "generous" — the faces of mothers and fathers and friends, teachers and doctors and fundraisers — transmogrify into the look of hard, almost sadistic suspicion that I so often see through windshields and above steering wheels when I am a hitchhiker. They're the kind of faces that you imagine nowhere else than at a witch trial. Our culture condemns staring. That social sanction evaporates when a woman requests a ride. They stare. Oh, they stare. They stare at me as if I were food and they were starving. But they do not stop.

I walk a lot. As I walk, I note and attempt to memorize unfamiliar street names, landmarks, and traffic patterns. I don't do this for myself. I don't have a car, and I rarely drive. I do this because so many drivers pull up and ask for directions. I'll be walking along, and a car will suddenly appear beside me; the passenger-side window will descend.

"St. Joseph's hospital?" the driver barks, quizzically, importuning.

I stop, remove my Walkman, and approach the car. I must focus closely. I'm going to be using words like "left" and "right," and I will be estimating distances and mentally rotating objects in space. These tasks are very challenging to my dyslexic brain. I have mastered them, to the extent that I have, exactly because so many drivers ask me for directions. "Go straight on this road about another mile. This lane will divide and become two lanes. You need to stay in the left lane. At the first traffic light, turn left. That's Hamburg Turnpike. It's four lanes. You need to get into the right lane. The hospital will be up ahead on your right, after an auto dealership and a strip mall."

"Thanks," the driver shouts, as he speeds away.

When drivers need directions, a woman alone on the side of the road is their best friend. When that woman sticks her thumb out for a ride, she is obviously evil.

I was there for an hour when a taxicab pulled up. I peeked inside. As I suspected, the driver was swarthy and not from around these parts.

"Hi," I said. "Thank you so much for stopping. As it happens, I am hitchhiking. This is an American custom that does not entail the exchange of fees for service."

"Get in," he said.

He was from Afghanistan. He showed me a snapshot of his wife and family that he keeps tucked into his sun visor. His wife looked sad, as Muslim women often do. You don't see a lot of bubbly Muslim women overcome by *joie de vivre*. "No one suffers as much as Muslim women," Aisha, Mohammed's favorite wife, famously said. The cab driver's kids looked slim and healthy but solemn.

"Thank you so much for sharing those photos," I said. "Your wife is very beautiful. Your son is very handsome." Both true. Afghans are among the best-looking people on earth. This is, perhaps, cold comfort. Afghans make up the largest number of the earth's refugees.

I rummaged through my backpack to find a photo I could share. I had a small snap of Uncle John in my wallet. Uncle John — *Strycko Janko* — was standing in front of one of his beehives in the Tatra Mountains. His cheeks were deeply cragged and his eyes crackled with the fierce unquenchable fire of a man who has watched Hapsburgs, Nazis, and Soviets advance and retreat through his village, each digging their own unique well of tears in the local emotional landscape.

The cab driver gave the photo much more attention than he should have while driving in heavy traffic. I finally tugged it out of his hand so that hand could return to the wheel.

"Looks Afghan," the cab driver declared.

"Yes," I said. Uncle John, like me, is pale as old ice, and the blue of his eyes was riveting, even in a black-and-white snapshot, but I knew exactly what the cab driver meant.

"So," I said, "my country invaded your country. What do you think of that?" Given the language gap between us, I figured I should cut to the chase.

"When the Americans came in, they should have called a meeting. Invite all the warlords. Bomb it. Kill them all."

"But that would just restart the cycle of violence," I pointed out.

"What cycle of violence? Everyone will be dead," he explained.

He dropped me off near Dulles airport.

"*Tashakur!*" I said as I got out of the cab.

"You speak our language?"

"No," I said. "I just live in New Jersey."

I walked a very few steps, not hitchhiking but merely seeking an exit ramp, when Bruce Barton of the Virginia Department of Transportation pulled over. I entered his jam-packed vehicle. There were computers, tools, and manly-looking things I cannot name, many of them fluorescent orange, including Bruce's vest. He was blond and sun-worn. He spoke with a southern accent. He drove me to the ramp and handed me a folded highway map.

A buteo soared overhead. Buteos are raptors, that is, birds of prey like falcons, but they are chunkier and slower moving, reaching speeds of 120 MPH in their dives on mammalian prey like rabbits and squirrels. It had wing windows. These "windows," made up of light-colored primary feathers, are translucent: they let light through. A few buteo species have wing windows, but I also saw a belly band. This was a red-tailed hawk, a hawk so reliably glimpsed on long car rides along tree-lined superhighways that it is practically a passenger. One can measure distance in miles or in how many red-tailed hawks are sighted along the route given that their territorial demands affect how they space themselves out along the highway. Red-tailed hawks are movie stars. Eagles have rather sissy-sounding voices. They sound like the stereotypical cartoon blonde who has just seen a mouse: "Eeee!" Red-tailed hawks sound exactly like humans want a hawk to sound, and their vocalizations frequently accompany onscreen images of just about any bird of prey, wilderness scene, or Native American in popular movies and TV commercials.

I unfurled my sign. Almost immediately an African-American man in an eighteen-wheeler pulled up. I had to push my body hard to climb the two steep, metal grill steps to the passenger-side door. He was listening to loud Gospel. There was a capacious bed behind his seat. I tossed my backpack onto his bed. He said he saw my sign and realized he was going right by the monastery. Wahoo!

Jamie looked to be in his thirties. He was transporting mulch. Fully loaded, he guessed he weighed eighty thousand pounds. He had the most elaborate dashboard I've ever seen in an eighteen-wheeler. It told him his cargo weight, tire air pressure, and many other facts. He said that many of the displays were useless to him.

He never stopped talking. It was hard to hear him, as I am deaf in the ear on the driver's side and because his truck was very noisy. I wonder if he realized how loud he had that Gospel music going. Truckers lose hearing to their engines and teeth to the amphetamines they take to stay awake.

Jamie said he liked the job well enough, but he wanted to give it just a few more years, sock away X number of dollars, and then try for something else. He said truckers used to enjoy the freedom of the road; they could just go and go and earn what they could. But there were so many regulations these days that it had become a pain.

He had been married for a while, and he liked it, but he had been divorced for a year, and he had no idea why his marriage hadn't succeeded. He missed his wife.

"Maybe you'll get back together?" I asked.

He was noncommittal.

Jamie said he'd grown up on a 180-acre dairy farm. His family worked it; they didn't own it. He came from a family of nine, with seven sisters. His father had a family of ten. His mother a family of twenty-one. His grandmother, eighty-one, comes to family reunions and kicks off her shoes and plays volleyball.

We drove through gently rolling hills being sacrificed to characterless McMansion-style suburban sprawl. As we drove past a shopping mall, he reminisced: it had once been a field where he played ball. He pointed out a swimming hole that would soon be more exurbs.

He said that at a certain point on his daily route, "The gates just open up. People smile and wave at each other and let each other pass. It's a whole 'nother world." That's the Virginia he remembers from his childhood, real country, as yet not buried by the advancing army of "progress."

We mounted a pass. My ears popped. We crossed over the Shenandoah River. We drove uphill and parked at a small store. Behind the counter, a white woman greeted Jamie. She had the kind of skin that I associate with the American South. It's the skin of a woman who has spent many long hours in full sun, with full make-up, while smoking unfiltered Marlboros and drinking beer. The skin has lost its elasticity and has broken into a net of tiny polygons. Still, she wears a lot of make-up, dyes her hair blonde, and wears it in a girlish style: bangs and a bob.

The light was very dim. Waxy-looking, roughly rectangular, fist-sized blobs in plastic wrap were stacked on a table near the door. Bacon fat? I lifted one and smelled it. Nothing definitive. I asked Jamie. He said they were "old hunks of meat for flavoring soup." There were bags of pork rinds and three sinks full of fingerlings in graduated sizes. "Bait?" I asked the woman. "Yup," she said.

Jamie kept trying to buy me something. I declined, out of politeness. I did want a Coke, and would have bought it myself, but I didn't want to risk offending him. He asked the store personnel for directions to the monastery. They gave them.

Jamie said, "We overshot it. You need to go back to the bridge over the Shenandoah and up a wooded road. I can't get my truck up that road." Jamie looked around. "There's an old man who is usually here. He might give you a ride."

"Jamie, you are so very kind," I said. "Don't worry about the old man. I can do it on foot. May God bless you for your kindness to me," I said.

"God blesses me every day," Jamie said with a smile.

I wrestled my pack out of the back of the truck and began the trek downhill.

The East Coast was in the grip of a heat wave. Back in Jersey, I had cut the sleeves off an old, white man's shirt. I had been wearing that shirt for so long that the sweat stains in the armpits were stiff even as the shirt soaked in hot water.

I have to discipline myself to get anything still usable into a garbage can. Surely, my inner survivalist insists, this item you are about to throw away forever has some use left. Surely someone poorer than I is suffering somewhere for want of this item. Surely, when the shit comes down — when the marauding Cossacks return to finish me off, a descendent of the inhabitants of a village they pillaged in 1648; or when the space aliens invade; or when the post-petro-Depression hits; or when the Zombie Apocalypse commences — surely I'll be in dire need of this sweat-stained shirt!

I went to the Salvation Army and bought two "new" used white men's shirts, expressly as part of an effort to convince myself, finally, to throw out this shirt I've been trying to throw out for years.

But I didn't throw it out. Just the sleeves. Kept the sweat stains. It is now a flimsy semi-sort-of-garment I soak in cold water and wear around the apartment, dripping, so I can take the heat. And I was wearing it as I walked down the road toward the Shenandoah River.

People who, like me, have never swung from its willow branches or dandled a lightly shod foot over its banks could, thanks to the river's eponymous folk song, grow up yearning for those happy days wearing a straw hat and chewing on a blade of grass. The folksong "Shenandoah" has always aroused in me a powerful nostalgia for that misty, pink-dawned, sun-ray-shot landscape everyone dreams of as if it were home, or else why would Thomas Kinkade paintings sell so well? That yearning feels like a newborn baby's yearning for its mother, a newborn that knows damn well it is going to spend the rest of its life being, more or less, an arrow shot from mother with only one trajectory — away.

The singer of the folksong that carries the name of the river, "Shenandoah," never spends so much as one single moment actually on the Shenandoah. The song is all about longing to see and hear and feel and live something you've definitively, and of your own free will, forever left. The river is given human substance. The singer bids it off, "Away, you rolling river." And, "rolling"? A word used to describe the hips of a woman wantonly deploying her charms to keep someone she knows she's already lost. And yet the singer yearns for this river he orders "away."

> Oh, Shenandoah, I long to hear you,
> Away, you rolling river.
> Oh, Shenandoah, I long to hear you,
> Away, I'm bound away 'cross the wide Missouri.

I choke back tears. I want to apologize to the Shenandoah. And I want to keep moving, to get away. Because that is life: leaving — and losing — paradise. Through an LP I heard at home as a child, I fell in love with the Shenandoah River, sight unseen. I learned to yearn for it as if I had once had it. And here I was, walking along it. I felt full, as if an ancient soul hunger had finally been satisfied.

◆

I heard a car behind me. I turned and waved at it, my wave friendly and not importunate, but my body far enough into the road that going around me would be hard to do.

It was a compact car. The driver, an elderly man, did stop. I approached his window and asked, "Is this the way to the monastery?"

"Yes," he said. "You can have a ride if you like."

I was grateful that he had stopped and directed me, but I genuinely did not want to impose. "I don't want to impose," I said, attempting an air of casual relaxation so he wouldn't feel obligated. Like, "Oh, I had nothing to do this morning so I decided to stroll along this wooded road in ninety-degree heat while carrying a small library of Christian books in a poorly designed backpack."

He suddenly became crabby. "Suit yourself," he snapped.

Wrong answer, Bud. The correct answer is, "It's no imposition," if it isn't, or, "Well, I am going the other way, but you don't have far to walk; it's right up ahead," if it is. In lieu of sounding a buzzer, I walked in front of his car, which he was accelerating. The passage of my body in front of his car ceased his acceleration.

I opened the door and got in. I was offended by my chauffeur's headgear. His straw hat was too high on his head, and it was in the shape of a beehive. It was so ugly, it was an affront. I wanted to perform an aesthetic intervention and tear it off. I wanted to say, "How dare you wear that in my presence?" I see a new appeal of the cloistered life, especially for crabby old men: "Never again worry about whether or not your attire is socially acceptable!"

"I'm a monk," my chauffeur said, with a self-deprecating chuckle. He gave his name as Brother "Bernard." He came from New Jersey.

He had been middle-aged and working as a substitute teacher. He was content, debt-free, and healthy. And, he said, ruefully and with great conviction, "One day God just . . . I explain it this way," he began using an orotund voice to indicate that he was quoting himself. I got the impression he had told this story before, and he was reciting his own memorized account as much as spontaneously re-inhabiting a living memory. Monks, like all those with unusual experiences that others find mysterious or admirable, must often be called on to explain themselves, and that explaining probably becomes routine. "God opened a door, and a great light shown in my path. I could either follow it, or not. It was up to me. I followed it, and here I am."

Our ride couldn't have been much more than five minutes. We were traveling a mere couple of miles, and he did what rides do when they pick up a hitchhiker, or me, anyway. He told me the story of his life.

We arrived. He adjured me not to go to the retreat house, as it was not yet three o'clock.

I knew that retreatants were not to check in until three. But when you are hitchhiking, especially in a strange state, you have no idea what time you are going to arrive. I left DC early because I am a single woman, and darkness is the enemy.

Contemplatives live in out-of-the-way places. Someone shows up, chances are that someone has traveled far under less than ideal circumstances and needs a roof and a drink of water and a chance to decompress. Saint Benedict's Rule for Monasteries recognizes this in chapter fifty-three: "Let all guests who arrive be received like Christ, for He is going to say, 'I came as a guest, and you received Me.'"

Brother Bernard's story was a good story. I'm glad he told it to me. I'm glad I was his attentive audience. I wish, though, he had been a bit more aware of me, a woman alone on foot, soaked in sweat, under a hot sun, carrying a heavy pack. I wish he had shown the awareness that Jamie had when he offered to buy me something, an offer I felt courtesy-bound to decline. I wish Brother Bernard had said, "You look thirsty." When he cautioned me not to enter the retreat house until three, he spoke more like a suburbanite, someone who can assume that his interlocutor's physical needs are all met, than like a monk, manning an outpost for pilgrims who have journeyed hard and long in search of a physical and spiritual well.

My mother was imperfect, but not a single person ever entered her kitchen — and everyone entered her house through her kitchen — without being offered a cold drink, a hot drink, a hard drink, a soft drink, a piece of cake, some potatoes, and *oskvarky*. You've never had *oskvarky*? How have you lived this long? Or maybe you don't eat pig. How about some matzo brei? It's not a problem! Sit!

Gosc w dom, Bog w dom — A guest in the house is God in the house.

Jesus was visiting an important man. A sinful woman showed up and washed Jesus's feet with her tears and dried them with her hair. The important man was scandalized. Jesus is no prophet, the man concluded. He let a whore touch his feet. Jesus "overheard" this man's thoughts. "Look," Jesus said, calmly, just stating the facts, not bashing, not looking for a fight. "I showed up at your house, and you didn't give me any water. She gave me the water you withheld."

That's my God speaking. He is not the God of "do what people expect; perform some timeworn, predictable ritual the crowd have been conditioned to regard as holy." Jesus is the God of right-now. Jesus is the God of pay-attention-to-the-person-right-in-front-of-you. Right now, I am hot. Right now, I am thirsty. Give me a glass of water. My God is the God of see-what's-right-in-front-of-you, from a swallow-tailed kite to a sweaty, thirsty pilgrim, whether that's what you were expecting or not. That's my God.

CHAPTER FIVE

THE CONTEMPLATIVE LIFE

The Dudh Kosi or River of Milk drains Mount Everest. It glimmers in its gorge, turquoise and silver. I once trekked along it, to a spot where it joins one of its seven sister rivers. The confluence of rivers is sacred in Hinduism. I encountered a sannyasi seated in lotus position in the sand and gravel at the place where the rivers joined. Sannyasis' renunciation of the world is so severe that they perform their own funerals before taking to the wilderness. This sannyasi was naked except for ashes. His limbs were as slim and slack as jute ropes. His dreadlocked hair was piled atop his head. Once he took his vow, that hair was never again combed or cut.

There was nothing anywhere near him except for the fierce V of mountains rising up thousands of feet from the rushing river's bed. The rise of those mountains was an act of aggression to me. As I trekked, I felt the mountains to be my enemies, eager to cause me pain, thwart and humiliate me. And yet I adored their beauty. The Himalayas are active; they grow a couple of inches every year as the Indian subcontinent pushes into the Asian landmass. There were no people; I was the lone other. There were only the parrots down low in the gorge, winging, carefree, from river bank to river bank, their highway air, their concern with the pitch of the mountains minimal. Then, rising higher, there would be crows. Still higher were lammergeier, vultures that eat bone. The mountains bullied even sunlight; it visited only in slants.

The sannyasi said nothing to me, and I said nothing to him. I thought of everything he had renounced, from peanut M&Ms to romantic comedies to the contents of the *Encyclopedia Britannica* to crying over a broken heart to worrying about the future to telling a friend about last night's dream. What did he receive in exchange? I wondered what he knew, if anything. I kept walking. I was on my way to a Peace Corps conference, the closest thing to a Roman orgy I'd ever know. We'd eat till sick, dance, flirt, copulate. That sannyasi would be with me every moment. I'd be thinking of him. What does he know that I cannot access? I just googled "Dudh Kosi" to revisit this river in photos. I see that now it hosts organized whitewater rafters. I wonder what the sannyasi makes of them. I wonder if he ever thinks of me. No, not really. I know he has never thought of me. I think of him often.

I have long had this question: are contemplatives, the Desert Fathers, the Desert Mothers, and all those who leave society and go off on their lonesome — Tibetan monks, Hindu sadhus, Buddha, John the Baptist — are they truly holy? Or are they merely crabby misfits who couldn't get laid and are too lazy or soul-dead to engage in conventional hygiene?

Entering the wilderness temporarily to contemplate a difficult question or to realign yourself when you are off track is a necessary thing. In the Bible, Elijah left society and slept under a juniper tree. There, Elijah was commanded, "Go forth, and stand upon the mount before the Lord. And, behold, the Lord passed by, and a great and strong wind rent the mountains, and brake in pieces the rocks before the Lord; but the Lord was not in the wind: and after the wind an earthquake; but the Lord was not in the earthquake: and after the earthquake a fire; but the Lord was not in the fire: and after the fire a still small voice."

That's where God was. God was not in the special effects: not in the wind, the broken rocks, or the earthquake. God was in the "still small voice" that, to hear, Elijah had to leave society and enter the wilderness. A quote from the Desert Fathers and Mothers: "Stay in your cell, and your cell will teach you everything." I respect staying in one's cell for short stretches. It's the lifelong rejection of society that gives me pause.

We tend to stereotype urban life as stressful and country living in wide-open spaces as healthy and stress-free. My mother grew up in a village in Slovakia. I visited Kovarce in the 1970s, and it was postcard-perfect. Kovarce was surrounded by fields of blue rye and red poppies. Clouds of white butterflies rose into the sky. In the hills, wild boar announced their presence with heavy pants. And the cuckoo, such a tender punctuation to the drawn-out ripple of the breeze caressing leaves. Uncle John built an indoor toilet for our visit. Before that all he had was an outhouse. He didn't even have a refrigerator. When he wanted something to eat, he didn't stand in front of a cold, white light and stare at leftovers. He went into his backyard and dug up his meal, or picked it, or chopped off its head.

My mother grew up in that idyllic rural setting. She told me that there was one guy in the village who didn't fit in. He hung himself. She and her brother Joe peeked in the window. She remembered the corpse's black tongue sticking out of its mouth. The entire village came out for his funeral, as they did for all funerals. They marched in the funeral procession. They sang loudly, as they always did — Slovaks do love to sing — and they wailed loudly, as they always did. She told me that if anyone had paid that kind of loving attention to this poor misfit before he died, he probably wouldn't have killed himself.

I grew up on stories like that. Village beatings, murders, feuds, conspiracies, and chicken thieves — and this was just our own family. I knew that the perfect rural image is not what urbanites want it to be.

Contrary to what we moderns want to believe about our "stressful" urban lives, rural people are far more likely to commit suicide than urban ones. Young rural Americans are almost twice as likely to kill themselves as young urban Americans. It seems that there may be something salubrious about spending time around other people and something stressful about being alone in the back of the beyond.

I value Matthew 25 for its clarity. God gathers all people together and divides them into two groups. To those he invites to Heaven, he says, "For I was hungry and you gave me something to eat, I was thirsty and you gave me something to drink, I was a stranger and you invited me in, I needed clothes and you clothed me, I was sick and you looked after me, I was in prison and you came to visit me."

To the group he condemns to Hell, God says, "I was hungry and you gave me nothing to eat, I was thirsty and you gave me nothing to drink, I was a stranger and you did not invite me in, I needed clothes and you did not clothe me, I was sick and in prison and you did not look after me."

That's why I have done the work I have done. That's why I was a nurse's aide to pay for college and not a bank teller or a cashier. That's why I joined the Peace Corps. I wanted to feed the hungry and clothe the naked.

As I've matured, I've realized that bank tellers and cashiers do necessary work. I have also realized that I don't have the constitution to be a health care worker. When I gazed at the raw meat exposed in a patient's bedsore, when I realized that what I was looking at was no different, in appearance, from the cuts of meat on sale under plastic wrap in the butcher's case at the supermarket, I felt I was ministering to the wrong location. As a teacher, I feel like I'm addressing our hunger for knowledge, our need to differentiate truth from lies. I feel like I'm using my real skill, my inexhaustible drive to discover and share information. I want to look into people's eyes, not their anatomy. "Man does not live by bread alone." I am feeding people by teaching them.

It's neither necessary nor sufficient to escape to a remote fortress to experience spiritual peace. One can carry the monastery inside. When I heard NPR announce the news of 9-11, I was writing my dissertation. I resolved to take no break in my work schedule.

I kept to that vow. I never saw the footage of the planes hitting the towers till years later and then only by accident. I don't buy beef because I can't stand how cows are treated in slaughterhouses. I won't watch violent movies. After finally learning my lesson, I don't respond to bait in internet discussions. I could turn myself into the lady of perpetual sadness over my lack of family. I don't allow myself to do that. When I feel myself sinking, I focus on the positive. With iron discipline, I take other paths: I tell myself jokes, I encourage others who are down, I start up a project.

No matter how the world pressures you, you can carry the monastery inside. You can discipline yourself and what you listen to, what you read, what you see, what you consume, what pleasures you allow yourself, and even what pains.

This is hard for a Catholic to admit: I'm no fan of Thomas Merton, America's most famous monk. Ivy League, Protestant, agnostic Thomas Merton, self-described as the "complete twentieth-century man," converted to Catholicism in 1938, became a monk, and then a bestselling author. Merton's 1948 autobiography, *The Seven Storey Mountain*, was a publishing sensation.

William Carlos Williams, in his poem *Paterson*, wrote "no ideas but in things." Sarah Orne Jewett's father gave her similar advice: "Don't try to write about things: write the things themselves." I think of Williams and Jewett when I think about why I don't respond well to *The Seven Storey Mountain*. I dislike writing heavy with abstract nouns. Regret, repentance, justice, peace, love — these abstract nouns are pre-digested words that reflect someone powerful arriving on the scene before the reader and judging for the reader. I prefer concrete nouns: chicken, rain, wheelbarrow. These nouns name what the reader can touch, taste, smell, see, and hear. The writer's job is not to interpret the chicken or the wheelbarrow or the rain. The writer's job is to give the chicken, the wheelbarrow, and the rain to the reader. They affect the reader. The reader decides how he feels about them.

"No ideas but in things" isn't just a dictum on how to write well. "No ideas but in things" is a dictum on how to live well. Jesus says that being a Christian isn't about spouting holy words

(Matthew 7:21). It's about action verbs. Jesus listens. Jesus cries. Jesus teaches. Jesus multiplies loaves and fishes. Jesus stands up to authority. "*Talitha, koum.*" One concrete noun. One action verb. A two-word sentence that reduces me to tears. "Little girl, get up." No ideas but in things. No poetry but in things. No spirituality but in things.

There's one episode in *The Seven Storey Mountain* that moves me to tears. In this episode, Merton isn't writing about things; he is writing the things themselves. Merton describes being a swaggering boy, self-confident and competent enough to build, with his buddies — all of whom were older siblings of their own younger brothers and sisters — a fort in the woods. Merton was nailing shingles all over his new hut. Merton's younger brother John Paul wanted to join him. Merton felt "demeaned" by his younger brother's presence. He and his friends threw rocks at John Paul to chase him away.

> Standing in a field a hundred yards away from the clump of sumachs where we have built our hut is this little perplexed five-year-old kid in short pants and a kind of leather jacket, standing quite still, with his arms hanging down at his sides and gazing in our direction, afraid to come any nearer on account of the stones, as insulted as he is saddened, and his eyes full of indignation and sorrow. And yet he does not go away. We shout at him to get out of there, to beat it, and go home, and we wing a couple of more rocks in that direction, and he does not go away. We tell him to play in some other place. He does not move.

Merton's childhood rejection of John Paul was, Merton confessed, the "prototype of all sin." Interestingly, Merton didn't, in this didactic coda, invoke Cain. In the fourth chapter of the Bible, in the Book of Genesis, Cain, the first human to be born of a woman, Eve, murders his younger brother, Abel, the first human to die, and the first human to be murdered in the first siblicide. After Cain murders Abel, God asks Cain where Abel is. Cain responds with bitter sarcasm and indifference. "Am I my brother's keeper?" I wonder if it crossed Merton's mind to mention Cain. I wonder if he decided not to do so because it would hurt him too much.

I don't know what it feels like to be the older, more loved, rejecting sibling hurling rocks at the younger sibling whose mere presence "demeans" his elder. My older brothers and sister could speak on this. I cannot. I do know how much older siblings matter to younger siblings who don't have perfect parents, because I know I will never love anyone or yearn for anyone more than I have loved and yearned for my sister Antoinette. Ruth Merton, Thomas and John Paul's mother, died when John Paul was only three years old and Thomas was six. After Ruth died, Owen, the boys' father, left John Paul with relatives and took Thomas on a trip to Bermuda. No wonder John Paul wanted so badly to play with his older brother. No wonder it hurt him so much when Thomas would not play with him.

The Seven Storey Mountain provides a coda to Thomas and John Paul's entire relationship. In its insistence on symmetry and redemption, the coda is a Hollywood ending. In March 1942, John Paul visited Thomas at Gethsemani Monastery. Thomas was twenty-seven; John Paul was twenty-four. Tom recognized that his younger brother was living an unhappy and aimless life. I find John Paul's unhappiness understandable. Both of John Paul's parents died in his childhood, and he grew up without stability, moved from place to place for the convenience of adults. Thomas prescribed the solution to John Paul's ennui. John Paul must convert to Catholicism as his older brother Thomas had before him. Merton spent days instructing his younger brother in the faith. John Paul was baptized. Thomas Merton later described their encounter. "In those last four days, the work of eighteen to twenty years of my bad example had been washed away and been made good by God's love . . . I was full of peace and gratitude."

On April 17, 1943, while he was serving in World War II, John Paul's plane went down in the North Sea. Merton wrote a poem, "For My Brother: Reported Missing in Action, 1943." Merton addresses John Paul:

. . . if I cannot eat my bread,
My fasts shall live like willows where you died.
If in the heat I find no water for my thirst,
My thirst shall turn to springs for you, poor traveler . . .

The poem continues in that vein. Merton will sacrifice his own comforts, needs, indeed his very life, and through this self-sacrifice, his kid brother will find his rest.

I suppose I should be moved by Merton's poem. I'm not. I can't help but notice that the emphasis is still on the heroic older brother. I get no sense of John Paul from this poem. No sense of what the world lost in that April 17, 1943, plane crash. Was John Paul tall, short, blue-eyed, green? What did his laugh sound like? What I get from this poem is that Thomas will justify and sanctify John Paul's early death through his, Thomas's, self-sacrificing suffering.

Eat a sandwich, Tom. Nothing you can do will bring John Paul back. Nothing you can do will redeem those shattered moments in his childhood when he yearned for you, and you not only rejected him, you humiliated him in front of your friends. Here's what you did: you described John Paul indelibly in his leather jacket, refusing to leave in spite of the rocks you threw at him, as you and your friends built your hut in the sumacs. No moral coda you attach to that story, no fasting, no theodicy will ever improve on the real-life details you have reported. Believe me, Tom. Believe me. I love your brother because you described him so well. In that passage, as Jewett taught, you didn't write about John Paul or sin or redemption. You wrote the things themselves. That's why I love John Paul and care about his death and your pain.

Or maybe I have a problem with Merton because Merton had a problem with "extremely brawny" Polaks. "There was a time when I and my magnificent friends, in our great hut, having formed a 'gang,' thought we were sufficiently powerful to antagonize the extremely tough Polish kids . . . we would shout defiance and challenge them to come out and fight."

When, in *The Seven Storey Mountain*, Merton moves on to

describing his wayward university years, full of women, booze, jazz, atheism, and intellectual arrogance, he loses me. I encounter too many figures of speech, too many abstract nouns. He's writing about things; he's not writing the things themselves. "I labored to enslave myself in the bonds of my own intolerable disgust," Merton wrote of his wild oats. What does that mean? Does it mean that he fathered an illegitimate child he didn't support and never saw? That's what his biographers report. If that's the case, then say it in concrete nouns and action verbs. Of course Merton couldn't say it. His superiors decided that it would be best for the church, and for the reader, if "the things themselves" were hidden behind abstractions.

The only Merton book I was able to get through, cover to cover, was *Preview of the Asian Journey*. I read it because it was short. There. I've said it. *The Seven Storey Mountain* is 467 pages. *Preview of the Asian Journey* is the 114-page transcript of Merton's 1968 comments to intellectuals at a liberal California think tank.

In *Asian Journey*, Merton sounds very much like any number of elite university professors. He is critical of America, the West, and Christianity. He is indulgent of non-Western cultures, especially Asian ones, and a Native American culture before Columbus arrived. Merton voices cultural relativism. He wants Christians to recognize the "truth" of non-Christians and the value of non-Christian religions.

Merton declares that the West is guilty of "unmitigated arrogance toward the rest of the human race." Christian missionaries "could not recognize that the races they conquered were essentially equal to themselves and in some ways superior." Christianity imposes a "repressive, partial, and fragmented" view of humanity. Merton depicts Americans as wanting to bomb other countries back to the Stone Age. He describes Kentuckians — the civilians who surround his monastery — as violent thugs who shoot doves in a cornfield. The gunfire disturbs him as he sits under a cottonwood tree at his hermitage. Merton compares Americans to Canaanites performing human sacrifice. Merton assumes he knows what contemptuous thoughts an American tourist thinks while visiting Mexico.

How on earth would Merton know what tourists think in

Mexico? Merton spent his adult life cloistered in a monastery in Kentucky. It's possible that Merton read trendy authors who were contemptuous of Americans, of Christianity, and of the West, as many tended to be in the revolutionary 1960s and as many are on elite campuses and in media today.

When I think of missionaries, I think of Father Damien, who went to Molokai to serve abandoned lepers and died of the leprosy he inevitably caught there. I think of Peter Claver, who entered the hellholes of slave ships. With tears in my eyes I think of Maura Clarke and Ita Ford, Dorothy Kazel and Jean Donovan, who worked with the poor. They were stalked, beaten, raped, and murdered by members of the El Salvador national guard. I think of Gladys Aylward, a domestic servant. A thirty-year-old spinster, she sank her life savings on passage to China. She rescued discarded female infants and was one of the "arrogant" Christian missionaries who played a key role in ending at least a thousand years of the crippling and torturous binding of Chinese women's feet.

Other "arrogant" Christians: William Wilberforce, who campaigned against slavery, and Sir Charles James Napier. They made it their business to end *sati*. Hindu priests insisted that *sati* — the burning alive of widows on their husband's funeral pyre — was a religious requirement. "All nations have customs which should be respected," they said. Napier replied, "Be it so. This burning of widows is your custom; prepare the funeral pile. But my nation has also a custom. When men burn women alive we hang them, and confiscate all their property. My carpenters shall therefore erect gibbets on which to hang all concerned when the widow is consumed. Let us all act according to national customs."

Merton never served overseas, so he never met missionaries in the field. I did. I met them in Africa, producing the first dictionary in a language with fewer than two million speakers, all poor. I volunteered with Mother Teresa's Missionaries of Charity. They put me to work washing lice out of the clothing of elderly and ill people whose relatives had dumped them on the street to die. These nuns lifted up vermin-ridden, contagious starvelings, bathed them, fed them, and put a roof over them as they died. I witnessed Christians in the Soviet Empire facing off against tanks.

At the same time he is bashing the presumed racism, classism, and lack of charity of American tourists in Mexico, Merton accepts uncritically Zen Buddhism's lofty self-marketing. In Merton's words about Zen, I don't encounter the objectivity of a scholar. I don't encounter a believing Christian. I'm not saying that Merton wasn't a Christian. I'm saying that in his unquestioning promotion of Zen, I don't hear a Christian. Zen insists that it is transcendent of thought; Merton accepts that. Zen promises an experience that can be achieved through no other route; Merton chomps at the bit to get to Asia so he can partake of that unique blessing. Accepting a belief system's public relations talking points about itself is the proper path for an acolyte. It isn't the proper position for a scholar and author who is not part of the belief system. Merton prescribes Zen to Catholics: "If Catholics had a little more Zen, they'd be a lot less ridiculous than they are."

Asian Journey closes with Merton's description of Shangri La, which Merton found through his reading in pre-Columbian Mesoamerica. Merton describes Zapotec culture, which began over 2,500 years ago in what is now Mexico, as civilized, peaceful, artistic, and timeless. Labor-intensive construction of the massive stone pyramids of Monte Alban, all done without the wheel or draft animals, was carried out by hand with "patience and love." In contrast to "aggressive" Americans, Zapotecs lived in "final perfection." Zapotecs "achieved self-realization" through their "awareness of a network of relationships in which one had a place in the mesh." They "fell in step with the dance of the universe, the liturgy of the stars." They were "peaceful, prosperous, aesthetic and religious." "There was no war." There was no slavery; people worked to enjoy the rewards of creating something beautiful.

I don't see a reflection of Shangri La in Zapotec art. In one stone frieze, a Zapotec ruler brandishes a human femur. He looks grim. I am not uplifted. I don't experience myself as falling in step with the dance of the universe. Call me xenophobic, but I'm always wary of grimacing figures who gesture vehemently using someone else's amputated body part to add emphasis. Femur-man frieze is not an outlier. Use of human femurs as status symbols was ritualized in Zapotec culture.

As in most Mesoamerican art, the favorite Zapotec facial expression is the grimace, as in the Zapotec funerary urns depicting Pitao Cozobi, the maize god. There's a three-thousand-year-old Olmec ceramic of a naked woman at the Met. She's grimacing. Her grimace is so intense you notice it before you check out her nekkid boobies, or her naked other stuff. You look to her eyes to see if anything else is going on there. Hers are the heavily lidded slits of a waiting gator. Two-thousand-five-hundred years later, Aztecs produced the turquoise mask of fire god Xiuhtecuhtli. Guess what? He's grimacing. Just like that naked lady two and a half millennia previously.

Mesoamerican mouths clench, expose teeth, stick tongues out of tight, tight jaws. Reptilian eyes hide or never contained any spark or joy or reflection or vulnerability. It's as if smiling had been outlawed, as if eyes had been mechanically drained of soul in one of humanity's most chilling and yet impressive engineering feats. These are images of people and gods who devoted a lot of energy to looking threatening. Either that or they wanted to show off their famous Mesoamerican dental work. Some Mesoamericans filed their teeth to sharp points and inlaid them with turquoise, jade, or cinnabar. Or maybe they wanted to display their tongues for religious reasons. Maya Queen Xook is depicted kneeling, running a thorny rope through her pierced tongue in an eighth-century stone relief. The flowing blood was collected on paper and offered to the gods. The gods thirsted for human blood to maintain their vitality. Another method to start a sacrificial flow of blood — stabbing the genitals with stingray spines. I'd grimace too. Or maybe these grimaces have a more mundane source. Maybe constipation was epidemic. Nah, couldn't be. Mesoamerica gave the world much of its beans, all of its corn, squash, tomatoes, avocados, peppers, chocolate, and vanilla. For these, we are grateful. For tobacco, not so much.

Smiles are so rare in Mesoamerican art that the few statuettes that do smile are intensively studied to understand why. Artists mass produced *Caritas Sonrientes* or Smiley Faces. Sounds good, no? Just wait. These "smiley face" figurines were decapitated and smashed. Some theorize that the repeated iconoclasm of happy faces was a ritual attempt to send to the dead the frivolity in the afterlife that was in such short supply in Mesoamerican art. My guess — maybe the statuettes were smashed for the crime of smiling.

Hundreds of years before the rise of the Zapotecs, Egypt gave the world the "Ramesside Smile," an exquisite, Mona Lisa facial expression. You can see this delicate, private amusement, or peace-of-mind, or hint of coy-flirtation-across-a-crowded-room in the three-thousand-year-old, seven-ton granite bust of Ramesses the Great at the British Museum. He was probably the most powerful man in the world at that time. He was manly enough to be portrayed in the movies by the swaggering, bare-chested Yul Brynner in the 1956 film *The Ten Commandments*. In his granite bust, Ramesses looks like a SNAG — a Sensitive New Age Guy. The Egyptians got it that you can be badass and also cultivate your inner poet, or at least look like you do. The Mesoamericans, in other words, did not grimace so much — at least in their art — because they lived a long time ago. They grimaced because their culture favored the grimace over any other facial expression.

Mesoamerican civilizations lasted for over 2,500 years. Mesoamerica produced significant, and indeed beautiful, awe-inspiring art depicting threat, war, fear, submission, agony, death, worship, and power. I don't know if, in all that time, their art produced one individual. Want to see an individual from the Ancient World? Look at Fayum mummy portraits from a Hellenized, newly Christianizing Egypt. These two-thousand-year-old faces are your neighbors. Your cousins. The person next to you on the subway. You. They're hopeful. Tender. Shy. Thoughtful. You can see their veins pulse. You can hear their hearts beat. You say, "Wow, there is no time between us," only the mysterious dimension of death, a death these portraits almost erase.

I wouldn't want to live in a world where artists aren't rewarded for seeing the heart's most tender moments, its most fleeting investments, and riskiest, most impossible dreams. My utopia would have to produce artists who can see what Johannes Vermeer saw in his 1665 painting *The Girl with a Pearl Earring*. She's a girl, just a girl. Not, in this painting, anybody's mother or daughter or wife. She's not cleaning or cooking or weaving or planting or entertaining a sugar daddy. She's not waving about a human femur that establishes her status. The painting forces us to confront the humanity of a girl. We don't have enough clues to pigeonhole her. She could be a nun or a streetwalker, a queen or the youngest daughter of low-status parents. The clothing is not hers; it is an "exotic" costume provided by the painter. What we think we know about her — that she is wearing a pearl earring — may be incorrect. The bauble is probably tin. All we have of her is her face and the soul shining through it. She appears to be lost in her own thoughts. The artist deems her worth seeing. The tribe assesses her as worth curating. In 2,500 years of Mesoamerican art, did any artist find one random, daydreaming girl to be worthy of his time? Did any tribe see that work of art and say, "this, this anonymous girl, this we must cherish"? The record we have suggests that the answer is no.

Cultural relativism is good as far as it goes, but you can't change this fact: art that reliably, century after century, gets back to the individual — rich or poor, male or female, young or old, beautiful or ugly — is a Western product, the fruit of the Western celebration of the individual, the individual who was born of Ancient Greek and Judeo-Christian parents.

I emailed Joyce Marcus, Robert L. Carneiro Distinguished Professor of Social Evolution and Curator of Latin American Archaeology at the Museum of Anthropological Archaeology. I described Merton's article. She wrote back. "Your doubts and suspicions are well-founded. I think none of us who work on Zapotec culture would agree with those characterizations. Zapotec civilization was not idyllic; their people did not live for art, and they did experience their share of raiding and warfare."

Why, then, did Merton advance Zapotec culture as Shangri La? I suspect it's because of a universal human tendency: the grass is greener on the other side of the fence. Idealists suffer this fever acutely. We want the world to be better than it is. I'm like Merton. Otherwise, I never would have gone to Nepal, the farthest place you can get from Wanaque, New Jersey, and still be on the same planet. The difference between me and Merton is that I discovered what Dorothy did in *The Wizard of Oz*. People far away are jerks, too, just like the folks at home. Christianity helped me in this. Jesus talked about letting the wheat and the tares, or weeds, grow together. His own crew were jerks. Peter denied Jesus. Thomas doubted Jesus. James and John's pushy momager demanded that her sons be made first and second in command. Jesus never kicked any of them out — not even Judas. As long as we are on planet earth, we are not living in an ideal world. We ourselves are jerks too. Maybe honestly confronting our jerkitude is the entire point of this dispensation.

Political correctness is grass-is-greener on steroids. Identity politics is the bastard spawn of political correctness. When you make all Americans, Westerners, and Christians bad, you make your other of choice all good. For Merton, it was Monte Alban and Zen. Prof. X adopted Zen as well. In his book, X compared and contrasted the Christian West and the Buddhist East. The Christian West is bad. The Buddhist East is good. Since he had adopted that Buddhist, Eastern identity, he adopted its purity too. He couldn't see how rotten he was to fire me when he did the way he did. Zen masters don't do anything bad. It's those awful Christians who do all the bad stuff.

In *Asian Journey*, Merton writes that monastic life is a Freudian family drama of "castration," of "power and subjection," of a "paternal type of authority" that "is constantly cutting down the kids, cutting down the sons and holding things back." Life in the monastery is typified by "futility and stupidity and triviality." Life is "restricted" "to a ludicrous limit." "Illusion is perpetuated." Tom, if you had ever had the chance to live in a Buddhist monastery, or a Zapotec city-state, or a factory town in New Jersey, or, heaven help you, if you ever spent even just one semester in the purgatory of adjunct professordom, you'd pen the same critique, and you'd want to put your fist through the same walls.

To his think-tank audience, Merton acknowledged, "It would be very interesting to write the book that one could really write about a Trappist monastery. I don't think I'd ever be able to get away with it." "Don't tell anybody I said this!" Merton warns. "I'm a member of the Roman Catholic Church in good standing." He's saying right here that he doesn't say, in his writing, what he really thinks. Isn't telling one's truth a writer's number one job? Write the things themselves? Isn't that how Jesus lived his whole life? In concrete nouns and action verbs. He encounters hunger. He feeds, and he eats, even on the Sabbath. He encounters demons. He exorcises, even though he doesn't have the proper credentials. He encounters mourners. He comforts, even if naming the source of the mourner's pain implicates the highly placed. Jesus didn't edit with the powers-that-be looking over his shoulder. He didn't change the subject because the subject might discomfit the Romans or the Pharisees or even his own crew. When he met a woman who had gone astray, he didn't use abstract nouns. Jesus didn't say, "Have you been laboring to enslave yourself in the bonds of your own intolerable disgust?" No. He said, "You have had five husbands, and the man you now have is not your husband." We have exactly one record of Jesus writing: when they bring him the woman caught in adultery. Jesus kneels and writes in the dust. The woman's accusers drop the stones they had intended to murder her with and walk away. We have no record of what Jesus wrote, but whatever it was, it was Nail — Head — Bang.

In a letter published after he died, Merton wrote that he was unable to conquer "continual, uninterrupted resentment. I resent and even hate Gethsemani. I fight against the place constantly. I do not openly allow myself — not consciously — to sin in this regard. But I am in the habit of letting my resentment find every possible outlet and it is such a habit . . . I am not kidding about how deep it is. It is DEEP." I love that guy. I love the all-caps Merton, seething with resentments, taking names and naming names. The "things themselves" writer. Him, I'd read.

"He couldn't," you're saying. "His superiors would not allow him to write the "things themselves." But you're saying that to me, and I write the truth as I see it, and I pay the price. So that's what I demand of anyone proposed as a potential hero.

Merton's choices and the success they brought him matter to me. I have a PhD. I want to find work. I want to produce scholarship that reflects reality, not scholarly trends like political correctness and cultural relativism. And everyone tells me that if I want to survive in academia, I must blind and deafen myself and sew my lips shut. Alan Dundes, the most outspoken man in history, tells me "Shut up till you get tenure." I've been told to shut up shut up shut up more than the princess lead in a BBC production set in Victorian England. An observation about facial expressions in Mesoamerican art — I'd be crucified for that on my campus. "Racist! Imperialist! White privilege! How dare you comment on Native American culture! You don't even speak Tequistlatec!" Yeah, but you aren't Christian and you don't speak High Church Slavonic, but you can say any awful thing about Christians, and that increases your chances of getting tenure.

I'm a Catholic. I'm trying to live my faith. I'm trying to read and also to write about my faith. Is this how it works? Do you become a big gun in Catholicism by going along with secular societal trends like political correctness? Or through crafty circumlocutions around anything that might upset the pious, from a bastard child to Freudian castration themes to having a gay Jewish atheist as a best friend?

I perform a Google image search of "Thomas Merton" so I may look at photos of his face and see if I can find there what I miss in his prose. What I accidentally discover: dozens of portraits. Not snapshots. Portraits of Merton, artistically composed, created with excellent lenses in the most flattering light. His whimsical eye crinkles are highlighted. Sometimes Merton gazes lovingly at the viewer. In these face-front portraits, Merton's direct gaze invites the viewer into intimate communion with the superstar.

Sometimes Merton stares into the remote distance. In response to these profile portraits, the viewer's assignment is to lessen himself, to envy Merton, and to hope that someday he can join Merton on an elite, rarified spiritual plane. Merton is framed against rugged Kentucky hills under sculpted cumulus clouds. One or two shots seem to benefit from a wind machine, almost like that iconic image of Marilyn Monroe on a subway grate; his tunic is tousled artistically. The portraits are in black and white to highlight the Cistercian color combination of white tunic and black scapular.

Merton did not commission these portraits. He chose, even craved, solitude and anonymity. Of his bestseller, *The Seven Storey Mountain*, Merton said, "It is the work of a man I have never even heard of." His superiors saw his gift and capitalized on it to proselytize. These portraits are carefully packaged and marketed charisma. Merton generously surrendered himself to fame so as to bring more to Christ. That's a very good thing. It's just not my thing. The most high-impact twentieth-century American Christians in my life were Bill W. and Dr. Bob, who cofounded Twelve Step. I don't even know what they looked like, and for a long time I didn't know their last names. In Twelve Step, I learned this salvific recipe: "Just show up, and tell the truth."

On December 10, 1968, in Bangkok, Thailand, twenty-seven years to the day after he entered Gethsemani Monastery, Merton was stepping out of the shower. He was electrocuted by a fan.

My biography and Merton's are polar opposites. I was not the firstborn male, not the son of cosmopolitan painters. I did not attend an Ivy League university. Ego is not my problem. Minute-by-minute convincing myself that I have a right to take up space is my problem. It's a battle I lose every day. Twelve Step was the one institution I encountered that gave me an inkling that it's okay if I keep breathing. I got the same message from Christianity, but only in empty churches, in silent communion with the statue of Mary. Full churches were always full of people who saw me get beat and never intervened and male priests whose gender exclusivity informed me that females are not good enough. I don't need to retreat to the wilderness to discover that I am nothing. I need to retreat to the wilderness to feel that I am something.

And I don't mind ego in others. If given a choice between interacting with someone who is struggling through trying to be humble and making mistakes at humility the way a beginner makes mistakes at speaking a foreign language, and interacting with someone who overtly celebrates himself, an Alan Dundes, say, I'd select the latter every time.

I love that Marianne Williamson quote about our deepest fear. Williamson says we ask ourselves: "Who am I to be brilliant, gorgeous, talented, fabulous?" She responds, "Actually, who are you not to be? You are a child of God. Your playing small does not serve the world. There is nothing enlightened about shrinking so that other people won't feel insecure around you . . . as we let our own light shine, we unconsciously give other people permission to do the same."

Rabbi Hillel, two thousand years ago, said something similar. "If not me, who? If not now, when? If I am not for myself, who is for me? And if I am only for myself, what am I?"

Alan Dundes was a loud, profane, obese, utterly unapologetic genius. I think Dundes was Dundes at least partly because he was Jewish. Jewish culture can encourage its sons to celebrate themselves in a way that Catholicism does not. I do like genuine, unadulterated Christian humility. I also very much like what strikes me as the healthy Jewish self-celebration that Williamson, who was raised Jewish, gives voice to. I think both are good for the soul and for the wider society. I know that when I am around people who are unsuccessfully trying to be humble, I feel I must "play small," and I'm never any good at that. When I was around Alan Dundes, I felt I could think and say anything I wanted because he was thinking and saying anything he wanted.

I once heard a folktale about a monastery that was going downhill. The monks were sniping at each other and slacking at their tasks. One night a Jewish traveler sought refuge in the monastery. Before leaving the next day, the traveler imparted a secret to the monks. "I have received a vision from God. One of you is the Messiah." He wouldn't tell them which one. Then he went on his way. They all started treating each other better, thinking, hey, this monk could be the Messiah. The Jewish traveler saved the monastery.

My Polish father inspired me always to see the other side. Of course he would. Poland was attacked by Nazi Germany and Communist Russia at the same time. We have to look both ways.

I have my questions about monasteries and convents, about humility, anonymity, and isolation, but they are questions, not conclusions. I need to learn more. Meanwhile, I instinctively value the encounter that is the heart of the cloistered life. The Judeo-Christian tradition recognizes the individual, apart from the mob. That individual is invited to meet and talk face to face and utterly spontaneously with God, without interruption from any earthly authority. That encounter is the life spark of Western civilization.

We define, and recognize, by contrasts. I learn much about Christian prayer and Christian monasticism by comparing them with their opposites. I think of Michelangelo's *Creation of Adam* and what it says about my faith, specifically, what it says about the Judeo-Christian concept of God, of man, and of prayer. I think of how that artwork and its implications contrast with other belief systems: modern atheism, ancient Paganism, and Islam.

Between 1508 and 1512, on the ceiling of the Vatican's Sistine Chapel, Michelangelo depicted the spark of life in the fingertip-to-fingertip, eye-contact encounter between one loving creator God and one human being, not a teeming mass, just one person. In Michelangelo's fresco, we see Adam's full naked form from head to toe. God looks like Adam, and Adam looks like God. They are the same size. Every detail here matters: Adam is just one man, he is naked, he is anatomically detailed, he is the same size as God, God and Adam are fundamentally structured the same, Adam is making eye contact with God, and God looks upon Adam with fiercely attentive love. Every detail here has an impact on the life anyone can live in a Judeo-Christian society.

Organized Christophobes have targeted Michelangelo's *Creation of Adam*. They call themselves The Church of the Flying

Spaghetti Monster. They blather, "Oh, you Christians and Jews are so stupid; you think God is an old man in the sky with a long, white beard." Swedish artist Arne Niklas Jansson created *Touched by His Noodly Appendage*, a parody of Michelangelo's *Creation*. God is a plate of spaghetti and meatballs. One strand of spaghetti reaches Adam. Their point: it doesn't matter what story a society tells itself about its origins. The Judeo-Christian God may as well be a flying monster made of spaghetti. These atheists are ignorant and childish enough to believe that if we told ourselves their story, we'd be able to have the same society that we have now. They are wrong on every count.

"God created man in his image; in the divine image he created him; male and female he created them": Sofers, ancient Jewish scribes, committed these words to print in the Book of Genesis thousands of years ago. Each individual person is the image of a loving God — *"tzelem elohim"* in Hebrew, *"imago dei"* in Latin. Michelangelo used the language with which he was fluent, his gift for accurately depicting anatomy and physiology, to communicate the essence of the relationship between the Judeo-Christian God and each individual person.

Adam and God meet face to face, eye to eye, in the Sistine Chapel fresco. Exodus 33:11 tells us that "The Lord spoke with Moses face to face, just as a man speaks with his friend." Deuteronomy 5:4 tells us that "the Lord spoke to his people Israel" face to face as well. In Numbers 6:25, God blesses thus, "The Lord let his face shine upon you." The Bible repeatedly adjures us to seek God's face. "My heart says of you, 'Seek his face!' Your face, Lord, I will seek," Psalm 27:8. "Face to face": this metonym has meant intimate connection — human and spiritual — for the past four thousand years. "To face" means "to meet." The sixth amendment to the US Constitution guarantees the right to face one's accuser. "Face" often means "dignity," e.g. "to save face." This is true not just of English, but of many languages. In Medieval Slavic languages, "without face" means "shame." In China and other Asian cultures, face is reputation, honor, and dignity.

Adam is an individual, apart from a mob. The Talmud teaches that God created only one Adam, rather than a group of men at once, to emphasize the value of each individual life. One man, in himself, is an entire universe. Folklorist Nathan Ausubel paraphrases the Aggadah. God created one Adam . . .

> . . . to demonstrate that one man in himself is an entire universe. Also He wished to teach mankind that he who kills one human being is as guilty as if he had destroyed the entire world. Similarly, he who saves the life of one single human being is as worthy as if he had saved all of humanity. God created only one man so that people should not try to feel superior to one another and boast of their lineage in this wise: "I am descended from a more distinguished Adam than you" . . . When a maker of coins does his work he uses only one mould and all the coins emerge alike. But the Kings of Kings, blessed be His name, has created all mankind in the mould of Adam, and even so no man is identical to another. For this reason each person must respect himself and say with dignity, "God created the world on my account."

The Bible teaches: you matter. Not some ideal you, not you as a cog in a big machine. You who you are, right now. The God who created the universe wants contact with you. Bring your moment-by-moment concerns to God. Suffering? Pray. Rejoicing? Pray. Sick? Pray. Worried about someone else? Pray. Anxious for yourself? Pray. (James 5:13-18, Philippians 4:6). David, Mary, and Jesus model candid, spontaneous prayer. David nags God in the Psalms, Mary spikes the ball in the Magnificat, and Jesus on the cross holds back nothing. No prayers are as poignant as the prayers of desperate women. Hannah is reprimanded for the intensity of her prayer — "Lady, are you drunk?" — and the woman with a hemorrhage prays her tentative, tiny prayer silently: "If only I can touch the hem of his garment."

St. Alphonsus Liguori wrote, "Speak with familiarity and

confidence as to your dearest and most loving friend. Speak of your life, your plans, your troubles, your joys, your fears. In return, God will speak to you, not that you will hear audible words in your ears, but words that you will clearly understand in your heart."

Historians of the Catholic sacrament of confession theorize that this ritual helped to give birth to the individual, the concept of progress, and the novel. To make a good confession, Catholics had to pay attention to themselves, their own thoughts, words, and deeds. They did so because they were convinced that the creator of the universe was paying attention to them. Confession promised that things could go from bad to good over time. You sinned. You confessed. You were forgiven. Progress and a teleological worldview were born, or at least reinforced. Confession demanded the organization of sins into a coherent narrative — a story — that would be understood by one other — an audience. Confession shaped life into a teleological, linear format, one that served the invention of the novel. Tell people that the gods must drink human blood in order to keep the world running smoothly — you create a society of genitalia stabbers. Tell people that God wants to hear from them — you create a society of novel-writers, of people who believe in progress.

Yes, yes, yes. I know what Prof. X would say. I know what Thomas Merton did say. "Christians fight wars." News flash: Merton's Zapotecs fought wars. Prof. X's Zen masters provided Imperial Japan's justification for being every bit as evil as Nazi Germany during WW II. Read Brian Victoria's *Zen at War*. Everyone fights wars. Not everyone produces a society in which a girl's face matters. I was once a girl. I want to live in that society.

In the Bible, men and women pray in a variety of postures: standing, sitting, kneeling, lying down, and, rarely, prostrate. The signature Jewish posture for prayer, though, is standing. The Amidah is the central prayer of Jewish liturgy. "Amidah" in English means "standing," and it is prayed while one is standing. Standing in prayer imitates the posture of the angels. In the Jewish Bible, angels stand in Ezekiel 1:7; in Christian scripture, angels stand before God in Revelation 8:2.

Jesus repeatedly tells people to stand up. "Jesus said to him, 'Get up! Pick up your mat and walk!'" (John 5:8) "Lazarus, arise!" (John 11:43) "Little girl, get up!" (Mark 5:41) Most significantly, Jesus re-establishes collegiality with his disciples after they have seen him certified as the Son of God. In Matthew 17, God's voice emerges from a heavenly cloud and states, "This is my beloved Son, with whom I am well pleased; listen to him." It's only natural that Jesus's disciples "fall prostrate." It's what Jesus does next that is remarkable. He touches his prostrate friends and says, "Rise, and do not be afraid."

The example set by Jesus, their role model, is not lost on the disciples. After Jesus's death, an angel of God visited Cornelius, a Roman centurion. In a vision, the angel told Cornelius to summon Peter to hear about Jesus. Cornelius did so. As soon as he saw Peter, Cornelius fell down prostrate at Peter's feet; what else would Cornelius do? But Peter raised Cornelius up and said, "Stand up. I am only a man myself."

There is an entity that demands worship from prostrate humans who have fallen on their faces — Satan (Matthew 4:9).

What was going on in the rest of the world when the sofers were recording the story of Genesis? In one of the most influential civilizations on earth, Egyptians were worshipping ibises, crocodiles, and dung beetles. In Egypt, no one looked at man as being the image and likeness of one loving creator God. Gods and man were very different. This difference is reflected in the care shown to real live people. During the First Dynasty, when a pharaoh died, his retainers were killed so that they could be placed in his tomb with him to serve him in the afterlife. The tens of thousands of Egyptian workers who erected the pyramids were not mummified. Mummification was required for a good afterlife. Egyptians mummified perhaps seventy million animals. Ibises were mummified in their millions. Ibises received attention, care, and the promise of a fine afterlife that was denied to human workers because ibises have curved beaks, and Egyptians took that curvature as a sign that these birds were magically connected to the Moon. Thoth, the Egyptian moon god, is depicted with the head of an ibis. The Moon was sacred because the Moon provided light at night and a way to measure time. Non-royal humans, those pyramid builders, were not sacred.

In one funerary papyrus, an Egyptian noblewoman prostrates herself — she lies down on her face in worship — before a crocodile. Crocodiles lived in the Nile. The Nile flooded. Floods fertilized Egyptian soil. Therefore: crocodiles are Sobek, god of fertility. In an ancient Egyptian pyramid text, Sobek says, "I urinate and copulate with my penis. I am lord of semen who takes women from their husbands to the place I like according to my mind's fancy." And so an Egyptian woman prostrates herself before a crocodile.

Dung beetles roll mammal poop into a ball and drag it under ground. Female dung beetles lay their eggs in the poop balls. Egyptians thought the poop balls themselves were actually the eggs and they thought the dung beetles didn't require females to reproduce. They associated dung beetles with their god Khepri, who fertilized himself by swallowing his own semen. Egyptians wore scarab jewelry in the shape of dung beetles to ensure their own immortality. And Egyptians buried their dead in underground chambers with vertical shafts and horizontal passageways not unlike the poop ball burrows dung beetles made for their eggs.

Egyptians elevated the peregrine falcon to divine and monarchical status. Horus, the falcon-headed god of hunting and the sky, struggled for dominance with Set, the desert god. Set was a chimera, those scary beasts that are more than one thing. He was part aardvark and part fennec fox, or maybe part jackal and part wild ass — all animals that live in the desert. Horus-versus-Set plots are like superhero comic books. An evil genius wants to destroy the world; the superhero must use cleverness and power to thwart him.

Horus's origin story: conflict with Set began before Horus was born. Horus was the son of Isis and Osiris. Isis and Osiris, in addition to being husband and wife, were also brother and sister. Pharaohs practiced brother-sister and father-daughter marriage because no one but a royal was good enough to marry a royal. Pharaohs are gods, so of course the gods do what pharaohs do — they marry their sibling or their parent. This inbreeding led to birth defects, infant death, and lifelong health problems.

In a dynastic struggle, Set, who was Osiris's brother, chopped up Osiris. Isis managed to find all the pieces except Osiris's penis, which had been swallowed by fish. Isis made a golden replica of Osiris's member. She turned herself into a falcon — or maybe a kite, another bird of prey — and hovered over Osiris's corpse. The wind from her wings revived him, or at least enough of him for her to copulate with him. Isis fulfilled the Rolling Stones' fantasy lyric: she "made a dead man come." She, thereby, gave birth to Horus, her falcon son. In commemoration, Isis's pious worshippers paraded with replicas of Osiris's sacred penis.

Set turned his attention from dead Osiris to living Horus. In one of their contests, Set tried to rape Horus. If Set can "perform the labor of a male against" Horus, Horus is nothing more than a woman, someone who has received a man's semen in a body cavity and therefore is not fit to rule. Horus cupped his hand and collected Set's semen.

Horus showed the semen to his mother, Isis. Isis cut off Horus's defiled hand. She then masturbated her son Horus, collected his semen, and gave Set some lettuce with a Horus-semen garnish. In those days, lettuce was a notorious aphrodisiac because Egyptians thought it looked like a penis. Set ate the lettuce, and was, thereby, feminized. Horus "penetrated" Set. Horus won and Set lost, until the next episode. In one subsequent episode, Horus will chop off his mother Isis's head. Kids can be so ungrateful.

When I teach mythology to college freshmen, on the first day, as I describe the subject matter and the theorists they will be reading, I have to say the word "penis" a lot. That and "poop." I'm acclimatizing them. The other thing they have to get used to is the chopping. There is lots and lots of chopping. Body parts all over the place.

Neo-Pagans insist that Paganism is pro-nature, pro-woman, pro-sex, and pro-the-body. I am not attracted to the attitude toward nature, women, sex, or the body that I encounter in authentic Pagan scripture or rituals. I don't want to chop up anybody. I don't want to have sex with my brother in order to maintain a royal lineage. Neo-Pagans also insist that Mary the mother of Jesus is just another Isis; after all, there are images of Isis breastfeeding Horus. Wow. Because every baby in the Ancient World was breastfed, this "coincidence" is several degrees of enlightenment short of mind-blowing. These Neo-Pagans never point you to more typical depictions of Isis as a bird of prey, hovering over her dead husband's green-skinned corpse from which a rather large penis stands erect. In some versions of this image, Isis's and Osiris's siblings stand beside the lovers, egging them on. The idea of my siblings watching me during sex — sex with my sibling — who happens to be dead — is not an aphrodisiac for me. Remember, for erections lasting more than five thousand years, see your doctor. For erections caused by a fluttering bird who happens to be your sister who has made a new penis out of gold for you, page Dr. Freud.

Look. I'm not making fun. I get it that when you live on a strip of land surrounded by desert and fertilized by a flooding river, the hotness of your women and the studliness of your men are all-important. It's just that all my life, I've had the sense that there is something greater out there. I seek that numinous something in myth, and in most myth, this is what I find: penises are very important, and a woman's job is to make them hard. And if all else fails, start chopping. It's cheerleaders, football captains, and cafeteria food fights all over again.

I was never the pretty girl. I did find reflections of myself in the Greeks, of all people, in Sophocles' Antigone, in her pain-in-the-ass, kamikaze independence, and in Leah, the Old Testament matriarch who wasn't loved by her husband because she was uglier than her superstar sister, Rachel. God saw Leah's pain and consoled her, allowing Leah, according to the rabbis, to be the very first human in history to praise God. I like that god. A god who cares about a woman who hurts because she is uglier than her sister and gives her a chance to redeem herself through words about the transcendent.

Back to Egypt. The God Ra was also a falcon. Human beings were the "cattle of Ra." Yes, cattle. Human beings as cattle of a bird god. Once a year the Coronation of the Sacred Falcon took place. A live falcon was elevated to monarch status. Sounds like a good time for falcons, no? Think again. Falcons, like dogs and other animals, were bred to be mummified. Falcons were mummified in the hundreds of thousands, if not millions. There are at least eight million mummified dogs. All this mummification did threaten some species with extinction. Ironically, the sacred ibis was eventually driven to extinction in Egypt, though it lives on — where else — in Florida, where everyone retires eventually. The mummified creature's job was to communicate, on the buyer's behalf, with its divine equivalent. Dogs were to mediate with Anubis, the jackal god, falcons with Horus. At least one mummified falcon died of forced feeding. X-rays showed that the bird had had several animals shoved down its gullet, all in an attempt to ingratiate the human purchaser with Horus. The poor falcon choked on the final critter: a house mouse. Mummified ibises had their necks broken. They were fed — snails — even after they were dead. The humans purchasing these animal mummies were sometimes gulls themselves. A third of the time, the mummy-maker filled the mummy with nothing but filler. How would the buyer know the difference?

Egyptians weren't keen on all animals. They mistreated — you guessed it — hyenas, hunting them and force-feeding them to fatten them up to be eaten for dinner.

And of course Egyptians worshipped other humans. In a 3,300-year-old letter, Yapahu, a mayor, verbally prostrates himself seven times on the front and seven times on the back before he may speak to his god-king pharaoh. In Egyptian art, in papyrus scrolls, in carvings, statues, and paintings, in aesthetic standards that go back at least to the Palette of Narmer and that lasted for three thousand years — until Egypt became Christian — "important" figures are depicted as being large, and "unimportant" figures are depicted as being small. Gods are depicted as being larger than humans. Pharaohs are depicted as being larger than everyone else. Males are larger than females. Parents are larger than children. Again, in the Sistine Chapel, God, Adam and Eve are the same size. This is . . . well, it's huge.

In ancient Persia, commoners had to cover their mouths and noses when near the monarch so as not to pollute him with their breath. Zoroastrian priests held veils in front of their faces so that their breath did not defile the sacred fire. It is possible that the Magi who visited Jesus, if following their own custom, covered their mouths in his presence. In Michelangelo's fresco, Adam and Eve require no such face masking when addressing the Judeo-Christian God.

Genesis gave us a God who created us in his image, who invited us to address him with our most intimate concerns, who chatted with us as we stood, not as we prostrated ourselves on the ground. This is all a very big deal. You know who agreed with me on this? Millions of Pagans in the Ancient World.

Jesus died the most ignominious death the Romans could concoct. His low-class, ethnically marginal followers had to meet in secret, in underground tombs — the catacombs. They were killed off in diabolical ways: dipped in tar, burned, used as torches to light parties; wrapped in animal skins and then killed by dogs. Three hundred years after Jesus's death, Christianity was the dominant religion of the Mediterranean world. Rabbi Shaye J. D. Cohen, the Littauer Professor of Hebrew Literature and Philosophy at Harvard University, said that explaining the rise of Christianity is "a monumental historical problem . . . historians have been trying to understand what it was exactly that pushed Christianity to the top. I can't fully answer that question myself."

Celsus, an Ancient Greek critic of Christianity, said that it was a religion of women, children, and slaves. Guess what, Celsus. There were a lot of woman and children and slaves in the Ancient World. Your Paganism did not serve them. Christianity did. Thecla was an Ancient Pagan woman who chose Christianity because through it she could become a full human being, as good as anyone else. In Paganism, she was a daughter and would soon be a wife. Alexander, a nobleman, wanted to buy her. She fought him off. He had her thrown to the lions. A lioness protected her. It's a great story.

My favorite story comes from the Venerable Bede. He offers an account of how Anglo-Saxon warriors converted in the seventh century. King Edwin and his men were debating accepting Christianity. A chief compared human life to the flight of a sparrow in winter through a banquet hall.

> [Man's life] seems to me like the swift flight of a single sparrow through the banqueting hall where you are sitting at dinner on a winter's day with your thegns and counselors. In the midst there is a comforting fire to warm the hall; outside, the storms of winter rain or snow are raging. This sparrow flies swiftly in through one door of the hall, and out through another. While he is inside, he is safe from the winter storms; but after a few moments of comfort, he vanishes from sight into the wintry world from which he came. Even so, man appears on earth for a little while; but of what went before this life or of what follows, we know nothing. Therefore, if this new teaching has brought any more certain knowledge, it seems only right that we should follow it.

◆

When at prayer, all Muslims must assume the exact same regimented poses at the exact same time. They kneel, touch their foreheads to the ground, and conspicuously elevate the one part of human anatomy universally associated, through idiom and metaphor, with lower bodily functions. We speak of "stupid ass" in English and "*dupa*" in Polish and "*esser un culo*" in Italian and "*Du hast wohl den Arsch offen*" in German. In Chinese one "flatters," "talks nonsense" "is scared witless" or "grovels" with the buttocks. In Arabic, "His buttocks missed the hole in the ground" — he is a failure. "Histoires des fesses" in French is "dirty jokes." In Hinduism, the buttocks are represented by the Muladhara, or root chakra. It is the chakra associated with basic instincts, raw survival, animal nature, greed for material things, and fight or flight.

On one campus where I worked, my Muslim coworkers and students would hang out in the cafeteria for hours debating.

"What does it say about your Allah that he demands that you assume this posture five times a day? Have you thought about that at all?"

They were usually quick with a comeback. Their blank faces revealed that they had no comeback for this one.

"It's good," said one, finally. "It is the posture of humility."

"No," I insisted. "It's the posture of humiliation."

They wanted me to clarify. English is not their first language. Humble, humility, humiliation: related words they could not differentiate.

"All these words come from *humus*, earth. But they mean different things."

"Humility," I said, "comes from inside of you. It is a personal decision that springs from wise consideration of available facts. You recognize that God is greater than you. You, out of awe, respect, and a rational recognition of your own lesser status, lower yourself in prayer.

"Our God, the Judeo-Christian God, takes our hand and bids us to rise up. He loves us so much he wants to see our face, and he wants us to see his. He wants us to feel in our bodies his love for us when we pray. His love for us elevates us — literally and metaphorically. We achieve what we achieve because we have been invited to rise and stand and look God in the face.

"Even as we do so, we feel humility. We know that we are not God, but we are loved by God. So when we re-enter everyday life, in our interactions with others, we try to do what God did for us. We look others in the face. We elevate others, even if we recognize that they aren't as smart as we or as rich as we. That's humility. It's in our founding document. 'All men are created equal.'

"You can't make a choice because you are offered no choice. Your prayer is corporate. The muezzin calls publicly and your every move is dictated. The force pushing you down comes from outside of you, not inside. That's not humility. That's humiliation. It's hierarchical. When you finish praying and re-enter profane, day-to-day life, you do the same. The man is higher than the woman. The Muslim is higher than the kafir. You have been pushed down and you push others down."

"If you knew how powerful the *sujood* is, you would never lift your head off the ground," Mohammed promised. *Sujood*: the posture of complete prostration, the forehead touching down; the face tucked under. Devout Muslims develop a *zebibah*, a permanent discoloration on the forehead, from repeatedly hitting the ground with the face. "You would never lift your head off the ground": what kind of god would want never to see a human face?

The face, the anatomical feature most associated with emotion, thought, vision, awareness, communication, intimacy and expressiveness, the brow, the eyes, the lips, the nostrils, the mouth — the features we monitor to recognize, empathize with, heal, love, and know one another — is lowered to the very ground. The face, the one true map of human individuality, our unique anatomical signature, is denigrated as low as it can go. In Muslim prayer, and where women wear the veil, the face is eradicated.

It's remarkable how many Koranic verses that do mention the face describe Allah disfiguring human faces as part of punishment in Hell or faces showing despair when they encounter such punishment. Faces turn "black" in the Koran. If you disbelieve, your face will turn black as punishment. Allah can also turn a face around to the back as a form of punishment. Angels will hit unbelievers in the face. In one disturbingly unique punishment, unbelievers' "faces will be covered, as it were, with pieces from the depth of the darkness of night." Who thinks up such a punishment? Such total obliteration of a human face? Again and again, angels or others say to unbelievers' faces, "Taste the punishment." In Hell, unbelievers' garments will be made "of liquid pitch, and their faces covered with fire." Thus both darkness and light will be used to destroy human faces. Thirsty unbelievers will be given drinks of molten brass that will scald their faces. On Judgment Day, Allah will gather unbelievers together, throw them down on their faces, and blind and deafen them. People hear the Koran and fall on their faces, weeping and humbled. Unbelievers are dragged on their faces into Hell. Unbelievers' faces will be stained with dust. Parents' faces become black with wrath when a daughter is born, instead of a son. A woman is hit in the face for being old and barren. (Koran 3:106, 4:47, 8:50, 10:26, 10:27, 14:50, 16:58, 17:97, 17:109, 18:29, 51:29, 54:48, 80:40 and many more verses not cited here.) Allah also reminds Muslims to wash their faces before they pray (4:43, 5:6).

Of the five world religions, Islam is the most emphatically opposed to solitary withdrawal for spiritual purposes. Islam is the most insistent on man's relationship with God being carried out in public, in a large group of others all behaving in exactly the same way, using highly choreographed scripts and rituals that do not allow for spontaneity or individuality. As Al-Islam.org puts it, "Islam has vehemently denounced" monasticism. A "well-known tradition" in Islam states, "There is no monasticism in Islam." "Man is an entity that has been created for a life within a society, and his material and spiritual development can only be achieved within a social life." Mohammed, in one hadith, declares that the only "monasticism" available to Muslims is "jihad."

A Muslim might live his entire religious life as a cog in the midst of others, whose every prayer is a rigidly systematized routine, commanding rote physical movements and rote words performed in public and monitored for conformity. Muslims and even non-Muslims can be whipped or jailed for possessing alcohol, revealing too much flesh, or being raped, which is a crime because it involves sex outside of marriage. Christians who eat during Ramadan have had their lips burned by the authorities. Even prayer within a Muslim's own room is publicly commanded by a muezzin. A Muslim woman once told me that when her daughter was ill, she recited Koranic verses. This woman did not speak a word of Arabic; she recited sounds from memory. She voiced no spontaneous words about her dying daughter to God. The idea of God as a father who was interested in what she had to say was scandalous to her.

A Muslim friend expressed to me her inner turmoil about wearing fingernail polish. Water must touch fingernails before Allah will hear Muslims' prayers. A Polish chemist, Wojciech Inglot, invented porous nail polish. Allah is satisfied, as is my friend. An online Muslim prayer guide stipulates that during prayer, "Your left leg should be bent. Outside of left femur should also be on the floor and your inside of your left tibia and foot should be protruding underneath the front of your right tibia. Also the right foot can be placed upright with the toes pointing toward the qiblah or it can be placed on the ground." Of course a Muslim woman cannot pray when menstruating. If a woman, a dog, or a donkey passes before a Muslim man as he prays, his prayer is annulled. Canonical Islamic guides to prayer, such as *Reliance of the Traveler*, go on for over a hundred pages detailing Islamic criteria for prayer.

Mohammed, the founder of Islam, *was* allowed spiritual retreat. Mohammed founded Islam after retreating, alone, to a cave, and speaking with an angel. For all other Muslims, relating to God must be public, monitored, collective, and rote.

The Pact of Umar is a seventh-century Islamic document that outlines how Muslims can continue to ensure Christians' "humiliation, degradation and disgrace." The Pact lists many requirements: Christians can't show crosses in public; they can't ride on saddles or wear belts; they can't refer to Jesus as the son of God; they must house and feed Muslims; they must surrender any seat they occupy to a Muslim on demand. The first item in the Pact of Umar is very telling. Christians, to be allowed to live, must agree never to build monasteries or convents, or even a single room for a monk or a nun.

Islam did whatever it could to silence, for Muslims and for Christians living under Muslim control, the "still, small voice." That the Pact of Umar places a prohibition on monasteries and convents at the top of its list of taboos speaks loudly of what powerful places they are.

CHAPTER SIX

THE MONASTERY

I lay down under a tree but knew I'd fall asleep if I stayed. I did not want to fall asleep because I didn't want to feed ticks and have bugs fall into my open mouth. I entered the church. It looked like a poorly lit borough hall. Dead bugs and spider webs littered the windowsills. Ahead were wood-paneled walls and a crucifix. There was a wooden bar across the aisle four rows up; I'm guessing to separate monks from guests. To tell the truth, I've never been in a Catholic church where anyone has tried to rush the stage. The barrier seemed excessive.

I went to the gift shop as soon as it opened at 1:15. The opening time struck me as a bit odd. Why not 1:00 or 1:30? There were paperback, palm-friendly, thirty-day meditation manuals based on the writings of St. John of the Cross, Therese of Lisieux, Catherine of Siena, and the anonymous author of *The Cloud of Unknowing*. Lots of shelf space devoted to C. S. Lewis. Jams, honeys. A slice of monastery fruit cake dipped in chocolate for $2.75. Rosaries. Not as much shelf space devoted to rosaries as to C. S. Lewis.

Clean, shiny, new, pretty, sophisticatedly packaged stuff that I could drop a wad on, had I a wad and a different approach to stuff than I do have. Books, to me, are things you get from libraries; this is easier on the pocket and on the trees. Buying a book can be a good thing, but only if you know you will keep it and need to highlight it, which you don't do with library books. My rosaries are flimsy plastic. I get them from "free rosary" internet sites. I send a donation, but no more than five bucks. I keep my rosary in my pocket as I walk, and I've lost too many to invest in jeweled beads and precious-metal links. Fruitcake is not something on which I would shell out $2.75 per slice, though, for the monastery's sake, I'm glad that there are those who do. I generally spend about $2.75 per day on everything I eat, total.

The cash register was manned by a short, fortyish, blond, plump monk with a high, round paunch. He was in full garb: white robe, black scapular over that. There were just the two of us. I felt uncomfortable with the silence, and so I commented, "You have many books by C. S. Lewis, and he wasn't Catholic."

"But he's a better writer than many Catholics writing today," he said. He went off on the standard rant about the poor quality of writing today.

I rushed to agree. "Yes, language use is often substandard in published books today." My agreement earned me no points. He still looked at me as if I were there to ruin his day. I wondered how I would ultimately disappoint him.

Again, trying to make conversation and genuinely curious, I said, "I note that you have a thirty-day mediation guide based on the works of Catherine of Siena. You know, she was a very assertive, outspoken woman who told male church leaders and secular leaders, as well, what to do. She was very beloved in her own day and is today, as well. In short, her behavior contradicts what the church demands of women today."

"I can't comment on that," he said, looking genuinely fearful. "I would be putting myself at risk if I did so. Anyone who has questions about these matters should direct them to the church leaders who are making these pronouncements about women's status."

I was stunned.

I backed away from the cashier area, back to the shelves of meditation guides. I grabbed one at random. I tried to look and feel inconspicuous.

A pretty, well-dressed woman and her male companion entered the store. The woman looked so proper. Her shirt was pristine and her hair looked like the kind of hair a child would draw on a stick figure woman. A neat flip. I could never look like her. Not in a million years. I nervously fussed with my road-dust-coated clothing and tried to suck my sweat back into its glands.

Suddenly I felt, "I am not one of these people. I don't believe any of this. These authors keep talking about abstractions that may be illusory. They have no proof for them. God's love. God's love. God's love this, God's love that. Where is God's love? Show me evidence. If we are going to talk about feeding hungry children, I need to see food. We can't talk about hunger without laying hands on food. Medicine, housing, bombs, suppurations — these are all concrete, visible phenomena. How can you, how dare you, write an entire book about God's love, act as if that is the starting point, the *sine qua non*, if you don't even demonstrate that there is such a thing? I experienced human love once in my life, while visiting Uncle John. And he was a Communist and an atheist who denounced all priests as *blazons* — fools — maybe because one of them tried to seduce his sister, my grandmother.

Yes, these sudden, violently wrenching thoughts were terribly strange. Yes, I have identified as a Catholic all my life. Yes, I had just traveled far to spend a week being a hardcore Catholic. Yes.

Rabbi Levi Yitzchak of Berditchev once said to an atheist, "The God you don't believe in, I don't believe in either."

I left the bookstore and went in search of the monastery's retreat house.

The one-lane road to the retreat house was lined, on the left, by a single row of young tulip trees and silver maples and, behind them, a field of corn. The corn grew noticeably taller during my five-day stay. On the right was a fifteen-foot-wide sward of lawn grass bearing the distinctive corduroy pattern left by machine mowing. There were intermittent trees, a power line overhead, then a barbed wire fence, then a fallow field, or maybe it was cow pasture, although I did not see any plops. Ahead were weedy patches punctuated with thistle plants now producing bulbous purple heads on their armored, six-foot stalks. Thistles, explosive as Fourth-of-July fireworks, shoot forth dozens of rays of perfect purple filaments. These radially symmetrical flowers are surrounded with pointy spikes that can puncture skin. Thistles spell out, in prickles, spines, and barbs: *noli me tangere*Latin for "touch me not." Other translations: "Don't cling to me" and "Don't hold me back." We speak thistle's warning in Latin because Latin was once the language of the universal church, and Jesus spoke these very words when Mary Magdalene clung to him after his resurrection. Theologians interpret Jesus's comment as a warning against clinging. Mary can't stop the clock. Jesus must ascend to his father. Mary must become the first apostle. She cannot linger in her sweet and awesome reunion with her once dead "rabboni," or "dear teacher," any more than a seed may linger in its comfortable flowerhead. Mary must leave to spread the good news of Christ's resurrection. Scots hear *noli me tangere* as the cherished memory of one of their bristly thistles wringing a cry of pain from an otherwise stealthily silent invading Viking. His thistle-wrung cry warned the Scots to rise and defend their homeland. Poles embroider thistles onto bride's bodices. If you think "thistle" is as hard to say as it is to touch, try this: *dziewięćsił*. That translates roughly to "nine powers." Three is the divine number. Nine is three threes. Poles see thistles as imparting awesome gifts to the bride. What I'm saying is that I'm looking at weeds and thinking of a phrase associated with these weeds, and being drawn into a tightly woven web, each spoke reinforcing the other, encouraging my love and knowledge of each, and my sense that I am part of something big and long-lasting. I feel not that plummet through the void that Prof. Wiles felt as he fell from the roof of the parking garage. Rather, I feel that if I moved too far from my place in it all there'd be a tensile twang snapping me back from the brink. God, flowers, armies, brides, homelands; not too long ago, we inhabited these integral webs of meaning. We have torched the libraries of our ancestors' lore, surrendering them to progress, political correctness, or *sola scriptura* purity. Our memories now scrubbed, we assume that we must turn other-ward if we are to find intimate encounter with God, nature, or powerful women, from the first apostle to Polish brides in embroidered bodices. In fact, all we need do is turn our heads and gaze at a field of grasses and thistles under hot sun.

Beyond the thistles was a field of uniformly tanned wheat. Beyond that, a greenish yellow plant that took the wind like silk takes a breeze. Then more trees, and, not visible beyond them, the Shenandoah.

The presence of the Shenandoah was certain. Even if one were not familiar with the terrain, one would know there was a river of some size down there because immediately beyond the column of sycamores, cottonwoods, and willows marking the river's bed, new hills rose. Given the lushness of the foliage, a complete newcomer would know that it rains here. Given that the hill one was standing on descended sharply and cleanly, and given that new hills rose up sharply just beyond this clean line of drop, one would gather that an unseen river marked this landscape.

Though they were maybe a bit less than half a mile away, I could identify the trees following the river's path; I could see that they were different from the trees near me on this dry rise. Trees, no less than bluebirds and peregrine falcons, have silhouettes; even the colorblind, from a distance, can identify them. The sycamore has a sculptural crown, accommodating its man-hand-size leaves. The cottonwood crown is messy, and the branches droop. The willow is a forest sprite's seductively entangling tresses. Though individual leaves were, of course, too far away to diagnose, they, too, wrote their signature, even from a distance. Greens really are quite different. Observe the woods someday and quiz yourself: how many different greens can you count? How many shapes? The shapes of visible forms, the shapes of shadows?

The emerald green of the sycamore, the long, lance-shaped willow leaves, the shaky cottonwoods on flat stems that make them the wind's best dancing partner—all these take light differently and create different shadows than do the leaves of beech and chestnut oak that prefer higher, drier ground. And all three—sycamores, willows, and cottonwood—do love water. Even among property owners uninterested in nature, willows and cottonwoods are notorious burrowing boa constrictors who siphon water from city pipes. Devout Bible readers who have never gone on a nature hike will associate willows with rivers. In Psalm 137, the Israelites, in captivity by the rivers of Babylon, hang their harps in willow trees. Inspired by this verse, Linnaeus named the weeping willow *Salix babylonica*, the willow of Babylon. It's really from China. Centuries ago, its beauty guaranteed its passage west on the Silk Road. The Israelites most likely hung their harps on *Populus euphratica*, the Euphrates poplar.

Yes, there is a river down there, and those trees are drinking deeply from it. And where did I learn to focus on topography and to regard it as so communicative? Probably Nepal, where I was constantly scanning the horizon to see how much of my thigh muscles I was about to shred, and how much forehead sweat I was about to rain down on those trails.

The retreat house was around a bend in the road. It was brick and accordion folded. These folds allowed the chapel, placed at the end of the building, to be walled by individual-sized pockets of windows and light. A person could claim his own little space, walled, however shallowly, on two sides, inside this eight-pew-deep chapel. Such a tiny space allowed for individual isolation.

On the retreat-house porch, determined not to bother anyone till three, I sat in an Adirondack chair and put my feet up on a leather ottoman. A plastic bucket full of sand and cigarette butts sat next to me. Smoking? A bad sign. Why not a stack of porno magazines? I blame the Mesoamericans. A black, gray, and white striped tabby and a much fatter ginger cat wandered and lolled. I would eventually learn that the sizeable front mudroom was entirely given over to houses, food, and water trays for these two.

In front of the retreat house stretched an umbrella-shaped weeping cherry, and beyond that was a patch of green with a maze of dry twigs sticking out. On the most prominent twig erupted an indigo bunting, persistently bugling his paired-note song, even though the better part of the mating season, and the day, was over. His posture was defiant, his chest expanded, his throat so full of song he had to deliver. His extravagant indigo plumage was rendered hallucinatory by the visible heat and the very blue sky.

I fought sleep hard. Though I was sitting down, I could feel myself striding, coming upon a crack in the sidewalk, tripping over it, plunging. To keep from falling, I shot out my palms and shook myself awake. I was so tired, it hurt to do so. At three, I went to the door of the retreat house and knocked. No answer. I opened the door and went in. Perhaps it had been open the entire time. I ran into a fiftyish man, fleshy, with a look of surprise on his face. I would learn from the bulletin board that this was "Eddie." "Do you work here?" I asked.

"No. I'm on a retreat."

He was with another man, also short and fleshy and around fifty, dressed in shorts and shirt. They struck me as a couple.

Signs were posted in our paths. "Please check in on the bulletin board in the front room. Please see your room assignment." We were directed by invisible guides, as was Belle in the Beast's castle. I wanted a wall sconce to hand me an iced diet cola.

I put a checkmark next to my name on the bulletin board. I would be in room A-6. I found it and dropped my stuff.

Because of the accordion design, and perhaps to accommodate the extreme privacy the monastery advertises and provides, and seekers hunger for, one could not see into the rooms from the hallway, even though the rooms were quite small and the doors to the empty rooms were open.

Room doors opened into an entranceway so truncated that its only purpose could be to separate rooms from the hall. The bathroom, including toilet, sink, shower stall, and full mirror, was to the right. Towels were plush and a Franciscan shade of brown. Ahead, around a bend formed by the closet and the bathroom, was the bed, situated between a nightstand with a lamp and, tucked into the corner created by the bend, a desk. There was a light imbedded in the ceiling above this desk, a crucifix hanging above the desk, and a New American Bible. There was an alarm clock on the nightstand. Just an alarm, no radio. A chair tucked under the desk, and a garbage can tucked under the desk.

Laminated pages instructed and informed. Retreatants were not allowed to play musical instruments, and radios, newspapers, and magazines were not allowed on the grounds. Earphones could be used to listen to recorded music. We were asked not to bring fast food or other road debris into the rooms. There was a 3:30 A.M. Vigil service, Lauds at 7:00, mid-day prayer at 2:00, Vespers at 5:30, and Compline at 7:30. "Rising time is a matter of personal preference." Breakfast was self-serve and could be eaten any time before 9:30. Lunch was at noon. Plainly, all these were not-weird times. No Vigil at 3:32, for example. But dinner was at 6:25, not 6:30. This struck me, like the gift shop opening time, as a bit odd.

I peed brown. No wonder I felt so beat. I needed water. I showered and took a nap, being careful to keep an eye on the alarm clock so I wouldn't miss dinner.

The mattress was the most comfortable I'd slept on in years. Before I left Indiana, Doris Beasley, a Christian and a librarian, gave me the bed I sleep on now. It is so narrow that, even as I sleep, I must play tightrope walker to keep from falling off. There was wall-to-wall carpeting in my retreat-house room. In Paterson, I don't have carpets because I can't afford a vacuum cleaner and soot constantly drifts in through my windows. The bottoms of my feet and the inside of my nose are always black. There were five lights in the room, way better than I enjoy in Paterson where I have to tote around my one lamp. It doesn't flicker or shock me if I handle it gingerly. I found it on the street. The retreat room was air-conditioned. My Paterson apartment is a box of hot air from June to September. Once I bought some chocolate chips for cookies; in one day, on the cupboard shelf, they melted. In other words, in every respect, these digs were cushier than I enjoy. Would that whatever vow of poverty I took before I shouldered this incarnation guaranteed the luxury that can be found in a twentieth-century American monastery.

◆

The dining room had three long tables with settings for six, six, and three; the six and six tables against the long walls, the setting for three along the back. Windows opened on one long side, the southwest, and one short side, the west. A floating ball thermometer sat on a shelf in a glass case in the corner farthest from the entry door. In that case, there were also a couple of small monk dolls and a couple of animal dolls, including a reclining cat. There was a three-part steamer tray in the corner closest to the kitchen door, a door that had two halves so the lower half could be closed and locked during the day, leaving the upper half open. Cabinets for glasses and drawers for silverware were in the front near the entry door. The air conditioning was on full blast.

Table settings included plastic placemats; plain, heavy-duty china dishes; heavy-duty, heavily streaked drinking glasses; butter knife; two forks; two spoons; and paper napkins.

Every knife, fork, and spoon I own I found on the street. Before I became this poor that sentence would have sounded unbelievably bizarre to me. Even my immigrant parents had silverware with a graceful "G" monogrammed on the handle. A wedding gift? A delivery truck that got "lost" as sometimes happened in our working-class neighborhood — wink wink nudge nudge? My dad finally placed a bet on the right horse? Dunno. Didn't ask. These days I gaze at my full, if mismatched, silverware drawer and contemplate what Americans throw away onto public streets. I've had my very best, sharpest knife for ten years. It slices tomatoes without squishing. I found it while walking on Preakness Avenue in Wayne, NJ. In fact, I find so much cutlery that I am selective. I don't take anything made of low quality metals. I don't take anything that has been distorted by being run over. I have found so many soup spoons that I don't take any of those, not even the really good ones. I mention this because the retreat house silverware, cups, glasses, and dishes matched. To me, that's not vow-of-poverty. Not condemning. Just observing.

The laminated instructions told us that we were to maintain silence. As far as I could make out (which isn't very far, because I was doing this, too), everyone in the dining hall stood for grace before the meal with their hands folded and extended down front as if we were cradling basketballs: this is typical at-ease, at-prayer posture for Catholics. Our heads were bowed, and our eyes were on our plates. We were cloistering ourselves with our posture and our gaze. For the most part, these attitudes were maintained throughout the retreat.

A tall, thin, elderly man shuffled into the room. This was Brother "Andrew," the "Guest Master," as identified on the laminated sheet, but not by Brother Andrew: he did not introduce himself. Only retreatants ate in this dining room; Brother Andrew was the sole monk among us. He had a helmet of thick, industrial gray hair in a bowl cut and a salt-and-pepper beard and mustache. He wore a striped shirt and white pants. He wore these throughout the week. His shuffle was pronounced; his feet dragged along the ground, and he moved slowly.

He spoke. "Sometimes, you think, 'I'm going to make a retreat.' And, then, you make a retreat." He went on in this vein for some time. He told us he has cats. "I call them my rodent patrol. They are people-friendly." The cats did not wear bells, and they roamed freely in a natural area. Domestic cats kill between one and four billion birds annually. They do more damage to American wildlife than wildfires, oil spills, or hunters. Just by being aware of these facts, I was highlighting for myself why I am a weirdo and have no friends. I'm sure most retreatants regarded the cats as purring, picturesque, warm-and-fuzzy fringe benefits.

Brother Andrew shuffled over to the steamer tray and said, "It looks like we are having Monday night soup for dinner." He reached a ladle into the pot and stirred from the bottom, chanting, "Friday, Saturday, Sunday, Monday. Yes, it's Monday night soup." I could see that Brother

Andrew was a nice guy. His patter wasn't working for me, though I could see how some might find it to be charmingly unassuming. For me, unassuming words from any adult sound assuming, as if the person is thinking, "I will be credited with humility if I talk like Forrest Gump," which is a pretty calculating thing to think.

In addition to soup, we had packaged salad, one of the most expensive things you can buy in terms of cost added to the actual price of its constituent ingredients. Dessert was a vanilla bundt cake with chocolate frosting. I later asked the cook — she didn't make it from scratch, which would have been cheaper, and she didn't make it from butter and real eggs, which would have been more wholesome. She made it from a box mix, one of the most nutritionally shabby things you can buy.

There wasn't any protein at this meal. The lack of protein at the meal was a play at poverty. It wasn't poverty. Dried beans are the budget shopper's best friends. I eat them pretty much every day. Peasants in Nepal, a "food deficit" nation, know enough to serve roasted soybeans with roasted cow corn kernels. The beans plus the grain makes for complete protein, something humans require. Even John the Baptist was sure to combine high-protein locusts with his wild honey. The protein-free meals we retreatants were served might pose prettily for a magazine spread on poverty, but they have little to do with real poverty.

Breakfast — packaged, name-brand cereals like Fruit Loops. The grains on which these cereals are based cost pennies per pound. The cereals themselves cost more per pound than steak. Their second ingredient, after grain, is sugar. They often include hydrogenated oils, making them more fatty and less healthy than meats and cheese. Their excessive packaging is toxic to the earth. So, no, I didn't like the food.

Thomas Merton, of course, had it worse. "There is no point," Merton wrote, in reliving the monastery life as he lived it back in the 1940s. "With sign language, no heat, and bad food. In Lent you get up, you have no breakfast, and you go out and break rock on the back road like a convict . . . Of course, by now, we've had a certain amount of renewal. You get a decent breakfast. You can get cornflakes if you want them. The cornflakes are there and you can pick them up." Thomas Merton loved the cornflakes. Would I ever see eye-to-eye with Thomas Merton about anything?

◆

At that first meal, I hoped that Brother Andrew would go around the room and have us all introduce ourselves. Something like, "Hello, my name is Fred, and I'm here for a quiet retreat, so I won't be engaging in conversation, but I'll be keeping you all in my prayers." In my experience, having a human body so close without a basic introduction renders everyone in the room much more intriguing than they have any right to be. Sidelong glances and throwaway utterances like "excuse me" and what they reveal — for example, the Irish accent of the man next to me — become entirely too riveting. I'm still curious about Eddie and his partner in a way that I normally would not be.

I knew this man's name was Eddie because I had seen it on the retreat house bulletin board. One day Eddie approached me in the dining room as I was eating my otherwise solitary self-serve breakfast and said, "Me and my mumble-mumble drove down from Brooklyn together." Really, that's what he said. It wasn't a word I didn't hear, it wasn't a word. It was "mumble-mumble."

I assumed that Eddie was gay, that the man he drove from Brooklyn with was his partner, and that neither wanted to say that directly because they feared sanction. I would have not sanctioned them.

I wanted to say, "Eddie, there is no need for the word 'mumble-mumble' with me. Yes, I am Catholic. Yes, we are in a monastery. You know what, Eddie? In the same way that some people stereotype homosexuals, some homosexuals stereotype Christians. I don't care if you are gay, and I don't know any Catholics who do. I've been Catholic my entire life, and I've never heard a Catholic say a single negative thing about gay people.

"You know who gives gay men a hard time, Eddie? Lots and lots of straight men, utterly independent of Christianity. Eddie, some day listen closely to the comedy of atheists like Bill Maher.

I've never heard him do a routine that didn't include a gay bashing joke, however subtly disguised. It's the great church of macho that threatens you and me both, Eddie. Let's be comrades." But I didn't say that. This was a retreat. I was supposed to be silent.

"Suzi" was a pretty, painfully thin, heavily made-up bottle blonde. She spoke to me only once. In that silence, I made up a backstory about Suzi. I wasn't trying. It just popped into my head, into the vacuum of information.

During lunch on Tuesday, Suzi and I approached the steam tray. I wondered if the mystery meat, swimming in a thick, milk-colored sauce was chicken, pork, or fish. "Does anyone know what that is?" I asked.

"Chicken breasts . . . maybe?" Suzi ventured. She placed food on her plate, but she did not take a seat. Rather, she walked rapidly into the kitchen, and then just as quickly she walked out, with nothing in her hands. She then zoomed out of the room.

About twenty minutes later, Suzi re-entered in skimpy jogging clothes. She was covered with sweat and breathing heavily. She draped herself across a chair in the corner. If you're prostrate, why be prostrate in a dining room? She wasn't asking us for help. She was just lolling there, panting and dropping sweat onto the floor. This was a heat wave. It was high noon. What was going on? One thing was clear: Suzi was announcing, silently, that she had not eaten and gone jogging instead! After lunch, I saw Suzi sitting on the green lawn, talking into a cell phone with great concentration.

The mind craves detail and narrative. My mind invented its own. My asking if anyone could identify the meat triggered Suzi's anorexia. She ran outside and indulged in her addiction to exercise. Then she collapsed in jogging clothes in the dining room, in front of us, to demonstrate her virtue. Then she phoned her therapist. I have no idea if any of that is true, and I don't care. I'm reporting, merely, that when we witness our fellow humans, even if we don't speak to them, it's hard not to fill in any blanks.

Just as I had been making silent assumptions about him, Eddie had made a couple about me — accurate ones. I'm guessing he saw me birdwatching. He approached and said. "I was here fifteen years ago, and I saw a bald eagle as big as a Piper Cub fly right over the retreat house."

I replied, "Eddie, may I call you Eddie? I saw your name on the bulletin board. Listen, when addressing a birdwatcher, you do not compliment a bird by comparing it to a plane. You compliment a plane by comparing it to a bird. And, by the way, I don't care if you are gay." No, I didn't really say that, either. I said, "Oh, wow!" and I scanned the skies the rest of the time I was there seeking that bald eagle.

A mere facial expression can be the opening scene of a short story. The man with the Irish accent looked not just sad, but torn. I heard a fife and drum dirge every time I caught sight of him. What was his woe? Why didn't he unburden himself to me as I walked along the bucolic roads worrying about him? I could have solved it all for him! Instead, I had to stand there, meal after meal, staring at my hands folded in front of me, sending him healing vibes.

Of course, it's right that he did not share his woe with me in words but only in his troubled face. "Solving" other people's problems would just be a distraction for retreatants, a way to escape from confronting self.

◆

One of the first things I did was sign up on the lobby bulletin board to speak with the monk-priest. I took the very first slot, Tuesday morning at nine. After breakfast, I waited in the library. Attached to the library was a sun porch with a spectacular view of the fields and hills beyond.

I was surprised, given the high quality of everything else, that the library books looked moth-eaten and not very interesting. These were not the same sleek, sexy, consumer-friendly books found in the gift shop.

I was waiting for my 9:00 A.M. meeting with Father "Justin." The man with an Irish accent waited with me. He seemed anxious, as if he had a bomb under his shirt. I knew I would be conscious of him waiting outside as I chatted with Father Justin.

Father Justin didn't show by nine. Or nine-oh-five. Or nine-ten. I was crying. This was proof. This retreat was all just a formality. God hates me. I would kill myself. There is no balm in Gilead, only for the kind of people who'd frequent the gift shop.

Father Justin showed up at nine fifteen. He was in that stage of elderly that comes right before death. The first thing he did was tell me to move, to sit in the other chair in his office. The office was as big as a closet. It was not clear to me why my moving a matter of inches was necessary. I did. He then turned his back to me and began to fiddle with venetian blinds. Then he sat down. He told me he was late because he had forgotten to mail a graduation card and backtracked to mail it so it would arrive in time. There wasn't much of an apology in what he said, if there was any.

He asked my name. I had to repeat "Danusha" several times. When he finally got it, he said, "Now I've heard everything." Danusha — Danusia in Polish spelling — is a perfectly respectable name. It's Lech Walesa's wife's name. There was no call for a priest, in such a sensitive setting, after arriving late and not apologizing, to mock a supplicant's name. He demanded, in a rushed, loud way, "What did you come to talk about?"

I glanced at the clock. "We've got only ten minutes."

"Oh, no, we can take the full half hour."

"But there are other people —"

"They'll just have to wait."

I thought of the Irish guy outside. His face looked like it had escaped from a monument to the Potato Famine.

I pulled out the bag of books I'd been carrying. I explained, again, what I'd previously explained in emails about my finances.

Father Justin said, "You will have to speak more distinctly."

I never do that to people. I say, "I am hearing impaired." I put the onus on me, not on them. And, "more distinctly"? No one speaks more distinctly than I, someone who has taught English to students in Africa, Asia, Europe, and North America.

Father Justin flipped through the books. "Since you are Polish I doubt you have brought anything heretical."

I didn't know how to respond to that.

"Now, what is your concern?" he asked.

In a silent monastery, I was hesitant to begin shouting, "I HAVE NO MONEY. I AM ALONE. I AM CONTEMPLATING SUICIDE."

I sat with my arms tight across my belly.

"Don't look so tight and tense," he ordered.

"I can't talk." I said.

"I can respect that," he said, in a voice that finally sounded compassionate. "Don't read anything you've brought with you. Read something you find in our library. Do you like chant?" I said that I do. "Listen to us chanting in the chapel. Perhaps a line from a chant, or from a sermon, or a biblical reading will speak to you. Meditate on the Blessed Sacrament. Let Jesus be all you see. You may see more. You may have a vision. Go for walks around the grounds. God speaks in silence."

Too wounded to travel far, I stumbled into the library. I saw Roger Tory Peterson tapes of the birdsongs of North America. We were not supposed to listen to broadcast radio, but we could listen to recorded music, and apparently, also, recorded birdsong.

I fiddled with the library's cassette recorder. I stuck the jack for my Walkman headphones into the hole marked "microphone." I had progressed from the call of the red-tailed hawk through to the bald eagle when Eddie poked his head into the library, saw me, smiled indulgently, and left. I was confused for a second, then realized that the birdsongs were not going through my headphones at all but were being broadcast. Good grief, what a dyslexic faux pas, to broadcast birdsongs into a silent monastery. Red-faced, I turned off the machine and left.

I returned to A-6. Time was warped, or time was . . . different. In that tiny room, with no TV, no radio, no telephone, no other person present, in a minimum amount of time, I had been whipsawed into the kind of turmoil that it normally takes a major life loss to conjure.

I really, really wanted to eat something sweet, to watch TV, to call someone, to do anything that would erase Father Justin and that encounter and what that encounter meant. I had come here to give God a chance to guide me, and God had just thrown a pie in my face.

I decided to leave the next morning. It was too late in the day to start hitchhiking back to DC now.

At lunch, I didn't stand in "Catholic at prayer at ease" position. I stood with my arms folded tightly across my chest. I didn't bless myself or participate in the grace before meals. I stared out the window.

A new guy had shown up. His lower body was normal, but his shoulders, neck, and head were outsize and aggressive-looking. In fact he had the proportions of a hyena. His head was shaved. He didn't look at all like Bruno, but my little voice told me that this was the guy who would somehow remind me of Bruno.

Brother Andrew read as we ate. I could barely make out what he was saying over the air conditioning. He was reading *Lifesigns: Intimacy, Fecundity, and Ecstasy in Christian Perspective* by Dutch priest Henri Nouwen. Nouwen was probably gay. I mention this because of the term "mumble-mumble." The entire retreat, all the readings were from the work of a gay priest. So much for Christians being the alleged source of homophobia. We aren't.

Nouwen was talking about how important it is for peacemakers to be willing to risk their sense of security. "Nations," Nouwen wrote, and Brother Andrew read, "cling to old ways and prefer the security offered by preparing for war to the insecurity of taking risks for peace." Well, yeah. If you keep your focus on what nations are doing wrong, that can sound very deep. But if a monk who hears that read over his dinner is not willing to risk his sense of security and say why he profits from books by an outspoken Catholic woman in an era when women are told that to behave as Catherine of Siena did risks excommunication, then what good is it having a monk read to you over dinner?

After lunch, the new, bald guy argued with Brother Andrew about Nouwen. I was shocked. Here we had all been working so hard to be quiet and self-contained, and here was this man with a hyena-shaped body being loudly argumentative and self-assertive.

Nouwen had used the phrase, "The God of Jesus." "Jesus was God," this man protested, as if he were arguing with a door-to-door Jehovah's Witness rather than with an elderly Catholic monk.

I detected an accent. I asked. Yes. Not only was the new guy from the same small Eastern European country as Bruno, he was from Bruno's hometown.

The new guy's name was Brother "Hugo." He was a monk.

CHAPTER SEVEN

THAT IS HE

That night at dinner, a man walked into the room. Another new guy.

Given the self-containment and quiet we were all (except Hugo) practicing, there was no way to get a good look at this new guy. I peeked and the little voice announced, "That is he."

Suzi was standing next to me silently. Suzi was never the first to say "Good morning" to me during the retreat. She scrupulously observed silence. The only time she initiated conversation with me was right then, after the new guy walked in.

She leaned over and whispered, "That new guy's a theologian."

I was astounded. How did she know? I was pissed off at myself that I am always the last to have cool inside gossip in any group.

He was about six feet tall. Like Hugo's body, this man's was normal enough until you reached the shoulders. Straight up from the feet and then a sharp bend forward, like a willow tree, as if he were carrying the weight of the world, and it was crushing him. Some tall people develop a stoop when they are trying too hard to accommodate shorter people when talking with them.

Maybe late thirties or early forties. Dark hair with some gray; a pleasant face with some lines. He was wearing a pink Izod polo shirt and baggy taupe shorts over thin calves. He looked just WASP, with no additions, the way vanilla is just vanilla, no crushed-up cookies in the mix. The kind of white man that has been invisible to me, and I only realized how invisible this kind of white man has been later when, after the retreat, I visited the National Museum of the American Indian. There, I was, for want of a better word, "missing" this man. I kept "seeing" him, but what I was seeing, of course, were other men who are also just plain, WASP, tall and thin, wearing girly-colored polo shirts and baggy shorts over very thin calves. The world is full of these men. "That is he." I didn't know what my little voice was telling me, but I listened.

After meals retreatants are to bring their dishes into the kitchen, where they are rinsed and placed in a dishwasher. Then retreatants are to help re-set tables. "This is all voluntary," Brother Andrew reminded us. We didn't have to do anything we didn't want to do, he said.

I collided with the new guy in the kitchen. "I need guidance," he said, as he was new, and he didn't know yet what was going on.

"I think we all do," I said in a way that I hoped would come across as gracious and witty. I was trying to make a double entendre. Guidance — get it? Get it? We're on a retreat. We're in someone else's kitchen. We need guidance! He didn't laugh. I tried again. "I don't like being in a kitchen unless I have complete control," I said. He didn't smile. I thought, what, you don't think that's an interesting comment? Well, who cares, I'm leaving tomorrow.

Brother Andrew approached me. "Do we have you all week?" he asked.

I thought, hallelujah. God is here to intervene. Brother Andrew saw how upset I was. He could tell from my not participating in grace before meals. Father Justin had had the humility and the presence of mind to tell Brother Andrew that he, Justin, had failed miserably with me, and to tell Brother Andrew to try and pick up the slack and reach out to me. I'd forget about hitchhiking back to Paterson tomorrow.

"Yes," I breathed, solemnly, fully committing myself to this light-shining-through-a-stained-glass-window moment.

"Well," Brother Andrew said painfully slowly, as if he were thinking about something weighty, "There's something I'd like to ask you." I assumed that since there were people around, he was being discrete and just putting out a feeler.

"You can ask me anything you want," I said.

He said that the next day, Wednesday, would be his day off, and he would have free time to talk to me. "How about before breakfast?"

Hope sprang within me. "Before breakfast it is!" I said. There is a balm in Gilead!!!

◆

That evening I went to the retreat house chapel. It's beautiful, and I hope always to carry it in my heart. It's a virginal place, white, pure, antiseptic. You can't imagine an elderly, mustachioed woman in a black mantilla mumbling her beads through smoke and incense there. In other words, unlike the churches of my youth. That is not a criticism. I love the churches of my youth, and the Italians. When I have lived away from New Jersey, I have missed Italians, though they are not my people.

The walls of the retreat house chapel were white cinder blocks. The windows were clear glass; there was no stained glass. The air bore no trace of incense. There were no stations of the cross, no altar, no organ. It could almost have been a Shaker structure. There was merely a white box with a cross on it; that is where the Blessed Sacrament was kept. The sanctuary candle, symbolizing Christ's eternal presence, was white, hung in a clear glass tube, suspended from the ceiling. The beeswax represents Christ's body, the wick his soul, the light his divinity. Always three — the number of the divine. At certain times of day, fumes from the candle flame cast sinuous, writhing shadows on the white cinder block walls.

Next to the candle hung a simple bronze tube; this served as a gong. In back, near the entrance, was the font for holy water. As my fingertips dipped into it, I thought of all the other hands, all the other foreheads, and how we were joined in a flood of faith. There were simple pine pews, and the view out the window was of pastures and then the mountains.

I liked praying in there. I was usually the only one there.

Tuesday evening, in that silent, white space, with the purest of intentions, I was haunted by celebrities. Catholicism has a rich tradition of monastic mystics. These are my favorite Catholic words outside of the Bible: "All shall be well, and all shall be well, and all manner of things shall be well." Jesus spoke these words to Julian of Norwich, an English anchorite. Anthony of Egypt, while living alone in the desert, was attacked by wolves, lions, snakes, and scorpions. Anthony commented, "If any of you had any authority, only one of you would have been sufficient." Teresa of Avila experienced God as a thrusting arrow of sweet, excessive pain. John of the Cross created art that, four centuries later, inspired Salvador Dali. Hildegard of Bingen produced one of the largest oeuvres of medieval music. I couldn't help myself. I wondered if in silent retreat I would come to know however small a portion of what they knew: the esoteric knowledge, the intimacy with God, the gifts to pass on to all humanity.

I struggled to release any expectations or desires. I poured it all out. I listened quietly. I felt I was maybe making some progress. Suddenly my little voice said, quite distinctly, "Pray for people who have rosebuds for ears," and I found myself praying for and seeing in my mind's eye people who have rosebuds where their ears ought to be. I thought, I'm hallucinating. This is all nuts. Here I was feeling all spiritual, and really I am just losing my mind.

I felt like William Hurt in the visionary 1980 science fiction film *Altered States*, though, of course, not as good-looking as William Hurt was in 1980. I didn't feel, at that moment, as if I were gaining insight. I felt I was, like an errant hot air balloon, losing whatever modest tether I have to consensus reality. I didn't see a future as a revered mystic ahead of me; I saw a future of peeing and mumbling on street corners.

◆

Wednesday morning I woke eager as a puppy for my meeting with Brother Andrew. Outside the retreat house, Eddie and his mumble-mumble were conversing animatedly with Brother Hugo. "*Al dente*," Brother Hugo was pronouncing, with an accent I can think of only as "affected." He was delivering the definitive disquisition on the subject of the monastery's cuisine. It would cause a riot in a prison cafeteria. If children ate it, they would be fat and pimply. With rickets. The cook didn't need to worry about pests in the kitchen because even bugs wouldn't touch that slop. He, Brother Hugo, could cook so much better with less equipment and fewer ingredients. Eddie and his mumble-mumble listened to Brother Hugo as if they were acolytes. Their faces shone with what looked like admiration and accord. It was the first conversation I saw any of the "silent" retreatants have with any of the other retreatants. It was about pasta pesto.

"I am a gourmet chef. I have cooked for Fidel Castro, Benazir Bhutto, and Jimmy Carter."

"Oh, wow!" I said after Brother Hugo made eye contact with me. I mean, what else could I say?

Hugo turned to me. "Other than the food, this is the best retreat house. You won't find a better retreat house. I've been all over . . . Pennsylvania, Kentucky . . . do you know about Kentucky?" And he sounded just like some Brooklyn hipster asking me if I'd heard of the latest, hottest, most obscure band so he could use my knowledge, or lack of same, to judge my coolness level.

"Yes," I said. "Gethsemani. Thomas Merton."

I didn't win any prizes from Brother Hugo for my awareness of what his name-dropping referred to; I just didn't immediately lose any points or present him with an opportunity to behave in a superior manner toward me. He went on, ready to challenge me with the next shibboleth. "Yes, this retreat has the best facilities you will find anywhere: private rooms, wall-to-wall carpeting, and a decent shower.

In some other places, the tile on the floor is just so crude. And it is in a very beautiful setting. I am looking for a new monastery."

Whoa. Brother Hugo's jump from a critique of monastery floor tile to his announcement that he was seeking a new monastery shocked me, and not just because of his abrupt change of subject. St. Benedict required monks and nuns to take the vow of stability. One community, Our Lady of the Mississippi Abbey, states the vow this way:

> We live together, pray together, work together, relax together. We give up the temptation to move from place to place in search of an ideal situation. Ultimately, there is no escape from oneself, and the idea that things would be better someplace else is usually an illusion. And when interpersonal conflicts arise, we have a great incentive to work things out and restore peace. This means learning the practices of love: acknowledging one's own offensive behavior, giving up one's preferences, forgiving.

I asked Brother Hugo, "Do you know where Brother Andrew is?"

"I thought that today was supposed to be his day off. Why don't you just allow him to enjoy it, rather than pestering him?"

We were a small group of people, together for a short time in a retreat meant to be silent in an institution meant to be built around love, and Brother Hugo was already making negative assumptions about me and punishing me for them. I could have said, "He told me to look for him today. We have an appointment," but I did not want to reward Brother Hugo with defensiveness. I just walked away.

I found Brother Andrew. I was, again, as I had been the day before with Father Justin, on tiptoe.

Brother Andrew stood very close to me when talking to me, spoke very loudly, and demanded I do the same, thus rendering any conversation we had both too intimate and too public. He began by asking me to guess his age.

I wasn't really sure where this was going, and I couldn't imagine anything I might say that might be the right thing to have said after I'd said it.

"What comes after 75?" he asked.

"76," I replied.

"That's the spirit!" he said.

I realized that was meant to be a joke and that I should laugh. I smiled as best as I could.

He told me his "straight" name — the name he had before he entered the monastery. I didn't ask.

"Okay," I said, again, not sure where this was going.

Finally, he told me what he wanted to say. He had learned that I had a vestibular disorder. The monks were all getting on in years, going deaf and experiencing vertigo, and he wanted insight.

How did he know I had a vestibular disorder? How did Suzi know that the new guy was a theologian? In any case, that's what Brother Andrew wanted to talk about. Not my struggle for life, both temporal and eternal, but his inner ear. What did someone say once? An expectation is a disappointment in the planning stage?

I had been sure that God would use Brother Andrew to convey guidance to me. But Brother Andrew wanted guidance from me, guidance about the one thing I hate to talk about, the catastrophic illness that had gouged a hole in my life.

"You wanted to meet with me to talk about diseases of the ear?" I said.

"Yes."

"Oh. Well, okay. That's something I know more about than most people, unfortunately. I'm happy to share what I know with you —"

"But not right now," Brother Andrew said.

"What?"

"Not right now"

"We had an appointment."

"I've got to go to town. I'm sorry, I know I made this appointment with you, and you showed up for it, but something has come up. Can we talk later?"

I couldn't believe it. Being blown off by the second monk in two days. And people always do this to me. Make appointments and break them. Always. Always. It's gotten to the point where I don't even make appointments anymore. It's another brick in the wall of isolation. People should just hand me a card. "You are an impoverished spinster, and if I tell you I'll be there Wednesday at 8:30, you can expect me six months from now at a time of my convenience. On my list of priorities, every other item takes precedence over you."

"Okay," I said. "We can talk later. Till then, can I ask you to think about one thing that might help your ears?"

"What's that?" he asked.

"Quit smoking."

"The smoke doesn't come out my ears," he joked.

"You asked me for information? You're asking someone who knows. I'm giving you information. I am someone who knows. Smoking is ototoxic. 'Ototoxic' means 'destroys the ear.' Smokers are seventy percent more likely to develop hearing loss than non-smokers. Check my information. It will stand up." God, how I wish being a woman who provides accurate statistics at the drop of a hat carried as many points as big boobs.

Brother Andrew, a cloistered monk with more on his schedule than I, went off to do whatever it was he needed to do, and I went to my room.

I put on my headphones and listened to my Walkman for two minutes. I was breaking monastery rules on purpose. Doing so did not satisfy me. I removed my Walkman, sat down at the desk and wrote down everything I learned from years of going from one doctor to another, of being on internet support groups, and from reading. I filled three pages with text. I began to obsess on how to rescue all the elderly monks who were now experiencing vertigo and deafness.

New vocations used to be a safety net for monks, but there are few new vocations. Numbers are declining so steeply that soon there might not be any monks left. I think the very best solution is to do what Buddhists do. They do not require lifelong commitment. In Thailand, or so I've read, almost all young males spend some time in a monastery. I am certain that a goodly percentage of Catholic males would choose a place like Holy Cross for a year, and I am convinced that the year that Catholic males spend at such places would contribute to making them better men and the world a better place. They all wouldn't have to bake fruitcake. There used to be warrior monks, banker monks. The Knights Templar were a force to be reckoned with. They pioneered international banking. They were so powerful they had to be destroyed.

But nobody's asking me, and I am a member of a church where the voice of a lay woman is without value to the celibate male hierarchy making the decisions. Decisions that, lately, always result in a smaller and smaller Catholic Church.

◆

I wanted to keep believing. I wanted to give God a chance. I wanted to give the monastery a chance. Father Justin had adjured me to read something from the monastery library, not anything from the outside world. The books in the library were largely dusty, moth-eaten, obscure texts by minor publishers. I didn't encounter there an abundance of the kind of crackerjack apologetics that modern American Protestants are so good at churning out. Books like *The Cross and the Switchblade, The Purpose Driven Life, The Road Less Traveled, The Case for Christ* are all slickly packaged, well-written bestsellers that present the Christian point of view in a way that sells millions of copies.

Modern American Catholics are weak at apologetics. Too many times I have heard a Catholic say, "Yes, yes, we Catholics are guilty of the Inquisition, the Crusades, and the witch craze, but, hey, the stained glass is pretty, and my priest is nice."

It took me a long time to discover the truth of the Inquisition and the witch craze and the Crusades, and nothing of what most people think is true about any of those is true. There are entire university-press books devoted to analyzing false histories built around all these events. Most Catholics don't know this and, I suspect, they don't care. "Always be ready to give an explanation to anyone who asks you for a reason for your hope," the Bible tells us. Vanishingly few Catholics heed this scripture; they just "pay, pray, and obey." And, more and more, leave the church.

How to communicate in thirty-second soundbites, which is all most people devote to the most important questions of existence? I do this: "Terrific! You're an expert on the Crusades? Tell me when they began. Tell me when they ended. Tell me what pope began them, and why. Compare the number of battles initiated by Crusaders, their rules of engagement, the size of the territory affected with the four hundred years of Islamic jihad on Christians that prompted the Crusades." I have not met a single "expert" who can answer a single one of those questions. And the thing is, before I asked them those high-school-level questions, they really thought they knew all there was to know about the Crusades. Their scholarly motto: "I learned everything I know about the Catholic Church from hip comedians' punchlines."

In the monastery library, I selected John Cornwell's *A Thief in the Night: Life and Death in the Vatican*. It was one of the newest, cleanest books by a well-known publisher. It was about Pope John Paul I, a pope I was curious about.

I could almost feel my hair burst into flames. *A Thief in the Night* is a gossipy, bitchy, libel-flinging attack on Catholicism, the Vatican, and even the figure it might be seen as protecting, Pope John Paul I. That pope, who died of a heart attack after serving only thirty-three days in 1978, wasn't, as is whispered, poisoned by cloak-and-dagger Vatican officials. Rather, he was an ineffectual fop who was worked to death by the hard-hearted careerists, doctrinarians, and cosseted capons around him.

Cornwell imputes ugly motivations to people, though he has no way of knowing what drives them. Cornwell uses a trowel to smear thick layers of degrading adjectives on every priest, nun, or merely any Catholic he encounters. These are trite and transparent writer's tricks. Again, telling the truth is all about obeying William Carlos Williams' dictum: "no ideas but in things." Telling the truth is not just a writer's discipline. It is a Christian's discipline.

"You gave me that gift I didn't like because you wanted to hurt me." Maybe not. Maybe the gift-giver just has lousy taste. Attributing that motivation to someone whose mind and heart the writer can't possibly read condemns him to the dark side. There's no appeal. As a writer, as a Christian, one of the most frequent obstacle courses I run is to limit myself to saying what I can observe with my own eyes and not to attribute motivations to people whose hearts I can't begin to read.

"The man gave his wife a gift." A writer like Cornwell can crank up the hate machine and report, "The ugly, spiteful man resentfully flung a cheap gift at his badly-dressed wife." In a word: spin.

It's maddening for me to witness writers playing these games and, worse, to see audiences fall for them. People are so naïve, or perhaps they are just so eager to hate, and they use writers as cheerleaders.

I marvel at how the Gospel writers didn't lather Jesus with adjectives. He isn't "kindly Jesus" or "righteous Jesus" or "helpful Jesus" or "woman-friendly Jesus." He is a Jesus of eyewitnesses disciplined and integral enough to record only what they saw: Jesus who lets children sit on his lap; Jesus who whips the moneychangers out of the temple; Jesus who turns water into wine at a friend's wedding; Jesus who has his longest and most interesting conversation with a woman, who saves a woman from stoning, and who appears, first, to a woman after rising from the dead.

Cornwell insults teeth. Holy See Press Office Director Joaquin Navarro-Valls has "big, fulsome teeth." "Fulsome" means "one who curries favor." Teeth cannot be fulsome. One physician has "a broad mouth with thick, womanish lips and a great row of strong-looking teeth." Another person has "teeth like a child's." Vatican officials clench their teeth, lie through their teeth, and smile through nicotine-stained teeth. Cornwell is also big on insulting eyes. Eyes "wrinkle." Really? It is the skin around the eyes that wrinkles, not the eyeball itself. Eyes can be "Irish and watery." One can have "the large, baleful eyes of a thwarted child set in a curiously wizened, bloodless face." Eyes can be "dull and obstinate," set in an "ill-shaven" face. Eyes can be "sardonic, almost drugged," "vacuous," "glaucous," "baggy," "protruding." Eyes can be "large, suffering, behind schoolboy spectacles." Eyes "smile glassily." Eyes "seem lidless." Eyes are "marbled with brown seams like aged mastiffs." And then there are the hands. "His hand felt as if it had been scrubbed in cold water and carbolic." How exactly does a hand feel that way? Hands are "blemished with dark warts around the thumbs." A maid has "rawboned hands." Her priest employer has, of course, "pale" hands. Lips are "prissy, little." A head is "steep at the sides, like a beehive." A priest has dandruff on his shoulders. A woman had once been pretty but is no longer so.

Pope John Paul II? "He would nail you with a sudden, upward, penetrating, beady eye — crafty, peasant-like." Make no mistake: "peasant-like" is an insult. John Paul II's "flesh" was "a little slack, almost feminine." Again, "feminine" is an insult. A homophobic one. John Paul II "seemed to cock his huge, bloodless, Slavonic ear toward me." When ears are bloodlessly Slavonic, that is a very bad thing. This overt, trashy, tabloid, scandal-mongering hatred is money-earning, prize-winning prose.

John Cornwell is also the author of the book with the 1984 title *Hitler's Pope*. Hitler didn't have a pope. Nazism's highly obvious goal was to eliminate Christianity and replace it with a system informed by atheism, scientism, nationalism, and Neo-Paganism. Dachau was full of Polish priests, the "largest monastery in Germany." Polish priests were used in obscene "medical" experiments or merely tortured to death. Twenty percent of Polish priests were killed. I know this because I wrote a book, *Bieganski*. A book I cannot get published.

My book — by a not famous, not powerful woman — would never find its way to the Holy Cross Abbey library, but John Cornwell's politically correct, bestselling hate would and did.

I was trying so hard to drink from the font of my church.

I just kept sucking sand.

I really couldn't take it anymore.

I needed to go birding.

CHAPTER EIGHT

BIRD-WATCHING

A s I walked to the Shenandoah, two large, loose, mostly lab dogs, one black and one yellow, ran toward me, barking aggressively. I tossed my walking stick, squatted, thrust my hand out, fingers down, and made friendly dog noises — mmm mmm mmm — descending from a high-pitch, from the back of my throat. They approached cautiously, sniffed my fingers, and responded enthusiastically to my scratching behind their ears. The property they policed, a colonial farmhouse that aroused eat-the-rich envy in me, was surrounded by the kind of fence I used to draw with crayons in childhood. Four-foot-high wooden uprights and two rows of cross beams hugged the contour of the earth. As the earth rolled, even through streams, this fence followed those dips and rises. I thought of what hard work it must have been to erect that fence.

Cliff swallows were winging under the bridge over the Shenandoah. Clinging to the bridge were their nests: gourd-shaped, pebbly-textured structures made of individual beak-sized pellets of mud gathered by both male and female. The intricate pattern of the cliff swallows' plumage, one I have to believe some artist's hand lingered over — buff forehead, striped blue back, light rump — was distinctly visible as they flew with effortless skill and grace, and perhaps also joy and daring, so very close to me. I watched them, and my eyes and heart took flight and participated in their beauty.

Beauty is not everyone's priority. "Methods for Excluding Cliff Swallows from Nesting on Highway Structures" is one government pamphlet documenting man's efforts to stomp swallows out of the sky. The swallows' presence may delay construction or maintenance of bridges. The government should reschedule any work delayed by swallow family life. Cliff swallows spend only breeding season in the US. We should welcome, not squelch, their visits and their all-too-temporary gift of beauty, and their dutiful vacuuming up of flies, wasps, and mosquitoes.

"My little friends, have a talk with the peregrines. They can advise you on how to thwart man's efforts to wipe you out. Chat with the sacred ibis, sipping an umbrella drink beside a Palm Beach pool. If you really want to go full badass, take a meeting with the hyenas, who, I swear, are soon going to start wearing suits and carrying briefcases to survive man's encroachment into their wild world. Life is a tough gig, and I want you to survive. I would be so much less without you."

I knew neither they nor anyone else would be less without me. I looked down at the river. Why not, God? Why not? You've denied me everything. Why should I not just jump?

A police car pulled up. At that very moment. Yes, really. No, I am not making this up. I approached the driver's side window and asked, "Are you going to tell me I can't walk on this bridge?"

"No," the officer said, "I'm going to tell you that you can't stand still on this bridge."

"What?"

"We had a guy stand still on the bridge a couple of weeks ago, said he was just out for a stroll, and then he jumped. So, we don't want people to stand still, as if they are thinking about jumping."

There were very few houses in the vicinity. I had to guess that the jumper was a monastery retreatant.

I informed the officer, "I am birdwatching. I have no intention of killing myself. So — may I please keep doing that?"

"Just to make my life easier, miss, could you watch the birds while walking over the bridge, rather than standing still on it?"

I was pretty sure that all this was unconstitutional. As a lifelong northerner, I assumed I had left the Constitution behind when I crossed the Mason-Dixon Line.

"Well, I guess I don't have much of a choice," I griped. I walked away, stiff and nervous, shooting backward glances at the cop. I tried to make sense of what just happened. Even as I was thinking what I was thinking, a police officer came out of nowhere and told me to stop thinking what I was thinking. Mere coincidence? Or . . . ? And if it was dot dot dot, God, why can't you just stop playing cute games and send me a job?

◆

Upon return to the monastery, I saw a striking, stubby-looking sparrow among the short grasses along a fence. I could not describe the pattern on the bird's back. I describe birds to myself. That verbal description, rather than a remembered visual image, is what I access when I later try to identify the bird. It matters much if a bird has one wing stripe or two, an eyebrow stripe or a stripe across the top of the head, yellow washing the sides or the rump. I can't remember that level of detail in images; I memorize it only in words.

My method for memorizing birds is similar to a supermarket ritual I resort to when I can't process the phantasmagoria of items populating the shelves — cough syrup or breakfast cereal, hair dye or canned vegetables. I talk to myself out loud while I am shopping: "Grapefruits. Celery. In-shell peanuts. Don't need. Tofu. Extra-firm. Need." There's this snotty term that women use, "male refrigerator blindness," for when men are staring at a refrigerator and can't see what is right in front of their eyes. I wish someone would devote serious study to the phenomenon. Such research might tell us something important about cognition.

Similarly, when looking at a bird, I'll say to myself, out loud,

"Red body. Black wings and tail. Northeastern forest. Scarlet tanager." Some part of my brain can decode the visual image, but can't do anything with that information, so that part of my brain communicates the information out loud, verbally, to the other part of my brain that can apply the information.

For the pattern on this sparrow's back, the word I was struggling for was "kaleidoscope." The colliding colors were black, white, gray, and buff. I did see a bold stripe across the center of the top of the sparrow's head. I heard its insect-like song. Grasshopper sparrow. A new species for me. Yippee!

There are birds on my life list because I have heard their distinctive and reliable calls, but I have never seen them: ruffed grouse, whose drum is actually the rapidly increasing percussion of air trapped by its wings; whip-or-will; bobwhite; barred owl; saw-whet owl; and the biggie, the one whose invisibility rankles even as I hear its eerie, exotic voice every summer, the yellow-billed cuckoo. Old-timers call them "rain crows" or "storm crows." They say their call predicts rain or follows thunder.

When I was a kid, frogs and toads were so common on the ground in my hometown on summer nights that when you walked outside — always in bare feet, because, summer! — you had to be careful not to step on them. All the civilized yards, like ours, had concrete splash blocks under the downspouts draining rain water from roof gutters. Lift up any given splash block and there he or she would be: the resident American toad. Clearly, "dirt under a splash block" was their home, their address, every bit as honorable and sacred a domicile as our house. These stately neighbors were one of my first awed awarenesses that life is everywhere, it comes in all shapes and sizes, and it is just as valid and worthy as I.

Boys are not known for their compassion to animals. Wanaque boys would catch frogs and toads, put firecrackers in their mouths, and blow them up. I remember passing boys doing that and realizing that there is evil in the world, that it's right outside my door, and that I would never escape, understand, or overcome it.

Phil was not like that. They say that when he was a toddler, he liked to play with dolls and wear dresses. I can't vouch for that. Before I was born. I can say that once I achieved consciousness, he was a young man, and every girl in town wanted him. There's a photo of Phil. He's wearing his eighth-grade graduation robe. He's standing alone. In our photos, people are not alone. Big family, near a bunch of other big families. The Salmons or the Andersons or the Mannings or maybe all of them had seven kids each. I think the Lotts lost count of their kids after thirteen. Mommy looked at this photo, and she suddenly knew. "He's alone. He's wearing a robe. He looks like an angel. He's too good for this world." And she just knew. And it broke her heart, and she couldn't tell anyone till after it happened.

So, when Phil was in the woods one day hunting and he stumbled across a yellow-billed cuckoo that had had an unlucky but not yet fatal encounter with what was probably a housecat, he couldn't kill it and he couldn't leave it. He placed it in a pail and carried it home.

How did a boy from Wanaque know about animal rescue personnel? We didn't have a library in our town. We didn't have a movie theater. We didn't have a ball field. We were the children of immigrants. We spoke Polish, Slovak, Italian, Yiddish, Spanish, Tagalog, Hindi, Chinese, Arabic — all in a town so small people driving through it didn't realize they'd arrived or left. We were terrified of any authority. I was into my thirties before I could walk into a restaurant and not fear that the proprietor and patrons would immediately rise up, point at me, and shout, "You don't have the proper papers; get out!"

How did he make the call? There was one phone in the house. It was black, and it was affixed to the wall in the hallway. Every call was monitored by my parents. If they heard anything out of the ordinary, they yelled and screamed continuously until the call was aborted. "What, are you trying to cause trouble? Who you callin'? How much is this costin' me? We don't want those people comin' here. We don't know who they are. Get off the phone!"

The animal rescue personnel were excited because, as a result of loss of habitat to humans, cuckoos are endangered, at least in part of their former range. If Phil had found a starling or a house sparrow — common, ugly, invasive species that birdwatchers hate — well, may as well stick a firecracker in its mouth.

Afterward, Daddy made a big thing of it. My poor parents. They couldn't see anything of value in their own children or in themselves, and this miniscule encounter with people my parents would understand as powerful and blessed — American-born Americans, animal rescue workers! — Phil's brush with a bird, even a rare bird, but still — made Phil, suddenly, someone to be proud of. "Yes, he found an injured bird. It's a special bird. No, he didn't kill it. He contacted the proper authorities and they commended him for his rescue." So I always associate Phil with yellow-billed cuckoos. And it drives me nuts when I hear them but cannot see them. They hide in the high canopy. They skulk, moving slowly or not at all as they eat hairy caterpillars. They hunch their shoulders to disguise their blindingly white breasts. Oh, well.

Is it wrong to have a crush on your brother? I used to ask myself that, but life solved the quandary for me by taking Phil away forever on my birthday.

When we were seeing each other around Mommy's death, Antoinette and Greg went out of their way to tell me that Phil had beaten them up. I don't care. He was trying to be sweet to me around the time he died.

Shit, that's probably why God killed him.

No, wait. God killed Mike too. And Mike was a real prick to me around the time that he died.

Phew. Dodged THAT bullet.

God is not B. F. Skinner — Ecclesiastes 9, John 9:2-3.

Yet it's hard not to note a pattern. Phil and Mike survived hunger, abuse, and deprivation. They were on the threshold of coming into their own. Mike told me he had put off having a kid till he knew he had overcome the abuse; he wanted to be sure he would never hurt his child as he had been hurt. And so he married a woman he liked and conceived Donnie. He was in a grad program he liked — theology, of all things. Being poised to overcome all the odds and actually experience happiness seemed to paint a target on his head. Same thing with Phil. He made it out of the house. He married a beautiful woman. They had a beautiful son. Bam.

And then there's me.

Sometimes being a member of my family feels like living in the waiting room for the next catastrophe.

♦

Did God cast a net under me at the bridge? Did God murder my brothers?

I try to get this one idea into my students' heads. A fish doesn't know it is in water. If, by the end of the semester, one or two students understand what I mean by that, I am astounded and grateful.

"Here's Bob." I say, holding up a photo. I found it by doing a Google image search of "ugly." The photo is a comically exaggerated Halloween costume of an ugly teen with large glasses, obvious zits, and distorted teeth. We can all feel confident that we are better looking than Bob, and that when we talk about Bob, we are not really talking about ourselves.

"Bob is alone. He has no friends. His parents don't like him. He is doing poorly in school. He has a chronic condition and knows he is destined not to live long. He decides to kill himself. Your thoughts?"

"No, Bob. It's wrong. You can't kill yourself." My students insist this. Semester after semester. I've never had a student, no matter how different or alienated, say that it is okay that Bob kill himself.

And I say to them, "You think it's wrong for Bob to kill himself because you and the society you live in have been affected by the Judeo-Christian tradition."

And they say, "No. I never go to church. I have not read the Bible."

And they have not. I reel off a quote I never even tried to memorize.

In the beginning, God created the heaven and the earth.
And the earth was without form, and void; and darkness was
upon the face of the deep . . . And God said, Let there be

light: and there was light. And God saw the light, that it was good: and God divided the light from the darkness. And God called the light Day, and the darkness he called Night.

That is King James. It isn't even the Catholic version. I certainly never heard that in church. Even so, it's in my head, forever. I absorbed it through osmosis; I grew up in a culture where it was wallpaper. Not anymore.

My students have no idea what I am talking about. "Genesis" means nothing to them. "King James" means less. "*Fiat lux*," "Let there be light" and all that phrase has inspired in Western Civilization, to them, as a cultural legacy, might as well be indecipherable scratches buried six feet under distant, foreign dirt.

I say to my students that the Bible, this book they have never read, is the reason they think that Bob should not kill himself. And they say, "No. Everybody feels that way. Human life has value, even if it sucks."

And then I hold up another picture: Ephialtes, the hunchback traitor from the film *300*. "Who's this?" I ask.

They know action movies. "Ephialtes," they say.

"Correct: Why did Ephialtes betray the Spartans?"

"Because he was a hunchback. Because they killed deformed babies. Ohhh . . . "

Some eyes in the class open wider. Some students are putting two plus two together. Maybe ten percent of the class.

I hold a still photo from another film. "*Apocalypto*," they say.

"What did the Aztecs do?"

"They practiced human sacrifice."

"Is that all?" I ask. "No," I tell them. "The Aztecs wore flayed human skin."

More students get it.

"So, you are saying that the Spartans and the Aztecs didn't respect human life. Well, the Aztecs and the Spartans were wrong and bad. Everybody respects human life!"

We talk about the ideas of Princeton's star atheist ethicist, Peter Singer, who reasons that since adult rats can think and feel more than human fetuses, killing a rat is a bigger ethical no-no than killing a human fetus.

I ask them, "Who are the first and last people the Nazis murdered as part of an organized program? What mass murder program did the Nazis use as their pioneer and their model for future mass murder programs? A member of what victim group did a Nazi kill on May 29, 1945, three weeks after Germany's surrender?"

"Jews," they always say.

"No."

"Communists," one or two students say.

"No."

"Homosexuals?" one student asks.

"No."

At that point, they stop asking. They just sit there, wondering why their understandings are being overturned. Am I playing one of those stupid teacher tricks?

"The first and last victims the Nazis murdered as part of an official program were handicapped people."

"Handicapped people? Why did the Nazis kill handicapped people?" They have no idea. And I realize that not only have they not been educated, they have been indoctrinated. Their brains freeze as thoroughly as mine when I am staring at the breakfast cereal aisle in a supermarket.

I lose a lot of them at that point. They become convinced that the entire purpose of the class, of all of education, is that "people suck," and the teacher's goal is to depress them and make them want to drink and smoke and wear all black and mock anyone who believes in anything.

I say, "Look. There is this thing called culture. And it shapes what you see and what you believe and even what you feel.

"If you were Bob and you lived in Sparta, you would never have to contemplate whether or not you should kill yourself, because as a loser, your parents would have dumped you in the *apothetae* — the deposits, a mountain chasm dedicated to infanticide — before you could even register the fact of your existence. If you were Bob in Aztec Mexico, chances are some priest would be wearing your skin. And if you lived under the Nazis, you'd be recognized as 'life unworthy of life.'

"But you aren't Spartan Bob or Aztec Bob or Nazi Bob. You are Judeo-Christian Bob, even though you don't go to church and you can't recognize the most famous verses from the Bible. You believe that every human life has value, even crummy lives. Judeo-Christian culture has affected you."

Through the internet I met "Crystal." Her website identifies her as an artist, healer, ritualist, storyteller, and steward of the land. I found her artwork to be superb: watercolor, monochromatic landscapes of mountains, forests, trees, and owls. Not many artists can capture that nameless, numinous something that turns the merely biological and geological into an inescapable evocation of the spiritual. Too many artists who try veer into Disney or Thomas Kinkade territory.

One day Crystal posted a "sacred" video of costumed Mexican dancers in New York City worshipping a faux-stone idol. The "stone" of the idol looked to be painted Styrofoam. A faux human skull occupied the center of the idol. I commented, "It's not really sacred till you rip out the still-beating heart of your sacrificial victim."

"Please respect what is sacred to me," Crystal said. Crystal's friends weighed in. They condemned me for being judgmental.

I pointed out that the Styrofoam idol depicted Coatlicue, the Aztec earth goddess. Coatlicue wears a skirt of writhing snakes and a necklace of human hearts, hands, and skulls. She is the earth, an ever-disgorging womb. She is a mouth, greedy and insatiable. She is an undiscriminating gullet, tearing up and swallowing down all the life she births in death. Her own daughter conspired to murder her mother; she is often depicted with blood spurting from the wound where her head used to be. Upon her death, her son, the god of war, burst from her loins and decapitated his sister. Remember? I told you about all the chopping on the first day of class.

The Aztecs kept captives in wooden cages to be fattened before being cannibalized. What remained of that human meat their fellow humans did not consume — flavored with tomatoes and peppers, those unique agricultural gifts for which we are genuinely grateful to Mesoamerica — was fed to animals in the local zoo. Priests dined on the brains.

The fury against my simply truthful statement that broke out on Crystal's website was just another New Age campaign to overturn the Judeo-Christian God. New Age wants to erase the God who took on all the woes of mortality in order that everyone "might have life and have it more abundantly." New Age wants us to forget the God who is a "good shepherd who lays down his life for his sheep." New Age wants us to airbrush out of the picture the God who said, "Let the earth bring forth all kinds of living creatures: cattle, creeping things, and wild animals." That God who saw how good his creation was, affirmed creation, and blessed it all. That God who said, "Let us make man in our image, after our likeness." New Age wants to reduce to dust the God who said, "Today I set before you life and death, therefore, choose life." New Age wants us to replace that life-affirming, loving, self-sacrificing God with gods who treated human beings as cuts of meat for their own narcissistic gullets.

I don't know the accurate answer to the bridge question or the question about my brothers' deaths. So maybe I am wrong. Maybe I am nuts, even. Maybe there is no God.

The red and black of a scarlet tanager almost elevates me physically. Registering it in the midst of wet, green foliage that surrounds it as a cloak of mist and mystery does something to me that I don't have the verb for. Behind that coloration, in that multi-dimensional, infinitely patterned web of life, I witness God's eye for color, God's rejoicing in beauty, God's generosity in sharing that beauty with me. I return home from birdwatching bouncing with love and renewed vigor. I have received. I want to give. I re-experience my own life.

Behind and in and through that tanager, I access John 1:1. "In the beginning was the word. And the word was with God, and the word was God." In the original Greek, John wrote that God was the *logos*. We hear that Greek word *logos* in "geology," in "cosmology," "biology," "ornithology," "physiology," in the words we have for "the study of," "the system of," "the reason of." God is the ecstasy of nature and the tick-tock science that generates ecstasy.

God occupies the location where there is no division. Where I can finally see, and feel, and understand a bird is where God is. When asked to produce his photo ID, God replied, "I will be what I will be." God is nature not as noun, but as verb.

I see a dying nestling on a brightly lit sidewalk. Ants swarm, gouging pincer-full by pincer-full of the nestling's naked pink flesh. This nestling is awesome potentiality; someday, it could do what I could never do: rise in the air and fly. Time would give it what evolution prepared it for: the sky. Not sidewalks. And its spill from its cup nest robbed it of time. It is paralyzed, helpless, its featherless wing stumps mere cruel jokes. Its gigantic blue-black orbed eyes behind translucent pink lids could have developed vision that would, in comparison, render mine feeble. Now they can do nothing. Potential wings, potential eyes, potential claws and bills are nothing against ants, against exposure, against sidewalks. As hard as it is to do, I am sure to bring down my heel on the nestling's head, to ensure that it experiences none of its final agony. My heart aches. As I walk on for the next hour, I go over and over the nestling's fate. Where is God? Why must there be suffering? During one such walk, I decided that maybe that nestling was offered the choice before coming to earth. Yes, you can go there. It is sometimes a place where you can fly; it is sometimes a place where you crash and hurt. It is a gamble. There are no guarantees. If you want to give it a try, I can send you. And the spirit of the nestling chooses to take a crack at life on planet Earth.

In my own teary face and troubled obsession with the fate of the fallen nestling, I see a reflection of the God in whom I believe. In my Bible, God expresses his concern for the ostrich's babies. Yes, they are vulnerable, plunked on the ground by a flightless parent, but God promises that these exposed chicks will grow up to outrun predators.

The God I find in the Bible, the God I see in nature is the God who taps on my shoulder and whispers to me as I interact with my fellow humans. I allow a driver to occupy an intersection that rightfully belongs to me. I write checks to St. Jude's Hospital and the Audubon Society even as I subsist on rice and beans. I visit a sick coworker though she's always been a bitch to me, knowing she will never repay the favor.

What if my god were Coatlicue, who consumed her own children? Would I not see black, charred soot and grimy viscera in the tanager's red and black feathers, the cue for more human sacrifice, no delight in beauty for beauty's sake? Wouldn't heads bouncing before being de-brained for priests' feasts make perfect sense to me? Wouldn't I interpret every setback in my life as a demand for more sacrifice? Wouldn't I become a despicable human being? Wouldn't I lose the very standard to judge what is despicable? If I am nuts to be a Christian, is it such a bad way to be nuts? Where there is no vision, the people perish.

◆

I stared at the wind playing with the grain behind the retreat house. Time had changed as soon as I got out of Brother Bernard's car. When I was sitting in that Adirondack chair, waiting for three o'clock, watching the indigo bunting have at the air with his timeless song, minutes didn't move. I had thought that was because I was exhausted and annoyed and I wanted to enter the retreat house, but I learned it was more than that. Without a digital clock display, computer, radio, or daily routine, a day becomes a landscape. I felt like a living experiment in the theory of relativity. Each day may as well have been a hundred years.

I stood behind the retreat house and watched the sun and wind chase the wheat and the yellow-green grass beyond it. The wheat rippled like ocean water . . . or ocean water ripples like wheat: light, dark, light, dark, light, dark. The yellow-green grass reflected a circular pattern of wind, round and round, an eddy. As I watched, I felt something unhitch itself inside me and rise and float away. Calendar printouts and internal boxes of hours and days evanesced. The outside world could have progressed through thousands of years even as I stood there watching the wind and sun on the grain. That watching was a palpable structure of time; it contained nothing else; it impinged on nothing else in my consciousness. It was an era.

Eventually I ran out of things to say to myself and turned back toward the retreat house. Suddenly, I was hit by that jolt, that rush, that bittersweet nostalgia that summer alone can flood through the human soul. There was a bright yellow flower among the weeds near the barbed wire. It had not been there the day before. It would not be there much longer. This five-pointed yellow star, with its central fireworks display of multiple yellow stamens, snapped my mind to attention. This flower is the child of the summer solstice. I see it only around then, and I always have to identify it every time I see it. I approached, plucked one of its tiny leaves, and held it up to the sun. In the leaf, the size and shape of a mouse's tongue, I could see the pinprick perforations that inspire the species name — *Hypericum perforatum*, a.k.a. St. John's wort. *Hypericum*, the genus name, is Greek. It means "above" (hyper) "the icon." People used to hang St. John's wort, a medicinal plant, over holy pictures. It is named after St John's Day because that is when it blooms, along with some days before and some days after, but not much longer than that. This yellow flower was reminding me that the summer solstice was almost here. In about a week, the days would begin to bleed light, and the year would begin its journey back into darkness. I must struggle to decode what I see on the faces of clocks. I understood this flower immediately. It zapped me with urgency. Whatever I wanted to accomplish this summer, from swimming to enlightenment, I needed to accomplish soon.

◆

I walked again to the bridge. I was returning to the retreat house, where the road was lower than the wooded land on either side, where heavy growth blotted out the sun, and it was, therefore, cooler; where I had heard a wood thrush. *He* was walking toward me. It was the man who had entered the dining room the other night. The tall, thin, white man in the girly-colored polo shirt and the weight of the world on his shoulders. When he had walked in, my little voice immediately had said, audibly, "That is *he*."

And there was another odd thing. The entire time I was in

the retreat house, from the first day, before he arrived, to the last, after he left, as if being pulled by a magnet, I kept *almost* entering the wrong room — A-8. Even after I noticed that I kept making this mistake, and would likely embarrass myself by walking into a stranger's room if I didn't check myself, I just kept almost walking in that door. I was in A-6; *he* was in A-8.

I had been praying for an opportunity during this silent retreat to speak, and to speak to him. I had been praying against the rules. The rules ordered silence; I was praying to speak. The rules ordered a public privacy. How could I walk up to him in public and ask for his private company without arousing scandal? Suddenly, here on this country road, we were the only two visible figures.

This was the only time during my stay that I ran into anyone from the retreat house that far away from it. In other words, our running into each other in a private spot was by no means inevitable. In other words, it may have been an answer to prayer. And, then, of course, you have to ask: if God can deliver, like a Fed Ex package, a handsome theologian to a wooded road, at a time of your choosing, why couldn't God have sent you a job, or a doctor, or parents?

In seconds, he would pass me and this chance would disappear with him. I hadn't much time to think. I came here to do this; it didn't work with Father Justin or Brother Andrew. Here goes.

As I walked toward him, I tried not to feel like a trap about to spring. As I walked toward him, I tried to calm and ground myself by focusing on the sounds of the birds coming from the side of the road. What was that I was hearing? It was a very familiar alarm call. *Gallus gallus*. Jungle fowl. Domestic chickens!

We had been working all week to prevent our feet from pointing in each other's direction. And here I was, against all of St. Benedict's careful rules, pointing my feet right at him. I felt like a bullet. Do bullets hesitate? Are they aware of their lack of choice?

We were face to face. Droplets of sweat stood out on his pale countenance.

"Excuse me," I said, sounding more urgent than I had planned, "I was told you are a theologian."

He kind of smiled, then a look crossed his face as if he were remembering something important and feeling the need to caution me. "I am an *Episcopalian*," he said.

"Okay. Then I'll try not to mention the beheading of Saint Thomas More." I wouldn't have cared if he had said, "Druid theologian." I think I would have stopped had he said, "Klingon theologian."

"May we talk?" I asked. "Am I interrupting you?"

"I was just trying to go for a walk after the hottest part of the day," he said. I noted the sweat on his face, and his slightly strained breathing.

"I understand," I said. We were just standing there. I needed to produce coherent speech. "Look, forgive me."

"You'll need to contact a Catholic priest for that."

I smiled. My smile felt, from the inside, like a miniature explosion of joy, like something I hadn't done or felt in a long, long time. But I couldn't luxuriate in that feeling. This was he. He. I needed to take care of business.

"Um, this is why I . . . I came here to talk about something. I tried to talk to Father Justin, but . . . well. I would like to propose a work exchange to you. I don't want to exploit you. You are on retreat too. If you want to turn me down, please, feel free. But, if you are willing to talk to me, in exchange, I am willing to listen to you, if you need an ear."

"No, that's fine," he said. Though he had been heading toward the road, he turned around and began walking in the direction I was going. "I've been wanting to talk to you too."

He'd been wanting to talk to me? Part of me was stunned. Another part of me felt, of course, of course, this is fated.

I didn't know the etiquette for seeking spiritual guidance from a stranger on a Virginia country road. I spoke the way an opened fire hydrant pushes out water. "I'm a complete failure. Worthless. I've never mattered to anyone, except my Uncle John, and he died years ago. At this point, I just need to admit that nothing's going to work out. I'm old, I'm sick, I'm alone, and I'm penniless. Every day hurts. I can't take it anymore. No one would miss me. Strictly by profit-and-loss, survival-of-the-fittest standards, I don't see the point of going on.

"As you already appear to know, I am Catholic. Suicide is a very bad sin in our church. The corpses of suicides can't even be buried in consecrated ground. There is no absolution. It's a one-way ticket to Hell.

"I live in a slum. The minute-by-minute human dysfunction is nightmarish. The other day I was just trying to walk in the front door of my building, and this ogress — three hundred pounds if she was an ounce — was abusing her little son who looked kindergarten-age.

"I said something to the woman — I can't even tell you what. I wasn't at my best, and I don't remember. It didn't do any good, and the monster just turned her wrath on me, denouncing me as a 'white bitch' who couldn't tell her what to do, and telling me she was gonna get me. I squatted down and said to the little boy, 'The way your mother is treating you is a shame. You don't deserve this.'"

"No one wants to live in a slum," he said quietly.

He mentioned the Biblical Job. Everyone mentions the Biblical Job. Yes, yes, Job lost everything. But God gave it all back to Job. I'm not Job. I'm one of Job's kids. The extra of the star's story. The one God killed in order to test Job. The one who was never redeemed, who gets no press. The one who is stuck in the limbo of abandoned subplots.

The Theologian told me that in next Sunday's Gospel, Jesus says, "Are not two sparrows sold for a penny? Yet not one of them will fall to the ground outside your Father's care . . . So don't be afraid; you are worth more than many sparrows."

Clearly, The Theologian knew how to talk to a woman with a pair of binoculars slung around her neck.

Christians always toss Job and the "two sparrows" verse at suffering people. These clichés were not why my little voice announced, "That is he." I needed to keep going, to feel out why I needed to talk to this man.

"I've tried applying for every kind of job —"

He said, "There aren't any academic jobs right now. Even if you get one, it's not permanent, and you have to move around. I know that. And low-wage jobs won't hire you. You could try hiding your work and education history, but just how you talk, how you carry yourself, they'll see you are not what they are looking for."

"That's right," I said.

"Can you try to go to a state employment office? Or is it . . . " he hesitated.

"Please feel free to say whatever you want," I said. Normally, I reject unsolicited advice. But I was willing to hear whatever a messenger placed in my path by God might feel led to say.

"Well, I don't know you," he said.

"I'm Polish," I said. "We appreciate bluntness."

"Maybe it's pride?" he said. "Maybe you feel you have to be doing a *certain* thing. But maybe pride isn't your problem at all. That's me. That's part of my problem. I have felt that I had to do certain, special work and that other work was beneath me. But I'm listening to you," he said. "Keep going. I didn't mean to interrupt."

He was aware of himself. He recognized that he was interrupting me, and he stopped and urged me to continue. I wanted to award him a Nobel Prize right then.

I went on. "When I get close—close to actually doing it—I have very vivid—you could call them dreams—about Artie and Benjie, family dogs. One morning I asked, why do I keep having these visitations—you could call them dreams, but they are just so vivid—at those moments? And my doggies answered, 'Because we're in Heaven, and if you kill yourself you'll go to Hell, and you won't get to be with us.'" I started crying then. I had not been crying before.

"Maybe you're not meant to be happy," he said. I was grateful. He acknowledged my pain and didn't promise me something that I know, at this point, I can't have.

He spoke in a way that was both didactic and gentle. "The new Catholic catechism's teaching on suicide is this." He quoted it. I was amazed that he had the quote at his fingertips. He summed it up as well. "We are told that we can't-second guess God. We can't put limits on God's compassion. Suicide is murder. It is a serious sin, but we don't know how God might handle it."

"I can believe in God for someone like you," I said. "I can believe that God exists for you and loves you. The God of the gift shop. A God as cozy and artfully patterned as a granny-square quilt. I don't think that God exists for me."

He smiled again, but in a way that seemed frustrated. (And, yes, I am reading into the smiles of a stranger I felt too intimidated to look at.)

I mentioned *Bieganski*, my dissertation on Polish-Jewish relations, and how it had been accepted for publication, and then how that acceptance had been rescinded.

He laughed a sweet, low-key laugh.

"This is a source of humor to you?" I asked, quizzical rather than angry, because his laugh was not at all cruel. It sounded like the rueful laugh of someone who has been ambushed by the very circumstance he thought himself escaped from.

He said, "I also wrote a dissertation about the Holocaust. I also tried, without success, to publish my dissertation. And I tried to kill myself."

"No way!" I shouted. At that point I considered that this encounter might be a hallucination or an elaborate psy-op even weirder than Area 51.

"Yes way," he said gently.

"What was your focus?" I asked.

He said, "I wrote my dissertation about Janusz Korczak — "

"You can't be serious!"

I adore Janusz Korczak. He was a Polish-Jewish doctor and champion of children. He was offered a chance to escape the Nazis, but he went with his orphans to Treblinka, where they were all immediately murdered. I invoked Janusz Korczak in my prayers every day before I began working on my dissertation. I know no one in my real life, my face-to-face life, who has ever heard of Janusz Korczak.

He kind of smiled. He got it too. That we were living an outlandish coincidence.

"My kids . . . "

Shit! He has children. He is married! Shit.

" . . . are studying the Holocaust now in school. I am wary for them. It can become a kind of pornography."

"Yes," I said. "But it contains its own antidote. It's like those lines from the first chapter of John: 'The light shone in the darkness, and the darkness did not overcome it.' There were heroes like Irena Sendler, Władysław Bartoszewski, Zofia Kossak-Szczucka, Maximilian Kolbe, Jan Karski, Jozef and Wiktoria Ulma."

He knew all those names. I have met Polish scholars who don't know all those names.

"Now," he said, "some of these are names I've only ever read. I haven't heard them spoken aloud."

Great Gosh Almighty! Here I was, the first to speak aloud the names of my heroes — whom he knows! — to a man who wrote a dissertation about the Holocaust.

"You mentioned pride. I'm not just upset because I wanted this for myself," I said. "I didn't want this for myself. I've never been happier than when I was a little kid hanging out in the woods, barefoot. I wrote this dissertation because I felt like I was doing something good for my ancestors, for my people, for all those folks who suffered in the Holocaust, like Arno's father." Yes, I told him about Arno.

"I try to work out ways that it could still work out for me. If I kill myself, maybe I'll get a better incarnation. You know, reincarnate as a big-boobed blonde who is loved and — "

He laughed again. "Reincarnation is a belief that negates the body," he said. "Christians care about the body. That's why we reject reincarnation."

"Wow," I said. I loved that he said that. It sounded so smart. It sounded like years of reading and study had gone into it. I could talk to him for hours about this topic alone.

"Well," I said. "What about Origen? He was a Church Father. He believed in reincarnation."

"He also castrated himself, which is a pretty anti-body thing to do," he observed.

I didn't have a comeback for that.

"You're single?" he asked. He rushed to add, "No family support?"

"Yes," I said. "I'm alone. Always have been. You know, I had a housemate once. She was stupid, sloppy, and mean. One night she and some other women were sitting around the apartment bullshitting. Talking about how they got men. She said — and this is something I have never forgotten — 'Whenever I want a man to come to me, I just show him my legs and my hair.' That's an exact quote.

"With that she removed the scrunchy rubber band from her hair and bent her head down, from the neck. And she hiked up her long skirt and crossed her legs at the knees. She instantaneously transformed into a Vargas pin-up. Her legs were spectacular. Her hair went on and on like Niagara Falls. This woman who couldn't be bothered consistently to flush the toilet. Never mind how the kitchen looked after she ate take-out. God knows she never cooked anything. She had to beat men off with a stick."

He laughed. I had made him laugh multiple times. I felt beautiful.

"The first time I had sex, I had waited for the guy. I really wanted it to be someone I loved. Bruno. Right after he was done, he told me that all the guys in our group had been having a bull session one night, and they determined that of all the girls in our group, I was the ugliest. Never forget that night. He later gave me a lecture on how I talk. He told me I should never speak while standing; I was too intimidating. He said I should always speak while sitting down."

"I wish I could tell you that men were different than they are," he said. "I wish I could tell my daughter that too. You know, I think lots of single women think marriage is the be-all and end-all. There's a grass-is-greener quality to such thought. Lots of married people are lonely."

I didn't respond. I know marriage is not perfect. I know it's harder to be alone. I didn't want to enter a suffering competition.

"How?" I finally had to ask.

"A bottle of aspirin," he said.

How WASP! I'll bet no one in Eastern Europe attempts suicide with aspirin. "Do you have tinnitus?" I asked. "Constant ringing in the ears?"

"No," he said.

"Sometimes when people take an overdose of aspirin, they get tinnitus," I said.

"I know," he said.

"I've done a lot of reading on the inner ear," I said. He didn't respond. He didn't want to talk about aspirin's effect on the inner ear any more than I wanted to talk about how hard married people's lives are.

"Why did you try to kill yourself? Did someone save you? Do you still think of it? Would you like to nestle your head in my admittedly inadequate breasts?" Why didn't I ask any of these more important questions? Talk about *esprit d'escalier*, that regret you feel when you miss the chance to say the right thing at the right time. I was trying not to impose on him; I was imposing on him. I was trying not to let my physical attraction to him rear its ugly, and certain to be thwarted, head; I was pathetically trying to seduce him. I was trying to have a socially appropriate conversation with a stranger, someone whose name I did not even know and whose entire life is alien to me, the life of a white-collar WASP on a high-rent country road in Virginia. I was trying to end my own life while saving my own soul.

We arrived at the fork in the road where going straight will take you to the monastery and going right will take you to the retreat house.

Afraid but eager, I asked, "Which way are you going?"

"Whichever way you're going," he said.

"My apartment in Jersey?"

He laughed. But I wasn't kidding.

We kept talking, but we kept moving too. We got closer and closer to the retreat house. This retreat, this monastery, this Virginia road, the very grass were all bending time. What would happen once we reached the retreat house? Would The Theologian suggest a continuation of our conversation? Would he be eager to get rid of me?

We arrived. He stopped moving. The sign he no longer wanted to walk with me.

"My name is Danusha," I said.

"I know," he said. "I was surprised when I saw your name on the bulletin board. That's why I wanted to talk to you." Oh! He had been aware of me before we ever met, just as I had been aware of him. "I used to date a girl named 'Danusia.' So I was surprised when I saw your name."

A girl named Danusia, the Polish spelling. Danusia is an unusual name. When I lived in Poland, I knew lots of girls named Gosia and Basia and Zosia but not a single Danusia. All the odds were against any of this.

The Theologian returned to his room. If he had said, "Listen, I need to go get a drink of water, but after that, wanna go get married?" I would have.

I was again alone.

I was at the edge of the retreat house. Someone had just listened to me. Someone had said my name. Someone had understood what I was saying. Understood the facts — knew the name Janusz Korczak. Understood the issues — why I can't find work. Understood the feelings — the utter despair. He even understood the spaces where he didn't understand, and he was humble and worked to understand, as best he could. Someone I liked. I was warm. I had just consumed the most powerful drug. I was terrified, heartsick at spending the rest of my life in withdrawal, without this drug, unable to obtain any substitute, and with only the memory of this moment.

I was looking toward the monastery, the Shenandoah at my back, and I saw a bird fly from a locust near the indigo bunting's twig into a tree right in front of me. The bird landed at the same level as my eyes. There was no foliage between me and the bird. It wasn't moving. I had all the time in the world to identify it.

Oh.

My.

God.

It was a yellow-billed cuckoo.

No, I am not making this up. Why would I make this up? Not a single person on Earth would understand but me. Phil's bird, the bird I was just writing about in my diary, a bird I saw just once before, in the bottom of a bucket, its ambulance. A bird I have never seen in the wild just flew past me . . . unless I am going crazy.

I clasped my binoculars.

Stared. Walked. Stared. Kissed the back of my thumb to make a bird-distress call. Stared.

It was a yellow-billed cuckoo. Though they are skulking, secretive birds, this one was in full sun, its length fully exposed, practically posing for its John James Audubon portrait.

Later, I was sitting on the front porch in the Adirondack chair. I was staring at the indigo bunting on its twig. The Theologian was walking up to the retreat house. He stopped abruptly. He fixed me with a gentle look. Without any preamble, "Two things," he said. "First, God loves you. Second, you have a gift. You know what you want to do. Most people don't."

I was looking up at him. I wanted him so much. I wanted to know, "Who was your Danusia? How did a champion WASP like you meet a Polak? Why did you try to kill yourself? What brought you here? Did your encounter with me mean anything to you?"

I wanted to have with The Theologian the kind of conversation I had had with Dirk. The kind of conversation you have when you are twenty-five and you and some backpacker you've just met are the only two English speakers on a man-powered craft plying the Ganges River just beyond the smoking cremation ghats of Varanasi under the Milky Way. I talked to Dirk for that one night only, and I have never missed him or forgotten him.

In my travels, there have been so many conversations that developed like a tale from *A Thousand and One Nights* and yet were aborted like a cheap TV show you just flick off and never revisit. But there are comforts, reassurances that though the contact was brief, it was significant, as worthy of its own status as a marriage. I was able to study the person's face so I could internalize it. Or hear his story. Something happened, some conclusion was reached so that I don't . . . the verb just isn't there . . . it's something like "miss" or "yearn for," but you can't really miss or yearn for someone you've met only once. But I feel that . . . that verb about The Theologian, and I wish he and I had reached . . . a destination. Maybe he did. But me? I did not.

I just sat there, looking up at him, making no polite effort to disguise my sadness or my curiosity or my crush or my awe.

He appeared to be awaiting a reply. "I wish it would feel like a gift," was all I could say, but I allowed my face to say so much more. I hope he saw it.

◆

A new woman arrived. The bulletin board identified her as "Becky."

Becky was slender and wearing an ankle-length, sleeveless cotton dress in an indigo wood-block print. She was the best of the humble movers among us. For the rest of us, moving slowly and quietly appeared effortful. Becky moved like a three-toed sloth, and that's a monastery compliment, as they are nature's slowest mammal. Her natural kindness came out in her body language, in letting others go first in hallway and dining hall near-collisions.

When I made accidental eye contact with the other retreatants, especially the Irish guy, I sometimes felt they were giving me the shamed, icky look of, "We both must be nuts because we are both in this asylum." Suzi never made eye contact with me. She was so scrupulous about this I felt like sneaking up and waving my hand in front of her face. Though Brother Hugo was shorter than I, his eye contact was always, at least metaphorically, looking down at me. Eddie offered a hail-fellow-well-met "Hiya" from a silent movie. Becky's eye contact offered the warmth of secrets only you and she were wonderful enough to share.

She had a way of cocking her head that was sweet and inviting. I thought to myself: this is the kind of person who, because she is so evidently kind and harmless, probably gets beat up a lot on the bully-run schoolyard playground of life.

◆

Earlier in the week, I had approached Brother Andrew. "I hitchhiked here from Washington, DC," I explained. "On Friday,

I need to get back to Washington, DC. Do you mind if I ask for a ride at dinner some night?"

Brother Andrew lowered his gray head and seemed to slow his speed. I took it that I'd asked him a more serious question than I thought I had asked.

"I need to think about this," he finally said.

His reply worried me.

Later he told me he had conferred with the abbot, and they decided to give me a ride to Winchester, ten miles away, where they would pay the fourteen dollars for a bus to DC.

He had conferred with the abbot? About my hitchhiking? And now they wanted to "rescue" me by giving me money that I never asked for? I knew their motives were beautiful, but I wanted to sink through the floor. I would have been mortified to accept cash from monks.

I was so frustrated. I had come to the monastery seeking guidance about my job search. That conversation never happened with a monk. It happened on the road, but with The Theologian, an Episcopalian. I have nothing against Episcopalians — who does? But I had hoped for guidance from a member of the clergy of my own church.

"I don't understand why you insist on hitchhiking," Brother Andrew said, and the thing is, he really didn't.

"I have no other choice," I said. "And I cannot take your money."

"What if it rains all day?"

I sighed. The sound was sharp enough to slice bread. "Brother Andrew, please understand me. I don't own a car. I can't afford a car. That means I walk everywhere, and, yes, sometimes I do hitchhike. I deal with rain on a regular basis. Snow. Wind. Hail. Heat. Stray dogs. Of course I have a Gore-Tex raincoat with me. Believe me, I take weather seriously. I paid more for that Gore-Tex than I pay in rent."

"What if someone tries to do you harm?"

"Again . . . I do this. It's how I got here. Look, Brother Andrew. Believe me. I am the person you want to have next to you the day you pull back the shower curtain and discover Norman Bates with a butcher knife. I know my self-defense! Yes, men have pulled guns on me. Oh, Brother Andrew, do we have to go through all this?

Please don't be difficult!" I couldn't believe I said that to a monk.

"Don't *you* be difficult," Brother Andrew came back, pretty quickly for a man his age.

Brother Andrew was genuinely concerned. I was touched by his generosity. I also felt sad and irritated because he wasn't hearing me. I did not want to interrupt Brother Andrew's cloistered routine by making him drive to town. I wanted it to be okay that I had chosen not to take his money. I didn't want to be labeled "ungrateful." And I didn't want to be looked down on for hitchhiking. I just wish he had heard me. I really didn't want to be misunderstood.

Two decades ago, Michael Blake was the director of my training as a Peace Corps volunteer in the Central African Republic, which is regularly ranked among the poorest countries on earth.

"Your students will be so poor that they wear the same clothes every day without ever changing them. They wear these clothes until they are rags. You will look at them wearing rags and think it is an affectation."

At the time Michael said this, we — me, Bruno, and the other volunteers — were in a room with a corrugated metal roof, a concrete floor, and no panes of glass or screens in the windows. We were surrounded by tropical jungle, moths as big as your hands, and random violence committed by machete-wielding tribesmen, off-the-chain uniformed mercenaries with automatic weapons, Muslim human traffickers from Chad and Sudan, and French tanks sent to protect diamond mines. Violence was so random and pervasive, from rapes and knifings to organized kidnappings for ransom to terrorist bombings, that the American ambassador had escaped. We regularly swam in his pool and partied in his abandoned mansion. Even the Marines had fled. Of course we were all at least twenty-one — that's how old I was — and we had all just received baccalaureate degrees, a requirement for Peace Corps service. We were fully prepared to, as one Peace Corps official promised me, and these are his real words down to the letter: "Have every man, woman, and child in the Central African Republic living like an American within twenty years." Funny thing. No one in the Central African Republic ever told me that he wanted to live like an American. Now, twenty years after this promise, the Central African Republic is one of the poorest nations on earth, and it is racked by chaos, violence, and disease, just as it was decades ago when the Peace Corps first arrived.

At the time, I thought to myself, "Michael Blake just used the word 'affectation.' It's a very fancy word to use in this setting." But as time went on, I came to realize that he had not just been correct, he had been insightful.

People really do use themselves as the standard against which they measure everyone else. They really do think of others who are not like themselves as somehow doing it wrong or faking it. National Public Radio star Garrison Keillor said once that when he was in Denmark, he appreciated how much effort Danes put into speaking Danish all day long. He thought about what a relief it must be for them to go home at night and finally relax and speak English. Because, of course, for Keillor, speaking English is normal. So it must be normal for everyone else. Just so — those African kids wearing those rags must be faking that poverty. It must be their costume for their performance that they put on for Americans. When they go home at night, they change into brand new Gap apparel.

There is some suffering we are trained to recognize and credit with our respect and respond to with our compassion. The word "cancer" gets a certain amount of respect. I sometimes see stories in the press about ill people receiving amazing rescues from goodhearted neighbors. Jennifer Dibble was a beautiful Fort Worth, Texas, wife and mother. In 2003, she informed her friends that she had been diagnosed with cancer. She received hundreds of thousands of dollars in donations, and a dozen trips to destinations including Cancun, Paris, Las Vegas, and Disney World. Dibble was faking. She never had cancer.

We're supposed to hate Dibble and think her friends are innocent saints. I say her friends are her co-conspirators. They wanted the feelgood from helping someone; they wanted the status that ostentatious do-gooders enjoy. They picked someone who didn't need help. "I hardly saw her cry," a friend said. Dibble's skin was "tan and vibrant "her arms were muscular" and visible in spaghetti-strap tops. Dibble never allowed anyone to accompany her to "treatments." Her friends weren't helping someone with cancer. They weren't inconveniencing themselves to be by the side of an overwrought person, ashen-faced, terrified, balding, melting into puddles of tears, and making bad decisions about the will.

When Dibble was confronted and asked why she scammed her friends, she replied, "Because the truth never got me anywhere." Jennifer, the truth isn't bus fare. It's not supposed to get you anywhere. Tell the truth, and they crucify you. The funny thing is, the alternative is even worse.

One can learn many lessons from cancer scammers. One lesson: audiences prefer the fake to the real. When I was vomiting uncontrollably every day and could not walk across a room, I was very alone. Fake sickness is more attractive than real sickness. Counterfeit sells. Consumers prefer the spread made of hydrogenated oils and sugar to the peanut butter that is just, simply, ground peanuts and salt.

People think, to use that fancy but accurate word Michael Blake used in that concrete shed, that my poverty is an "affectation." That whenever I felt like it, I could just stop "acting poor," cast aside my silly masquerade, and be at the exact same economic level as my interlocutor. Brother Andrew didn't get it that I hitchhiked because I had to hitchhike. He has a car; why shouldn't I?

Atheists sometimes wonder why believers who profess to adhere to creeds that recommend compassion don't show compassion, even to people right in front of them, whom they could help, just with one simple word showing awareness, kindness, or respect. I think one of the reasons is that human minds deftly eliminate from view any awareness of others' struggles.

"Mindfulness" is a necessary component of the Buddhist eightfold path to enlightenment. In Buddhism, you really have no excuse for not being aware of others' struggles. It's a requirement. I don't know if there is a Christian version.

At least one Christian understood this. The quote, "Be kind, for everyone you meet is fighting a hard battle you know nothing about" has been making the rounds lately. I've seen it on posters, coffee mugs, and t-shirts. The first person to pass it to me was a New Ager. She attributed it to Plato. I knew that had to be wrong. Plato was an ancient Greek Pagan, and they did not emphasize kindness or empathy with others' struggles. Turns out that the quote is from John Watson, a Christian minister. Of course. And of course New Agers would take a Christian quote and a Christian ideal, appropriate it, and fob it off as having been spoken by a pre-Christian Pagan.

◆

Thursday morning. The last full day of my retreat. God's last chance to whisper the number of a winning lottery ticket into my ear.

I could attend the full schedule of services. Matins, Lauds, Vespers . . . whatever else they call them . . . Happy Hour? Halftime? Afternoon Slump? Ladies' Night? Not holding my breath for that last one.

I could try again with Father Justin or Brother Andrew.

I could ransack the library in search of one book that might not make Gutenberg cringe.

I could hitchhike into town and buy that iced diet cola I had been craving all week.

Oh, to hell with it.

Just stepping out of the retreat house, it was easy to see the indigo bunting on its twig. On the barbed wire fencing and overhead powerlines slouched bluebirds: the heaven-blue-backed male, the shyly attired female, and the young, their mottled plumage a midden of fragments, some broken fragments of sky, some of clay pot. Many birds — mockingbird, brown thrasher, wood thrush, bobwhite — were still singing their mating songs.

I walked down the wooded road I had walked up on Monday. I passed a pawpaw patch. It was near the road edge and about as tall as I; pawpaws don't grow very tall. Its leaves caught my eye. They are about a foot long, toothless, arranged in a spiral, and obovate-lanceolate, that is, wide in the middle and pointed at either end. As I walk, worker-bee brain cells assess the leaves I pass. Usually the silent, background inventory runs thus: oak, maple, sweet gum, sassafras, beech, beech, sumac, locust, hickory, oak. Pawpaws merit the worker-bees sending up a little alarm.

Pawpaws—*Asimina triloba*—are the largest edible fruit native to North America. They grow wild and are delicious, tasting something like mango and something like custard. They are called "the poor man's banana." Most Americans don't know that pawpaws exist. That's partly because they hide in the forest understory, and the fruits are as green as the large leaves that shield them. Unlike other wild fruit, they don't call attention to themselves with bright red, blue, or black coloration. Manhandled pawpaws rot to discolored mush, making them hard to transport. That it's challenging to regiment or profit from these delicate fruits contributes to their hiding-in-plain-sight anonymity.

Pawpaws' mystery is deeper than the forest understory and their own easily bruised flesh. Pawpaw flowers are the color of open wounds, and they smell like rotting meat. This is a come-hither to carrion-eating beetles and flies. These bugs are supposed to pollinate the flowers, but pawpaws attract very few pollinators, possibly because their smell of decay is actually quite faint. It's as if this plant, that is at least fifty million years old, is, reproductively speaking, still clinging shyly to the wall of the high school gym at its first dance. The pollination rate is astoundingly low. Less than one percent of naturally pollinated flowers result in reproductive success.

Flowers are a universal symbol of beauty and life. Pawpaw blossoms surrender loveliness, their birthright, and camouflage as something ugly, a wound. Other floral essences — rose, frangipani, lily-of-the-valley — are sought, bottled and marketed for astronomical sums for use in human mating rituals. The pawpaw's come-hither perfume is an imitation of death. The pawpaw blossom's sacrifice is all but futile. It's an art exhibition with no patrons, a masquerade ball where vanishingly few of the dancers find a partner. They try so hard yet they, in futility, twirl alone. Mother Nature exerts herself, and sometimes she falls on her face.

Botanists wonder: how did these plants that can't seem to muddle through life's most basic requirement last for tens of millions of years? And once they do produce fruit, who broadcasts the seeds? The largest animals that inhabit our forests now, deer and bear, don't habitually swallow or poop pawpaws' extra-large seeds because they can easily chew around or spit out these seeds that grow to an inch and a half long.

One theory: pawpaws' extra-large, extra-durable seeds were designed to survive an amusement park ride that's been closed for thirteen thousand years. These large, thick-skinned seeds evolved, not for the guts of deer, bear, or humans, but to spring to life thanks to their passage through the digestive tract of a very large herbivore, to partner with that giant GI tract's unique movement and chemistry, and, finally, to be deposited in heaps of its fertilizing dung. Thousands of years ago, gomphotheres, something like North American elephants, did swallow and spread pawpaw seeds. Gomphotheres were driven to extinction, though, like the other megafauna, after humans arrived. But those same humans, who became Native Americans, cultivated pawpaws so they could eat their fruit. Nowadays pawpaws spread clonally, through roots and shoots, but when a patch is uprooted for a strip mall, it is not replaced by the absent gomphotheres or Native Americans who, like the rest of us, buy their bananas in the supermarket.

Pawpaws have an intimate relationship with a still living creature much smaller and finer than an extinct elephant. Zebra swallowtail butterflies lay their eggs exclusively on pawpaw. If you look at a distribution map of pawpaw and zebra swallowtail, you see they roughly overlap in the southeast of the United States. The butterflies venture out a bit beyond the pawpaw's border, but no farther than their black-and-white streaked, paper-thin wings can take them away from the plant they must return to as their nursery.

Now maybe you are thinking, "How do the butterflies differentiate one leaf from another?" and "Why bother making this distinction? All leaves seem pretty much the same to me." Check this out, you lowly human: 3-caffeoyl-muco-quinic acid (3-CmQA) and flavonoid concentration. That's what a zebra swallowtail can detect before she even lands on the leaf, and what you can't even spell. Zebra swallowtail mothers evaluate and contrast these chemicals' presence in several pawpaw leaves and select the best one. Why? The leaves are full of insect repellant; the larvae eat them and become toxic. Some leaves are better than others. The asimina webworm moth munches on older leaves, prompting the plant to produce new leaves, higher in toxins. That the swallowtail caterpillar can eat something that is toxic to insects is in itself another minor little mystery. The pawpaw-leaf-eating caterpillars are then less likely to be eaten by other insects, including their own siblings. So many puzzle pieces had to come together for this relationship. I could never be a zebra swallowtail butterfly. I failed high school chemistry. And I'm pretty sure my siblings would have eaten me before I could have stocked up on toxins.

Some view relationships like this and see Darwin. I see God. I've put these and similar complex biological scenarios to Darwinists. "Yeah, but really," I say. "We're not talking about a two-dimensional model such as the one you propose. Sure, if you take a furry mouse and a shaved mouse and release both in the Arctic, the furry mouse will survive longer than the shaved mouse. In real life, it's not that easy choice between two options for the hypothetical creature, and there's no hope of survival for the hypothetical creature that makes the wrong choice. We're talking about a multidimensional model and the need for a critical mass of hypothetical lifeforms to survive well past reproduction for any option to take effect. Tell me how all these millions of moving parts, with infinite variables in timing, shape, size, color, and weather, all fortuitously fell together, purely by chance, to result in the multidimensional web of life we are lucky enough to inhabit."

In response, the Darwinists recite a rote reply, usually involving the words "millions" and "billions" and "natural selection," a reply that has been passed down by the great men of their tribe, a reply that takes no notice of the specific question I asked. I point out the holes in their reply, and then they yell at me and call me an idiot Catholic who can't handle the truth because I find the idea of God comforting. And I say, "Yeah, but, I didn't mention Catholicism. I'm talking about colors and patterns and behaviors and timing—all of which have infinite variables, not the binomial choice between yes and no, furry versus shaved, that you posit—and repeated survivals past the point of reproduction in numerous organisms who made the same choice for one given option—out of infinite possibilities—to have any impact.

"Yeah, but," I go on. "I learned about evolution in Catholic school. The peppered moth photos. I still remember them. The darker moths did better during the Industrial Revolution, with its filthy air and trees, and they predominated, and the light moths, that lived longer on clean trees, dwindled. No problem.

"Here's my problem. Think about how you Darwinists use verbs. You use the passive voice. Do you even hear yourselves? 'Larger size *was chosen* as the better adaptation to the colder environment.' 'White color *was developed* as camouflage in the snow.' Darwin himself uses passive voice. 'Seeing this gradation and diversity of structure in one small, intimately related group of birds, one might really fancy that from an original paucity of birds in this archipelago, one species *had been taken and modified* for different ends.'

"Yeah, but, who's doing the choosing? The developing? The taking? The modifying? This ritualized reliance on passive voice removes the actor from the sentence. If you used active voice, all of the above sentences would have to identify an actor. I believe in evolution. Here's what I don't believe. If big numbers explain away evolution, here's a big number: fifty million, the number of people who pass through Times Square annually. Even given that huge number, I don't believe that, merely by chance, a random group of strangers, each of whom is perfectly honed to play Ophelia, Hamlet, or Laertes, somehow all find their way to Times Square. And purely by chance, they are all in period costume. Without any previous knowledge of the play, they spontaneously begin to speak the interlocking, iambic pentameter lines of *Hamlet* in perfect unison. Billboards and discarded rubbish and street furniture are all blown by the wind into curtains and sets and trapdoors. Again, purely by chance, there are accountants that know exactly what to charge spectators to turn a profit, and dialect coaches, and hairdressers. And an audience that loves Shakespeare stops and watches and applauds. Seems pretty far-fetched to me."

At that point the Darwinists get up and leave the room and go say mean things about me to other atheists. It gets old.

The more I learn about nature, the more I can't be an atheist. If you're not interested in the woods, you think they are placid or dirty or boring or random or merely just posing, waiting to be cut down and replaced by something worthy: a shopping mall or a tract of suburban McMansions. But if you know the woods, you realize you are stepping through a masterwork, through life and death, siblicide, lust, seduction, deception, betrayal, and always temporary triumph. The woods seem static to those not interested in them. In fact, in the woods, everything is moving all the time, interlocking, giving to and taking from everything else, creating a pattern that can't exist without its parts and parts that can't exist without this magnificently complex pattern.

That fluttering viceroy butterfly that is the picture of innocence and helplessness is shouting an intimidating, "No!" The birds hear, loud and clear. The viceroy is red and black. This red-and-black message is sent and received to and from plants, arachnids, insects, reptiles, amphibians, and mammals — including humans. Red-and-black snakes, frogs, and spiders like the black widow are often poisonous or successfully pretending to be. Just one of the red-and-black seeds of the crab's eye creeper can kill a man. The devil, Satan, Lucifer, is most often depicted in shades of red and black. The caterpillar of the red-and-black viceroy feeds on willows. If a bird eats a viceroy, the willows' salicylic acid upsets the bird's stomach. The viceroy, monarch, and queen butterflies all look similar to each other. The viceroy and the monarch both taste bad to birds. The queen butterfly is not that bad tasting. The viceroy and the monarch use their similar appearances to warn birds to avoid eating them. The not-so-bad tasting queen butterfly, by looking like these two, gets something of a free ride.

That black walnut tree that looks merely stately is actively poisoning the soil beneath it to snuff out any plants that might compete for sunlight with its seedlings. All this talk of poison sounds like a horror movie, no? But there's altruism too. That sugar maple, gorgeous in fall, whose sap is tasty on pancakes, benefits all the plants around it through a process called "hydraulic lift." Its roots redistribute moisture during both droughts and floods. Oh, and if hiking gives you sore knees, you can thank that willow tree over there for your aspirin. As long ago as Ancient Sumer, Egypt, and Greece, humans have been tapping willow's salicylic acid for relief from inflammation and pain, even though it upsets our stomachs, just as it upsets the stomachs of the birds who eat viceroy butterflies. Everything is interconnected, and we are part of this pattern too.

That very large crow overhead? Wait, is that a crow? No. It's actually a raven. And, no, "raven" is not just a word from fusty poems. It's not just the word that pretentious people use for "crow." The raven's very presence plots a tale on a graph of time and competition, horror and wit. Everything is moving, interlocking, depending, and enabling. There were no ravens here decades ago. Settlers targeted ravens just as they targeted wolves and cougars. Why the slaughter? Depends on whom you ask.

Here's the politically correct version. "Ravens get an unjustly bad press. Any big black bird tends to come down from history with a load of negatives attached. So the raven has a burden of cultural mistrust." So says Dr. Andre Farrar of the Royal Society for the Protection of Birds. That's what you'd expect to hear from a public relations man: you don't like ravens because they are black. But listen to Irish folklore: the raven contains three drops of devil's blood; they always do ill, but their master protects them, so you suffer if you kill them. Ravens play the villain in medieval ballads. "I'll peck out his bonnie blue eye," one announces, of a fallen knight. Ravens, shepherds will tell you, peck out the eyes, tongues, and entrails of newborn lambs, delivering them to a grisly death. "Attacks are so horrific that it's caused mental suffering to people who find the animals," says Johnny Hall, of the National Farmers Union of Scotland.

In spite of my shame, I cannot check my infatuation. Ravens

are the tricksters, not just of Native American folktales, but of YouTube videos: ravens tugging at the tails of eagles, ravens sneaking into hikers' packs and making off with their energy bars, ravens winkling dinner from sprung traps, ravens flying upside down. The raven's prime directive: "Just exactly how much of this shit will they let me get away with?" They just never stop, and they clearly don't give a damn. But here's the kicker. They fly for fun. Choke on that, Darwinists. For fun. Not a commute from meal to sex to death. Ravens fly the way you flew in your dreams in your footy pajamas before grownups explained that you can't fly. They luxuriate in the kiss of the wind on their black velvet bellies. They italicize air. There must be a Twelve Step group somewhere: "Hi, I'm Danusha, and I love ravens, the bad boys of the bird world."

When I was a birdwatching teenager, do you know how many crows I stared and stared at, trying to find the Roman nose, the fringed throat, the pointed tail, the massive size — as big as a red-tailed hawk — that set the raven apart? How many times I listened for that croak that makes you feel you've left daily life and entered a gothic novel? Hundreds of times. I never saw a single raven. They had been extirpated as a nesting bird in New Jersey. Now? A hundred years after their erasure? Raven chicks raise their open, red-lined beaks skyward on a campus roof where I teach. Like coyotes, ravens are slinking and dodging their way into backyards, parking lots, and garbage dumps that used to be forest primeval. The descendants of the men who once shot them out of our sky now have desk jobs. The raven is part of a tide that receded and now is rising. With the passage of time — and the absence of shepherds — everything is moving.

In the strictest sense, we can't say that coyotes have "returned" to the Northeast. Before 1700, coyotes did not live here; they were limited to the prairies of central North America. Coyotes could not move beyond their range because wolves would not permit them to. Man wiped out the wolves. Coyotes now live in forty-nine states. They arrived in New Jersey in 1939, in Virginia in the 1970s. I stumbled on a half-eaten deer carcass on Garret Mountain in Paterson, within the limits of the third largest city in America's most densely populated state. The deer's hind end was gone; only a ribcage, forelegs, and head remained. Clearly it had been taken from behind. I asked one of the guys in fluorescent t-shirts, the guys who have to nag me to leave the park at sunset. "Coyotes," he explained. "I hear them at night." The coyote has not returned; he has arrived. What has returned with him is wolf genes. Coyotes mated with their former competitors — wolves — and coywolves now claim what used to be wolf territory. Coywolves are also about ten percent domestic dog; Rover finally gets to answer the call of the wild and turn back the clock over tens of thousands of years to the time of his domestication. On the genetic level, everything is moving, seeking, and finding a new home, creating a new balance with the entire surround.

The red-bellied woodpecker is the edge of a wave moving north. Like mercury in a thermometer, this woodpecker is an index of rising temperatures. Again, I never saw red-bellied woodpeckers when I was a kid. The day I saw a red-bellied woodpecker was a red-letter day. Quite exotic! Now I see them all the time. I can remember the first time I saw a black vulture. It was just a few years ago. The once southern red-bellied's presence, and the black vulture's too, is evidence of a warming planet.

When you think of the woods and movement and life, you think of animals or maybe plants. Think again. It's all moving. It's all changing. It's all life-giving — even the rocks. Back in my hometown woods, I ran barefoot over gritty, gray-green boulders speckled with black and white stubble. When these boulders broke, the edges were jagged and crumbly. Me and my brothers used to find quartz and flint all the time; Mike could start fire with them. I tried to strike sparks with the quartz I found; never had any luck, so I just would gaze at its smoky translucence. I decided that appreciating the rocks' prettiness was the girl's job. Starting fires was the boy's job. Finding rocks that I could almost see through rocked my mind. It taught me that the line between this thing here and its opposite over there is blurry. Rocks are opaque barriers to light, except when they are not.

All those rocks we played on were the Wanaque tonalite gneiss, the oldest rocks in New Jersey. My hometown, Colombia, Ecuador, and Africa's northwest were all united near the center of Pangea, an ancient continent. Their massive rending pushed up the earth. The Appalachians are part of the same mountain chain as the Little Atlas Mountains in Morocco, four thousand miles and an Atlantic Ocean away. It was a giant traffic accident. Another metaphor by an Argentinian geologist: "North America was a dancer, doing a tango around us." I played on the fallout 1.37 billion years later.

When I first began hiking at Garret Mountain in Paterson, only eleven miles southeast of Wanaque, I noticed that the boulders there were not gray or speckled like those in my hometown. They were reddish, smooth, and when they broke, the edges weren't rough; rather, they broke as glass breaks. The broken bits tended to be polygonal, and some formed mini-columns. I never saw anything like that in Wanaque. Garret's smooth, reddish rock is basalt, lava from a volcano. This lava flowed and cooled two hundred million years ago. The column shape forms during cooling, and column size depends on the speed of cooling. The reddish color is oxidized iron.

Rocks, no less than breathing, flying, warm-blooded creatures, no less than Darwin's Galapagos finches, no less than Roger Tory Peterson's yellow-shafted flicker, no less than the missing-link Archaeopteryx fossil, move in other ways. Rocks move faith. In 1755, on November 1, All Saints Day, rocks moved near Lisbon, Portugal. Maybe ten thousand or maybe one hundred thousand human beings died. How could a loving God allow an earthquake — the involuntary movement of insentient rocks — to end so many lives? Voltaire, Rousseau, Kant and Adorno — the man who told us that there would be no poetry after Auschwitz — thought deep thoughts. About that Adorno line. What he actually said was, "To write poetry after Auschwitz is barbaric." And Voltaire, of course, argued that anyone who thinks that this is the "best of all possible worlds" is laughable, a fool. The Lisbon Earthquake proved to Enlightened Europe that faith is a farce. Just like the Holocaust, two hundred years later.

Reader, I give you Xavier Le Pichon. He survived a Japanese concentration camp during World War II. He pioneered the plate tectonics that helps humans understand earthquakes. He insists that a stable earth would be a dead earth — that without moving rocks — earthquakes and volcanos — not only would we not be here, we could not be here. And Le Pichon is a devout, lifelong Catholic who attends daily mass.

Those who have survived the worst get to decide whether or not poetry will continue. They have voted yes. Those who have plumbed the earth get to decide if science negates God. Many scientists have cast a "yes" vote; that is, yes for faith.

Every twig, every rock, every lichen flake in the forest is moving, interacting with everything else, and telling its own story, a story in which we are all also characters. We learn this story, in which we are playing a part, to our own benefit. Iron is heavy and gravitates to the center of the earth. Volcanoes vomit it up near the surface. Early New Jerseyans mined that iron. Did it matter to me, growing up, that I was playing on the oldest rocks in Jersey? In a way, yes. We didn't mine iron; Mike mined boyhood skills, bragging rights, and cool. I mined family pride. Wanaque's ancient rock is tonalite. Tonalite is twenty percent quartz. Mike found quartz, struck sparks, and made fire, without matches. I was wowed. Eons-old rock formations wrung little girl awe. My mother applied the leaves of plantain, a lawn invader, to bug bites. Spotted jewelweed, so thick near the river you had to fight to get through it to swim, was good for poison ivy. All my brothers hunted and fished and trapped. Our interaction with the woods, from its rocks to its mammals, communicated to me that I was surrounded by a living world that could meet my needs if I learned to practice self-reliance and to scan my surroundings with the eyes of a participant survivor.

Does it matter to me now, when I hike in Paterson, to know that I am standing on frozen lava? Beaten up by my worldly failures and human frustrations, I go to Garret Mountain. From the cliff edge I can see the entire Manhattan skyline, the Empire State Building and the Verrazano-Narrows Bridge. I can see the cranes of Port Newark-Elizabeth Marine Terminal. I can, if I lean out far enough to risk my life on the sheer cliff edge, see the spires of Newark's Sacred Heart Cathedral.

I am not at Garret Mountain for the view of man's accomplishments. I listen there for sermons I hear nowhere else. The now oh-so-solid, but once furiously liquid basalt, murmurs to me: "Everything is in flux. Nothing is permanent or immobile. No definition builds an absolute cage. Forces as subtle as wind and water can push and pull the heaviest of barriers. The earth sometimes disgorges its contents, turns itself inside out, raises the low high; even the outlines of continents change."

The burden on my shoulders suddenly seems manageable. I tell the rock that the villains and roadblocks in my life story are much less implacable, and the miniscule tools I have, as negligible as wind and water, will transmogrify into mighty weapons that can change my life into something better.

"Maybe," the rock replies. "But no matter what," the rock emphasizes, "know this moment, embrace this moment, live this moment, because this moment is moving, just as we, the permanent-appearing boulders on which you stand, change and are changing right now."

And what were the rocks of the Shenandoah Valley saying to me? I do not know. I can tell you about the pawpaw I saw there, but I know nothing of Virginia's geology. Another lesson: don't ever let the woods bore you. What you know about them is a page. What they have yet to teach you fills libraries.

I know about pawpaws because I lived in Indiana where I picked and ate pawpaws, as well as morels, oyster and sheep's head mushrooms, sulfur shelf, persimmons, chokecherries, mulberries, and shadberries. One day I was hungry, and if it weren't for a wild pear tree, I would have eaten nothing. A successful author and naturalist came to town. I provided her, in person and by mail, with pawpaw, Osage orange, and persimmons, and guided her to my favorite trees. Like the extinct gomphothere, whose legacy is still present in North American forests, I am in her book, and yet not. I am an unnamed presence, a "source" in Indiana.

She mentions me at least three times. I wonder why not by name. I wonder if it's because "Danusha" would have been too challenging to her readers — a wild guess. I did not feel myself to be her "source." I felt myself to be a "person" with a "name" helping another person with a name — a potential friend — who cares about nature as I do. I'd rather think about gomphotheres than about what happened to me at Indiana University: the whole icky business of campuses and scholars that adopt the camouflage of diversity, collegiality, and openness but that thrive on invisible competitions and cannibalism as much as any forest.

◆

I heard blue jays persistently squawking their version of head-butting the bully at the bar, writing a testy letter to the editor, or threatening a lawsuit. They were alerting me, along with smaller birds and mammals, that a predator was out and about. A really good naturalist can differentiate between alarm calls responding to a terrestrial predator like a cat and alarm calls responding to avian predators like hawks and owls. I'm not that good. I scanned the treetops. Sure enough, a red-tailed hawk was on the bare, white, horizontal limb of a sycamore. Other limbs of the same sycamore featured mere clumps of foliage, not an unbroken shimmering mass of summer leaves. The tree looked to have lost its leaves to the anthracnose fungus, yet another human-introduced threat like chestnut blight, Dutch elm disease, and gypsy moths. The hawk's claws were clamping something down on the bare white limb: a limp squirrel, a mere sleeve, no longer really a squirrel because the better part of a squirrel is its terrific, alert animation. I watched the hawk turn its head from side to side, at first slowly and shallowly, then picking up speed and momentum and moving further to the right and left with each spasmodic jerk. Finally, what the hawk was tugging broke free: the squirrel's surprisingly lengthy intestines. With one final yank the hawk eviscerated the squirrel and flung the guts off into the brush. I picked up the hawk in my binos. The feathers around its face were smeared with blood.

Atheists insist that I believe in God because the idea of God comforts me. A good part of the time the idea of God terrifies me. The woods make it impossible for me not to believe in God. I have never said that that inescapable God is nice.

Yes, God, I do feel like that squirrel, and you do feel like that hawk, and I pretty much hate you a good percentage of the time.

As a monotheist, I believe in a God who created, plays on the same team as, and actually *loves* both the squirrel and the hawk. That changes everything. The math of that equation overwhelms me. It would be so much easier to see the world through Pagan eyes, to divvy up all life and death into the mini-domains of competing gods who are sometimes kind and sometimes cruel and sometimes call in sick and get drunk and just need enough propitiation to deliver that winning lottery ticket. I've been thinking about how different the world would look to me, ethically, in terms of questions of right and wrong, suffering and the unequal distribution of joy, if I believed in Thoth, the ibis-beaked god of the moon, and Khepri, god of round things like poop balls and the rising sun. Different deities playing on the team of this or that slice of creation. We've got a god over here who is the god of hawks, and he sharpens their claws and preens their feathers to a fine, sleek sheen that dominates the wind and mocks oxygen's refusal to provide substantial support. This god crunches the numbers and engineers the exact aerodynamic shape that can transport a solid bird on insubstantial air as easily as a bike rides on a paved road. We've got another god over here who is the god of squirrels, and he is going to quicken their limbs to furred, grey lightning, their ears and eyes to expert traps that capture each shadow or breath of air created by a predator's stalk and spring into equal and opposite motion and elude any talon. The god of the hawks is out late partying and clocks in to work with bleary eyes; the squirrel is safe that day, and the hawk goes hungry. The god of the squirrels meets a hot number and loses focus; the hawk eats that day, and Mrs. Squirrel mourns.

During the war between Greece and Troy, the gods Apollo, Aphrodite, and Ares supported the Trojans. Divine Athena and

Hera supported the Greeks. The Greek commander, Agamemnon, wanted to transport troops to Troy by ship. Artemis withheld the wind that would move those ships. Earlier, Agamemnon had earned her wrath by killing one of her deer. Agamemnon knew the gods as partisan mathematicians, as rug merchants, as those who give to their own side and take from their opponents. Agamemnon called Ares the "lord of strife, who doth the swaying scales of battle hold, war's money-changer, giving dust for gold." When the winds would not move his ships to war, Agamemnon knew he had to cut a deal. He sacrificed his own daughter, Iphigenia, to placate Artemis, to compensate her loss of the deer, and to get her to grant favorable winds for his ships. Artemis accepted the life of Iphigenia in exchange for her deer. Artemis complied with Agamemnon's request. Pagan justice. Please note all those who insist that goddesses, as opposed to gods, are good for women. Iphigenia would not agree.

The trap continued to close, though, even if imperceptibly. Agamemnon moved his ships, commanded his war, and returned home to his wife, Clytemnestra, who threw a blanket over him while he bathed, chopped him up with a double-headed ax, and avenged her daughter with her husband's death. Remember — chopping. Always the chopping.

In Nepal, they told me that Saraswati, the goddess of learning, was married to Vishnu. Laxmi, the goddess of wealth, was also married to Vishnu. The two co-wives were jealous of each other, as co-wives tend to be. Thus, wealth and wisdom are rarely found in the same man. What an easy, ethical calculus the Pagan worldview can offer.

Here's a story about the one-God world:

Some time back, Cathy Sue needed milk. She got into her car and drove toward the store. But it had been a bad winter, and Cathy Sue hit a crater-size pothole. Tire went flat.

Cathy Sue's eyes squirted some tears. She punched the steering wheel and let out an atypical, for her, curse word. She hated eating Cheerios without milk. She was angry at God. "I need milk! You are making me eat dry Cheerios!"

If Cathy Sue had been a Pagan, she might have tried playing

the god of potholes off against the god of grocery-store runs, just as Agamemnon played the goddess of the hunt off against the god of war.

Jim was also angry at God. Jim was lonely. Jim was late for work. And here a broken-down car was blocking his route. Dammit!

Jim pulled over and changed Cathy Sue's tire. It's been ten years now, and their three kids are cute as buttons and doing really well in school and on their sports teams. To this day, Cathy Sue enjoys munching on dry Cheerios in memory of the anniversary of meeting the love of her life.

We can reduce this to a simple illustration. Point A is Cathy Sue. A straight, solid line charts her attempt to purchase milk for Cheerios. A broken line proceeds to her imaginary goal, the goal she never reached, a gallon of milk. An elevated line proceeds on a different trajectory, a lifetime of happiness. An intersecting line graphs Jim's collision with an unexpected gift.

At this very moment, some devout Christian is typing up her version of this story on Facebook. Her friends are clicking "like" and typing "Amen" and "I have to remind myself of this."

God loves his children. He can turn disappointments into rewards. God is juggling all these elements: milk for Cheerios, lonely men, harsh winters, flat tires. He's an artful juggler, and the elements fall in just the right way. "We know that all things work for good for those who love God, who are called according to his purpose." Romans 8:28.

My disappointments never end with Jim's arrival, or the better job / address / health outcome. I experience my life as being endlessly kicked downstairs by an endless succession of feet. Passing time charts no successes or rewards. I am older, sicker, poorer, more alone, thrust farther from my dreams.

Sometimes the illustration is not so simple as a few lines. Sometimes God is juggling story villains a bit less attractive than potholes.

There are worms. *Onchocerca volvulus* is a nematode. It can live up to fifteen years. It's about a foot long. It's just a long tube, mouth to gut. Imagine an animate strand of spaghetti, only finer. No beauty or personality to speak of. What this character lacks in physical attractiveness or intriguing mental life it makes up for in its gripping life story, one full of plot twists. *Onchocerca volvulus*'s biography is a can't-put-it-down page-turner. Even such simple creatures need to eat. *Onchocerca volvulus* eats humans from the inside. As part of its life cycle, this parasite migrates across the human eye. Want to gross yourself out? Do a Google search of "river blindness." You will see living nightmares that you can't unsee. These nematodes can't inject themselves into their all-you-can-eat buffet, the human body. They first parasitize black flies and live for a time inside of them. Black flies bite humans and drink their blood. The black flies that transport tiny, immature *Onchocerca volvulus* parasites to human hosts and inject them under human skin live near fast-flowing rivers. That's why the disease they vector is called "river blindness." Fish love black flies. Trout especially like to eat them.

After I returned from Peace Corps Africa, I didn't talk about it much. How do you tell Americans about these things? The ceremony during which naked tweener girls, their bodies daubed with white earth pigment, were genitally mutilated. The giant French tanks creaking past straw huts on their way to protect diamond mines. The old woman who turned herself into a pig and nearly killed that one Peace Corps volunteer with black magic. The Ivy League graduates who circulated and believed this story. The PCVs who took one step beyond that degree of crazy and needed to be "psycho-vacced": evacuated by helicopter after their psychological breakdown. And, actually how do you tell people about this: how all-over good you can feel, at the end of the day, when nothing has bitten you, or blown you up, or carried you off, and it's just you and a plate of manioc and mashed greens cooked in red palm oil, peanut butter and hot sauce, and the year-round, equatorial, six-o'clock sunset of orange disc into yellow dust kicked up from the encroaching Sahara. Oh, yeah — and a bottle of Mocaf beer, kept cool in a pool of water in a clay jug. How much that last little touch can make you smile — that in a land without electricity or indoor plumbing, on a hot day you can effortlessly cool down a beer thanks to the magical, inevitable properties of evaporation. How do you tell people with refrigerators about that? Not about how cold the beer got, but about how much its temperature delighted you?

A Pagan sees a god of fish who provides black flies for dinner and a god of nematodes who provides black flies as limousines and co-conspirators in the business of eating human flesh. Or maybe Pagans see one goddess, Gaia, who designed this whole ecosystem, orchestrates it all, and inhabits every feature. Gaia in black flies; Gaia in dung.

How could one God create humans capable of sight, a miracle so profound that many in the Intelligent Design movement point to sight as enough, on its own, at least to imply, if not prove, God's existence, and then destroy that very miracle with something so utterly Halloween, teen-slasher-movie puke-inducing as a worm that must, as part of its life story, migrate across the human eye?

Is there a way to illustrate God's redemption of this disappointment with a neat, straight line? The line Cathy Sue and Jim use to tell their story of how their disappointment transubstantiated to joy?

No. We're getting closer to a web-like illustration, now. But the Bible insists that God is still juggling, and juggling well.

"Rabbi, who sinned, this man or his parents, that he was born blind?"

"Neither this man nor his parents sinned; this happened so that the works of God might be displayed in him."

No straight line for this blind man. He wanted something all his life — sight — and for the better part of his life, he did not receive it. But something better came along. Vision for everyone around him. God was made visible through his pain.

In 1973, Betty Jean Eadie was a housewife, mother, and member of the Lakota Sioux Native American tribe. After an operation, she "died." She was later revived. In 1992, she published *Embraced by the Light*, a book about her near-death experience. Spiritual guides gave her a tour. She was shown a bum. Her guides said, "We will show you who he really is." The derelict was in fact "a magnificent man, full of light. Love emanated from his being ... The drunk had sacrificed his time on earth for the benefit of another." Why? To teach luckier people about compassion. All those involved in this exchange, the drunk and his students, were not conscious of the eternal ramifications of their temporal behaviors. "They would never know their covenanted roles here."

Xavier Le Pichon realized that revolutionizing scientific understanding of the earth's tectonic plates was not enough to make him a whole human. He applied what he knew about the earth's weak and torn spots, and their necessity, to his understanding of people. He needed to serve others, the weak and the torn. He worked with Mother Teresa's Missionaries of Charity and L'Arche, a French community built around handicapped people.

Le Pichon said:

> You can change the world, but it's up to you. God is a mystery, but it can be discovered only through the weak, the fragile, the part of us and around us. And then we discover that this has a power of transformation of the world. Not through very strong armies or rockets or whatever that is. . . . If we accept to be educated by the others, to let the other explain to us what happens to them, how they feel, which is completely different from what we feel, and to let yourself immerse into their world so that they can get into our world, then you begin to share something which is very deep.

If spiritual touchy-feely is not your cup of tea, consider cold science. Mitochondria are the powerhouses of plant and animal cells, including human cells. Their remote ancestor was ingested by one of our remote ancestors, a single-celled organism. At first, mitochondria were parasites. They sucked energy from the cell that had swallowed them. In time, they became not only friendly, but necessary.

Or consider the hygiene hypothesis. Decades ago, most American kids played in dirt, grew up in big families, interacted with animals and their poop, and got pinworms. Nowadays, American kids spend less unsupervised time playing in mud and muck, have smaller families, less animal exposure, and fewer American kids get pinworms. A good thing, right? Well, sure. But more Americans are now contracting asthma, type one diabetes, and multiple sclerosis. One treatment — helminthic therapy. Doctors purposely infect a patient with parasitic nematodes. These worms affect the human immune system in such a way as to help heal.

Billions of years ago, a single-celled creature swallowed a parasite and suffered. Today we rely on mitochondria for life. A blind man was healed by Jesus. Observers came to believe. Ravens are bad to the bone. And I can't stop staring at them. Leaves pump out insecticide that helps insects survive their cannibal siblings. I don't really know why God has to do this juggling act, but he does, or nature does, and we are the balls in the air.

It's not a straight line. It's more like those designs I used to make with a childhood toy. British engineer Denys Fisher invented the Spirograph in 1965, building on previous work by mathematician Bruno Abakanowicz. The Spirograph was a boxed set of multi-colored pens, pins, and toothed plastic disks, rods, and circles. You pinned the circle or the rod to paper mounted on cardboard. You put the discs inside the circle or along the rod. You put the pen's point inside a hole in the disc and used the pen to push the disc along as its teeth successively interlocked with and then released from the interlocking teeth of the circle or rod. It was much easier than it sounds. When you finished the route of the disc around the circle, you discovered that your captive pen had created a cool, geometric image on the page. You did that again and again, one image on top of another, and soon you had a really trippy, multicolored, intricately lace-like image, something like a snowflake, or the map of a planet's orbit, or the head of a daisy, or the inside of a star.

Those Spirograph designs, complex, hypnotic, and yet still entirely rational and reducible to a mathematical formula, more accurately plot the route from "this hurts" to "this is the one God balancing out the needs and wants, the blessings and curses of his vast creation."

Nothing is concealed that will not be revealed, nor secret that will not be known. What I say to you in the darkness, speak in the light; what you hear whispered, proclaim on the housetops. And do not be afraid of those who kill the body but cannot kill the soul; rather, be afraid of the one who can destroy both soul and body in Gehenna. Are not two sparrows sold for a small coin? Yet not one of them falls to the ground without your Father's knowledge. Even all the hairs of your head are counted. So do not be afraid; you are worth more than many sparrows. (Matthew 10 26-31 NAB).

And as I mention this toy, I'm realizing, right now, that I had a Spirograph because my mother bought it for me. She hurt me a lot. She was a bad mother. But she bought me a lot of toys and books and foods I liked. In 1977, the National Geographic Society published two books chock full of photographs: *Song and Garden Birds of North America* and *Water, Prey, and Game Birds*. One Christmas a bulky block was handed to me. I was not eager to unwrap it. I'd been given so many wrong, wrong gifts. Soaps. Lotions. Just, no. This Christmas was different. Mommy gave me two beautiful, expensive books about birds. I remember sitting on the bed gazing at them, touching the pages with such care, after washing my hands. I'd never been happier. I'm realizing, just now in telling this story, how hard my mother tried. And I tear up. Sometimes it takes a long time for a traveling object or story or noun or dream to reach its home, its resolution, its predicate, its prize. Sometimes the traveler takes a circuitous route. I realize, now. I'm grateful, now. Thank you, Mommy.

CHAPTER NINE

SOMETHING FUNNY

I returned to the retreat house. Brother Hugo stopped me outside. "How is your experience of your retreat?"

I could have ignored his question or given a false reply. I had decided that by being my honest self with Brother Hugo, by being present, and addressing his words at face value, I was being a Christian.

So often when I've been dealing with a hideous pile of crap, from the job search to chronic illness, someone has said to me, "I so wish I could solve all your problems. I can't."

And I've always wanted to smack that person. I've always wanted to say, "Please tell me when I asked you to solve my problems. Never. Got it? I have never asked you to solve one of my problems, never mind all of them."

What was I hoping for? That someone would look at my face while talking to me. Call me by my name, spoken out loud. Respond to what I say.

We can do this with each other. We can, minute-by-minute, choose to be a mensch, even with someone we fear may be a jerk. We can look at people's faces when we talk to them. We can address them by name. We can listen to what they say. It's a way to be a Christian in day-to-day life. Most people are actively doing something else: inserting their own expectations, drama, and baggage, and thus erasing the other. I cherish those who give others their presence. Like The Theologian.

I committed myself to being present with Brother Hugo. When he asked me about my retreat, I was frank.

"I feel more depressed than when I arrived," I said. "The absence of distractions here is bringing home to me how much pain I'm in."

Brother Hugo, who knew nothing about why I had made a retreat, said, "Stop feeling sorry for yourself. There are people out there who have no legs and can't walk. You should count your blessings. You should become a nun. Or you should get married."

I looked at him silently.

He looked me up and down. "So, I hear you plan to hitchhike to Washington." How did he know this?

"Yes, I do," I said.

"Who picks you up?" he asked.

"Long-distance, eighteen-wheel truckers. I think they have — " I was about to say, "a code of the road, so that they respond with concrete help."

Brother Hugo jumped in, "The idea that they are going to have sex with you?"

"No," I said. "They work hard, are often lonely, bored, or sleep-deprived, and they want someone to talk to. Or they have a knight-of-the-road's sense of chivalry, and they genuinely want to help. Another group of people that often pick me up are Grateful Dead fans. You see the dancing bear stickers on the car and hear the music. They usually — "

"Offer you drugs? Try something funny with you? Hasn't anyone tried something funny with you?" Brother Hugo asked.

I continued, simply because I had wanted to speak this observation out loud, and he had cut me off. "Women almost never pick me up. In my entire hitchhiking career, I think I've gotten maybe two rides from women. You'd think that a woman would want to help a fellow woman out."

"Because they don't want to have sex with you. So, has anyone ever given you drugs and then tried to have sex with you? Why don't you just buy a car?"

I wanted to change the subject. I searched for common ground between us. We are both Slavs. I asked Brother Hugo about his home country. His eyes brightened like a child's. "It's paradise," he said.

I was touched by his love for his Slavic homeland, sentimental to me because it was also Bruno's homeland. I liked this side of Brother Hugo.

"You have to understand, it's on the coast," Brother Hugo added. Something about the way he said that raised a red flag.

"Uh huh," I said. "Not like those other grubby Slavic countries, the landlocked ones. Like Slovakia."

"Slovakia, forget it, not like that," he said. "That's the Dark Ages."

I walked away. For ten seconds there, I had liked him.

◆

Dinner Thursday was rice, peas, and carrots. There was no protein to be had. I like to fortify myself before taking to the road; I need to be at my quickest and most aware. This protein-free dinner would not help. I chafed at the politically correct Henri Nouwen reading. Without doing dishes — not doing my dishes after a meal is one of the "loudest" things I can do, a scream in a monastery — I rose and began walking the road away from the retreat house.

As I reached the bend where the road forks to go to the monastery or to the highway, I heard a car behind me. I heard it decelerate, and then I heard tires on gravel. Someone was pulling on to the shoulder. I sensed it was The Theologian. I hoped against hope. As a pedestrian, when a lost driver pulls up beside me, I confidently provide the directions I have taught myself how to provide. As a hitchhiker, I summon all my courage when I inhabit the shoulder of the road. As a retreatant with a doomed crush, I was too nervous and shy to look up or even to slow my footsteps. The car accelerated and pulled away.

After walking to the highway, I returned to the retreat house. I sat on the very Adirondack chair I sat on when I first arrived. I again put my feet up on the ottoman.

The sun was setting to my left. I watched it collide with the horizon. The sun lingers impossibly in June; the days are long. The solstice would be next week. But nothing lasts forever. At one moment, a golden glow spilled beyond the boundaries of the possible and spotlighted every last item — the indigo bunting's twig, the weeping cherry, the cuckoo's locust, the corn — as characters in that epic production, a summer day. You glance at your watch. In winter at that same hour you'd be tunneled into an evening's hibernation. Now sun floods your sight and lures you outdoors, as once did your best friend's voice, announcing the start of a new ballgame, taunting you, "Get out here. Come on! What are you doing sitting on your can? We need somebody on first base!" When will this day end? Will it? Ever? And then, in a breath, eternity is snuffed out and replaced by temporality, summer is replaced by mortality. Everything that, a minute before, had been glimmering with the sun's own gold was now pewter gray. The sun had dipped below the horizon. The available foot-candles had not diminished so much; you could continue reading on the porch the same text in the same point of type. But there was no gainsaying it — a summer day was now over. Every opportunity for investment or action or pleasure that this summer day had once flaunted was now history.

Those tires on gravel that I'd heard. The decelerating car I was too shy to look up and see. The car that made me bite my lip. That had been The Theologian. He had wanted to say goodbye. I'd never see him again.

I remember a housemate noticing that I used to put chewing gum in my ears when I was writing. (I've since moved on to headphones.)

I complain that no one ever commemorates my birthday and that I always spend it alone. Once a housemate put a "Happy Birthday" Mylar balloon on the kitchen table. She noticed my lack of enthusiasm. She asked.

"Mylar balloons kill sea turtles," I said.

"*What?*" She was outraged.

"Sea turtles eat jellyfish. These balloons are filled with helium. They float with air currents out to sea, lose the helium, fall into the ocean. The sea turtles think they are jellyfish. They eat them. They die."

She never commemorated my birthday again.

But the thing is, I always did something for her birthday. I asked her first. She usually wanted some of my homemade cookies, and she always specified the type, and I always came through. Ghirardelli chocolate chips. Real butter. Real vanilla. King Arthur flour.

Is it so hard for people to notice that I care about the environment?

I remember a housemate saying to me when I was about to move out, "Oh, so now I can go back in the kitchen."

"I never told you you couldn't enter the kitchen!"

"You didn't have to say anything," he said. "You just radiate this vibe."

I don't want to be that person, that person who exudes a force field that keeps other people away. But I am that person. Whenever I fantasize about winning the lottery, I see myself hopping a plane and flying someplace distant, with lots of great birds, someplace under a very big patch of uninterrupted sky. The only human I inhabit this fantasy with is an anonymous masseuse.

Around other people, I am always bracing myself, waiting to hear, "You are doing that wrong." I probably am doing that wrong. I am a spaz. Retarded. Dyslexic. I was raised by wolves. Whatever it is I am doing, I am doing it wrong. The thing is, though, I am doing it the way it works for me. I cringe, waiting to hear, "You're fat. You're ugly. You're stupid. You're worthless." No, people don't say it straight out like that as they did when I was a kid. But the message comes through. How? Oh, here's one way. On those rare occasions when I am invited to share my photos, people skip past photos of me against Himalayan Peaks, photos of me teaching inner city youth, photos of me holding protest signs in Poland in 1989 as the Soviet Union crumbles into the dust of history. Then these same bored audiences stop dead at Dana's photo. She had hollow cheeks, a small nose, a severe jawline, and high breasts. "Wow! You knew someone who looked like *that*? Who is *she*?"

I am so lonely that it is a form of day-by-day, hour-by-hour, minute-by-minute torture. There's this phrase, "Even Hitler had a girlfriend." It's used to mock people like me who are alone in the universe. It's even worse than that. In 1966, Thomas Merton had to go to the hospital for back pain. His nurse was Margie Smith. She was twenty-five, half his age. Of course. They became lovers. Even America's most famous monk got more than I do.

◆

Long past the point when I thought there was any chance of anyone coming by, Becky walked around the corner of the retreat house. She was wearing that lovely indigo block-print dress.

"Do you mind if I sit down?" she asked in a voice as gentle as an old-school Disney princess.

"I don't care," I said.

Becky sat.

"Lovely evening," she said. "I hope you don't mind that I'm speaking to you."

"Please feel free," I said. "This has been the noisiest silent monastery retreat. I've had more conversations this one week than I've ever had in my own apartment."

"I hope I'm not bothering you," she said.

"Really, no, relax," I said.

"If I step on your boundaries —"

"I'll pull out my Glock," I said.

We both laughed. That broke the ice.

Becky talked. I was stunned when she told me her age.

"Whoa!" I said. "Did you sign a pact with the devil? You don't look a day over thirty."

She smiled and made no fuss. I'm sure she's heard that compliment before. "I thank my parents," she said. "Good genes."

Becky said that she is not Catholic, but, rather, is Unitarian, and that she has been a member of other Christian denominations. Her therapist, whom she has been seeing for twenty years, and who is a substitute mother for her, recommended Holy Cross. Becky repeatedly said that she felt "protected" at the monastery. She really liked the weeping cherry, she said, as it forms a "protective" umbrella shape.

Becky had met a man. He left his wife after their child died and she did not recover in "a few months." He made lascivious comments about his own sister's "assets." Becky didn't break up with him until after things got really ugly. Becky diagnosed her own problem. She ignores red flags and continues to pursue bad relationships because she has been programmed to believe that she is not worthy. She was sexually abused as a child by her uncle, a church official. No wonder she used the word "protect" so many times as a feature of the monastery that she appreciated.

"Listen, Becky," I began, certain I was about to lose another female friend before the friendship ever had a chance to begin. If being me loses friends, why don't I just not be me and fake being one of those pretty, vapid women who has lots of friends? If faking being someone else loses me, what good is my entire life?

"Becky, we just met, but I like you. I've been noticing how loudly body language communicates. I have to say, even before we spoke, I had a problem with —" I caught myself. I was about to say "Brother Hugo." I was about to say that his body language struck me as combative. I realized that doing so would be gossip, the last thing a monastery needs. "I mean," I tried again, "I sometimes have problems with people even before I speak to them. With you? You have such graceful, humble body language. I like you, even though we just met."

She nodded her cocked-head nod. So endearing.

"You know how they say that women talk to talk and men talk to solve problems? I'm thinking I must be part woman and part man, because I'm no good at sob-sistering. I don't want to say to you, 'Yeah, yeah, life sucks, boo hoo.' I want to offer a suggestion. May I?"

"I like you too," she said. I was tickled and thrilled. "Go ahead, say what you want to say."

"Thank you," I said. "'War is always,' Becky. 'War is always.'"

She nodded quietly as if I had just said the most profound thing in the world. I knew I had not, but I was grateful for her attentive presence. I wanted to bring her back to Paterson with me. Just writing about her, I feel warm.

"It's a quote from *The Truce*. Primo Levi was an Italian scientist. Jewish. Auschwitz survivor. He says to his companion, 'The war is almost over, and perhaps everything will be easier.' And his companion replies, 'War is always.' Yeah, the monastery is protective. But let's face it. The same tensions that exist out there exist in here. We have to learn to face them.

"You say you ignore red flags. That's a common complaint of adults who were abused as children. The abuse teaches us to become numb and passive. If we focused on what was happening to us, we'd be overcome with emotional and physical pain. If we fought for our lives, even if we just named what was happening, our abuser might kill us. So we learn to cooperate with destruction. I want you to check out a book called *The Gift of Fear* by Gavin de Becker. He's a personal security expert."

"I'll do that," she said. "There's a good library in my town. The librarians know me well."

I smiled. I don't know if she was just being polite. It's a great kindness to tell someone who has just recommended a book to you that you will check it out.

"So," she asked, "This author . . . "

"Primo Levi," I said.

"Yes, Primo Levi. Is he one of your favorites?"

"I can't really say that," I said. "I read him because . . . " what do I say? Because I've published on the Holocaust? My book remains unpublished. Because I'm a loser who devoted years of my life to work I can't publish? "Let's just say I admire Levi's work," I finally said, feeling more like a loose evolutionary strand than a substantial human being.

"I can see why. He sounds admirable," Becky said. "Holocaust survivor. People like that are role models."

I fidgeted.

"What?" she asked. Becky heard everything I said, whether I said it aloud or not.

"Some people say that he killed himself. It was 1987. He was found at the bottom of a stairwell. Elie Wiesel said, 'Primo Levi died at Auschwitz forty years later.'"

Becky looked really sad.

"But the thing is," I went on, "it might not have been a suicide. There was no note. And it's a stupid method; that kind of a fall is as likely to paralyze you as kill you. It could have been an accident. If he did kill himself, I wish he had not. I feel he stole something from me by killing himself. That he could survive Auschwitz and then kill himself . . . we can never know for sure . . . " I started to tear up. Becky's presence healed me quickly.

"One more thing, if I may?" I asked her.

"Go ahead," she said.

"Okay," I said. "I get it that you are Unitarian. I'm Catholic so this applies to me for sure, but maybe it applies to you as well. You talk about the monastery being protective. There's this opera, *Dialogues of the Carmelites*. Written by Francis Poulenc, Catholic and gay. It's about the French Revolution sending nuns to the guillotine. In the opera an older nun says to a younger one, 'The convent is not here to protect you. You are here to protect it.' Know what I mean?"

Again, Becky nodded her cocked-head nod, as if I really were saying profound and memorable things. I just wanted to hug her and squeeze her.

As we talked, and as Becky turned her head, my eyes were caught, as if on a hook, by her right ear, the one turned away from me. I thought I had hallucinated something. I resolved to look again when she turned her head again. When I did get another look at her ear, I realized that I hadn't hallucinated anything, and that I ought not to stare. Becky's right ear is deformed. It looks like a rosebud. In fact her ear looked exactly like the strange ear that popped into my head when I was praying in the chapel. That prayer had taken place before Becky arrived.

I think she saw me gaping, however briefly, at her ear, and she did not react. I guess she gets used to it. I didn't ask for an explanation, and she didn't offer one.

She asked about me. I told her my story.

She listened and said she hoped things would work out for me. She said I am a "very cool girl."

Night fell. The moon was waxing gibbous, ten days old; in four more days, it would be full. We heard Brother Andrew say, "Everybody in?" and thought we were about to be locked out. Becky jumped up and we went inside. Brother Andrew assured us that he had been talking to the cats.

I went to the chapel. Silent, empty and white, it was pure, clean, and receptive. There was no one there to compare myself to, no one to interrupt me, no one to tell me that I was doing it wrong. The chapel was empty of prayers for things I'll never have — job, husband, home, children. There were no pictures, no stained glass, no statues or oils, recounting no narratives I can never hope to inhabit, narratives of accomplishments, meaningful service, blessings, harvest fruit. In the pure, white light of the chapel, surrounded by dark, slumbering woods, I could almost believe that there is a God, and that everything was working out as it should. I left the chapel, and, one last time, almost walked into A-8, which The Theologian had vacated hours before.

I got up at five, focused on departure and prayers to St. Christopher for good rides and no psychos. I began to walk to the highway around seven.

I stopped to pee in some dense foliage. Realized after standing that the foliage was poison ivy. One curse that doesn't have my name on it: it doesn't affect me. My superpower: Poison Ivy Girl!

CHAPTER TEN

HEADING HOME

I stood on the sunlit shoulder of the Castlemans Ferry Bridge for almost an hour. There was a lot of traffic, and given the cars — Jags and Bimmers on a country road going very fast — I had to assume that many drivers were professionals commuting from their country estates into DC. No rides. Finally, a compact car pulled over. A middle-aged white man, smoking a cigarette, with cigarette packs all over the car. Loud rock and roll. I quickly examined the interior. As I did so, the driver glared at me as if I were his ex-wife and we were involved in a custody dispute. I politely declined that ride.

Within minutes, an official vehicle pulled over. A uniformed man in mirrored sunglasses with a shaven head got out. He was missing one of his lower front teeth. He had a deep voice, and he spoke *s l o w l y* . His words came out clipped and isolated, like bullets. "Good morning!" he said.

"Are you going to arrest me?" I asked.

He looked angry. "Why do you think I am going to arrest you?"

I shrugged.

He opened the police car door. "Get in," he ordered.

"Are you sure you're not going to arrest me?" I asked.

"Inside," he insisted.

I got in.

"Identification, please," he said.

I rummaged through my backpack and pulled out my university employee ID. He wanted more. I handed him my Indiana driver's license. I still haven't gotten a New Jersey license. Not having a car, it seems less urgent.

He studied it and handed it back. "Now, tell me why you are *hitchhiking*."

I gave him a truncated version of my story: chronic illness, the wrong dissertation, poverty, asking God about job, monastery retreat.

He gave no sign of hearing anything I said. "Don't you realize it's not safe these days to hitchhike? Back in the hippie days, maybe, but not anymore!"

Given that my words had had no impact, I didn't know what to say.

"I'm taking you to Leesburg. It's twenty-five miles from here. From there you can get a bus to DC. If you need bus fare — "

"Holy cow!" I said. "My God, you don't have to do that! I feel so guilty. I feel so grateful! Thank you!"

He appeared unmoved. How moved can a hard, uniformed, bald man in reflective sunglasses appear?

I sat back and relaxed as best I could. I chattered away, as is my wont, commenting on large cement structures that passed us on the backs of large trucks. Vic — his name was Vic — ranted against the suburban sprawl that those large structures represented.

"Everyone hates it," I said. "Every ride I've gotten has mentioned it and hates it. You guys should organize! Mount a protest — "

"Nobody cares," Vic said bitterly.

My ears popped. I asked the altitude. "A thousand feet," he said.

I noticed that Vic and I both use the same type of keychain, a carabiner.

"You climb?" Vic asked.

"Not a chance," I said. "I don't like to tempt fate."

Vic turned to me with the classic sarcastic face, lips pressed together, eyebrows high.

"I'm very careful when I hitchhike. I turned down a ride before you came along. The man was listening to heavy rock and smoking and his car was very messy."

Vic's look became even more sarcastic.

Vic wanted to know what I do. I said I teach, as I can find jobs. He asked what I teach. I said that I've taught anthropology, English, women's studies, and film.

He seemed to be trying to add up figures in his head and not reaching the expected sum. He asked, "Why are you wearing field glasses?"

"I'm a birdwatcher," I said, wondering what on earth he had been thinking.

Finally, Vic asked, as if it had been irking him for some time, "Why, when I said 'Good morning' to you, did you say, 'Are you going to arrest me?'"

"Because you scared me," I said. "You have a shaved head, a southern accent, and mirrored sunglasses. Haven't you ever seen *In the Heat of the Night*? *Deliverance*? And what was that one with Tony Curtis and Sidney Poitier where they are chained together?"

"*The Defiant Ones*. It's not as bad as all that," he said.

When we got to Leesburg, he pulled over and spent fifteen minutes waiting for a dispatcher to give him complete information on buses, bus stops, and ticket prices. "I'm sorry if I'm keeping you from more important work," I said. He shrugged. He didn't leave till he felt confident I was all set.

◆

The bus arrived forty minutes late. A uniformed black driver emerged, waving his arms and shouting, "No," at the people assembled to take it. Then, weirdly, he asked, "Where are you going?" given the arm-waving and the No-shouting, the question was a pointless tease. "Washington, DC," we said. What were the chances we'd say anywhere else? "No," the driver shouted in a real charm-impaired way. He had too many passengers, and he couldn't accept any more. "It's a legal thing! I could be sued!" He drove off without any of us getting on his bus.

Feeling like Miss Sadie Thompson returning to the docks, I walked back to the highway Vic had just rescued me from. My hope was to catch a ride before Vic saw me. That most anonymous of wastelands, the shoulder of a superhighway, had suddenly become the location where you can be seen and judged and cared about by someone it would break your heart to disappoint.

Just like that, an SUV that looked like a terrestrial version of the legendary black helicopters pulled up ahead of me on the shoulder. Big. Black. Shiny. Smoked windows. I ran up to grab the door, opened it. A woman! Just after I'd said I never get rides from women!

Blonde. Dyed blonde. One of those plastic holders for a picture ID slung around her neck, which the majority of people in some DC neighborhoods wear. (You have to wonder how many of them are fake, worn just for the sake of status.) She was maybe in her late forties or early fifties. A striking resemblance to Aunt Phyllis, only not as beautiful, but then who is as beautiful as Aunt Phyllis? Oh, no! This driver had a cigarette in her hand! I was ready to decline, but her resemblance to Aunt Phyllis won me over.

I got in. I thanked her profusely. Her no-nonsense demeanor put me in my place immediately. Her palpable personality was like the G-forces that smack you in your face and press you down when you're in a fast car or riding a roller coaster.

She had one of those South-Jersey-to-Maryland, middle-class, white accents. I don't know the official name for this accent. It's really strong in words like "on," pronounced like "oowen" and "water," pronounced something like "woodr."

"Yeah," she said, loud, fast, impaling the air mercilessly with her cigarette, monosyllabic, even when pronouncing multisyllable words. "I saw that movie last night, *Play It Forward*" — she did say "Play" not "Pay" — "and I decided I was going to do a good deed today."

I loved this so much I could have choked.

"My name's Doris."

I was amazed. Rides usually never tell me their names, and if they do, it's at the end of the ride when they can be certain I won't pull a knife on them.

"Wow," I said. "You may be the first Doris I've ever met."

"My mother was in a concentration camp. I was named after the woman who saved her life."

Now you see why I told you about the Arno coincidences. My father was in a concentration camp . . . my mother was in a concentration camp . . . were your parents in a concentration camp? Coincidences I couldn't ignore that sparked my dissertation.

I was so tired of holding back tears. I just let them flow.

Doris had the demeanor of a businesswoman, not a social worker. Trying, bravely but unsuccessfully, to make her voice suede rather than sun-bouncing chrome, she said, "Oh, I am so sorry. I said something that made you sad."

"No," I said, through tears. I told her some of the backstory. "And here I am on a country road in Virginia, and I'm picked up by a woman who has the Holocaust as part of her family history. It's the coincidence that made me cry."

Doris was unfazed. She just went on talking.

Doris's mother was a Christian Ukrainian girl in a concentration camp. There was a plan to allow a Jewish woman to escape. Doris's mother and the Jewish woman were both assigned to work near a forest. Someone was going to distract the guard. At the moment the Jewish woman was to escape, she let Doris's mother go instead. Doris's mother fled, and she later named her child after Doris, the Jewish woman who saved her life.

Doris's mother emigrated to the US and cleaned offices for over twenty years with the same company. Here her daughter is, as the business card she gave me attests, a project coordinator for a firm in Reston, Virginia. "My mother is a saint, the nicest person

I've ever known. She goes to church every day. I love her so much." I've never heard anyone from Eastern Europe speak that way about her mother. If I hear something positive, it's usually something like, "She was very tough but she always kept us fed and the house clean."

Doris's concentration camp story was unlike any I'd heard, or it was like all the others I'd heard; in that it was unique.

Doris dropped me off at a bus station in Reston where I could pick up a one-dollar shuttle to the metro. It was a bright, sunny day. What I saw of Reston made it look very modern, efficient, and prosperous. In fact, it is a planned community and often voted one of the best American places to live. Utterly out of place in this ultramodern setting, a wizened, tiny gnome with a caved-in chest and orangey tufts of gray hair, wearing a white shirt and dark pants, with no visible luggage or reason for being there, stood alone at the bus stop. Without any change of costume, he could have been a gatekeeper in a Tolkien-inspired film.

"Do I get the bus to the metro here?" I asked, stupidly.

He looked at me with a smile that could have been supremely knowing or idiotic. Really, this character would have been more at home in a dream than in this reality. Shiny new cars glinted in the park-and-ride behind him. Office towers rose before us, some under construction. Cranes rose in the sky.

He said something minimal. I forget what. I immediately noted, without surprise, the Eastern European accent. I guess I partly expected the Eastern European accent.

"So where are you from?" I asked.

"Albania," he replied.

"Oh, near Greece," I said, figuring that would rouse fewer sleeping dogs than "near Serbia."

He brightened. "You teacher!" he pronounced. "You teacher!"

Though I had undertaken this trip expressly to figure out what the hell I can be to earn a living, not wanting to disappoint, I nodded and said, "Yes, I teacher."

My bus was coming. He made sweeping motions with his

hands, as if scooping fodder into a hayloft, and then bending his knees and mimicking someone sitting down. He did not get on. He just stood there, alone, or folded into someone else's dream.

◆

A nice African American lady who complained loudly of suffering side effects from Novocain drove the bus to the metro stop; there I bought a ticket to the National Museum of the American Indian. This museum is only nine months old; it opened on September 21, 2004. It cost 220 million dollars. Half of that was raised from private donations and the other half came from taxpayers. Given its placement on the National Mall, near the Smithsonian and the Holocaust Memorial Museum, and its religious assignment, to help heal the wounds created by mistreatment of Native Americans, the NMAI has received a lot of attention.

The backstory of the National Museum of the American Indian is cataclysmic. Europeans arrived in the New World in 1492, bringing with them Old World diseases and overwhelming technological power. The Native Americans, lacking metal weapons, horses, the wheel, and immunological resistance, were no match. No one can ever know the exact numbers, but some estimate that diseases like smallpox and measles decreased the entire pre-contact population of Native Americans by ninety percent within 150 years after Columbus landed.

At the same time, Europeans were enraptured by Native American culture. Ever since Columbus, Europeans have collected Native American artifacts for display. I worked in a museum that did just that: the Phoebe Apperson Hearst Museum in Berkeley, California. The museum housed Native American artifacts, and it housed Native American body parts too. I used to have to don hazmat gear to fumigate human remains stored in an industrial drum.

Sometimes museums housed real-live Native Americans. Ishi, the last surviving member of his Yahi tribe, worked as a janitor at the Hearst Museum from 1911 to 1916.

Live Native Americans were sometimes put on display. Franz Boas, "the father of American anthropology," participated. The Eskimos that the Museum of Natural History put on display quickly died of tuberculosis. A little boy named Minik survived. Boas staged a funeral for Minik's sake. The funeral was fake. Boas had wrapped a log in fur to simulate a human corpse. The real bodies of the Eskimos were dissected and studied. Minik later discovered that his father's skeleton was on display. "Give me my father's body," he begged. The museum refused.

In the past, powerful Euro-Americans did very bad things. The National Museum of the American Indian is part of the effort to reverse the mistakes of the past and to do very good things. In the past, museum curators and directors were Euro-American. Now, at the NMAI, Native American architects and Native American curators are the decision-makers. The museum's founding director, W. Richard West, is a Cheyenne Indian. In the past, museums displayed historical artifacts from pre-Columbian Native American culture, like pottery and arrowheads. This choice, protestors claim, gave the impression that all Native Americans are dead. Now, the NMAI displays artifacts from Native Americans who are alive today, things like sneakers and baseball caps. That Native Americans still live is a good message. Sneakers and baseball caps, though, don't display the ingenuity of pre-contact cultures.

In the past, museums displayed ancient items like blades made from obsidian, a volcanic glass. That, protestors claim, gave museum-goers the mistaken notion that all Native Americans use outdated technology. It is important now to show Native Americans using modern technology, like metal knives, even though obsidian remains the sharpest cutting surface, sharper than metal.

In the past, museums extricated Native American religious objects from their ritual context. An Iroquois False Face mask might be put on display as an art object. Iroquois are scandalized by this; to them, a False Face mask is a religious object, not an art object. Many Iroquois want False Face masks removed from museums. The NMAI returned many False Face masks to protesting tribal members. The problem — if you hide the masks, fewer people will know the sophistication and power of Native American art. Besides returning art, there is another solution: Native American religious leaders sometimes perform ceremonies to bless museum exhibits. The Metropolitan Museum of Art owns many monstrances, the container for display of the Eucharist, the body of Christ. No one is bringing Catholic priests into the Met to say Mass with these monstrances. Two vital principles, separation of church and state and scholarly objectivity, are applied to Christian objects, but not to Native American ones. Museums must divorce Christian objects from worshippers and faith; museums must not divorce Native American objects from worshippers and faith. This is what's known as a double standard. In the past, there were other double standards that hurt Native Americans. Now we have double standards meant to help Native Americans. Our cultural leaders no longer suggest applying the same standard to all, regardless of their ethnicity.

The National Museum of the American Indian, that is, the building itself, is rounded rather than square. Rectangles and straight lines are linear, male, and Western. Curves are feminine, non-Western, beyond dichotomies of right and wrong. "See?" the museum's rounded shape announces, loud and clear. "In the past, we did bad things. We built buildings of straight lines. Now we are doing good things. We build our buildings with curves."

There's a problem, though. The inside of the NMAI is arranged as if it were a rectangular building. Artifacts and souvenirs are in square cases, and museum patrons follow linear paths. Rounding the exterior of the building, while it presents a lovely façade, doesn't enhance anything that's going on inside; it just makes the museum feel jumbled and chaotic, like a teenager's room that hasn't been cleaned in a while.

"It's a bad thing that Western males have been so in love with Indian culture for so long," the museum tells us. The collection of just one such man, George Gustav Heye, numbered one million Native American objects. This museum corrects that bad thing from the past. This museum has many exhibits with no artifacts at all, just, say, modern-day video footage and modern kitsch that you'd come across at an Indian casino. At times, I couldn't tell if I were looking at yet another gift shop or an actual display.

I'd get down on my knees and thank God if anthropologists of the stature of Heye, Alfred Kroeber, and Clyde Kluckhohn had dedicated their lives to preserving Slovak culture. I want to know what my grandmother saw, dreamed, and sang—and I don't. It's inevitable that humble people's culture will disappear. My grandfather wore a sheepskin cloak and listened to Slovak folk music played on a fujara, a six-foot-long handmade flute. My cousins in Slovakia today wear t-shirts and listen to Western pop. It's similarly inevitable that Native American kids wear the same uniform and wallow in the same pop culture. If a Native American wants to get in touch with his ancestors' world, he can, because all those demonized white males scrupulously preserved that culture when no one else was doing so. Love can be like that: obsessive, violative, imprisoning. Sometimes the only thing that holds you back from the brink of oblivion is the grip of a vise.

Here's the irony. Not just Native Americans like Minik were victimized. Henry Fairfield Osborn was the president of the Museum of Natural History for twenty-five years. In 1924, Osborn argued in *The New York Times* that Poles were racially inferior. Scholars like Osborn and his friend Madison Grant inspired Congress to pass the Quota Act of 1924 that stopped Polish and Slovak immigration to the US on the grounds that we are racially inferior. Franz Boas went to Ellis Island to measure immigrant Poles' and Slovaks' skulls. Neither my ancestors nor I were part of the group of powerful Euro-Americans doing very bad things. We were part of the powerless having very bad things done to us.

Here's another irony. Racism can't detract from the power of Native American artifacts. Since 1883, the Museum of Natural History has displayed a Haida canoe. The Great Canoe is sixty-three-feet long. It's carved from the trunk of a single red cedar. It's decorated with a painting of a killer whale in elegant, unmistakable Haida style. See that canoe and be, inevitably, wowed. After you've seen that canoe, you really don't need a politically correct lecture to inform you that Native Americans created exquisite design and objects of awesome power.

I spent a good part of the day in the National Museum of the American Indian. Not once did I have an "Oh, wow" experience. If I had known nothing about Native Americans before entering that museum, I would feel no inspiration to learn anything about them after leaving it.

I watched video footage of men in Western-designed and Chinese-made garments using Minnesota-made snowmobiles and guns to hunt. I heard a lecture about how the white man is evil because he forced Indian kids to go to schools to learn to function in American culture and not in their own traditional culture. If wearing outerwear from caribou hide is superior, why not wear outerwear made from caribou hide? Let me tell you. My grandfather wore a sheepskin cloak, but nobody is taking away my Gore-Tex. If hunting from dogsleds is a good idea, why not hunt from dogsleds? If your message is that the white man's assimilation is evil and traditional culture was superior, and you yourself are, for all intents and purposes, an assimilated American, doesn't that make you a hypocrite?

The NMAI displayed photos of people claiming to be Caribs, descendants of the original Indian inhabitants of the Caribbean Islands that first met with Columbus. The self-identified Caribs in the NMAI photos all looked plainly African American. There was a picture of a girl "reviving Indian customs" by wearing a tacky carnival-in-Rio-style feathered and sequined bikini. The captions said, paraphrase, "Yes, these folks look African American, but we accept them at their word. If they say they are Native American, to us, they are Native American."

I suddenly thought of Judith Neulander.

Sometime in the 1990s, when I was a graduate student at Indiana University, I wanted to watch Perseids, a meteor shower that comes around every August. Charlie Gaston, a dairy farmer I knew from walking out beyond the city limits, offered the hillside on his dairy farm. I asked fellow grad students if they wanted to come, and a woman named Judith Neulander did. We sat on the hillside with Charlie. Our conversation consisted of "Oh, wow, there's one! Hey, did ya see that one!" And then we all went home to our beds.

Later I mentioned to people that I'd gone stargazing with Judith Neulander and they gasped.

"She's so controversial!"

"She is?" I asked.

"Oh, but you are too."

"I am?" I asked.

"You both like to stir up trouble!"

"We do?"

I invited Judith over to my place and asked her why she was so controversial. She explained.

Back in the 1980s, some Latino Americans living in the Southwest claimed to be secretly Jewish — "crypto-Jews." A 1987 broadcast on crypto-Jews was one of NPR's most popular. People loved the crypto-Jew story. It proved that victims oppressed by evil white Christians could survive for hundreds of years by hiding in plain sight.

Judith fell in love. She wanted to become "the queen of the crypto-Jews." She investigated and discovered that the self-identified crypto-Jews' every claim was as substantial as Swiss cheese. She published an article systematically proving each claim false. The crypto-Jews weren't Jewish at all, Judith wrote. They wanted to be thought of as Jewish because they are really Hispanic, and people associate Hispanics with low-cost lawn care, nannies, and illegal immigration. Once they identified as Jewish, people treated them much better. Suddenly, they were survivors of oppression, romantic, dignified, invited on TV and university campuses.

One "crypto-Jew," Juan Sandoval, pimped a family tombstone with a Star of David on it. Turns out he made the tombstone out of Styrofoam, weathered it with spray paint, and used the photo as "evidence" of his Jewishness. He traveled nationally to synagogues and took money from, and romanced, naïve Jewish women.

Judith, on the other hand, had a hard time finding an

academic job. She paid the price that academia exacts from tellers of politically incorrect truths.

Gazing at photos of self-identified Carib Indians who looked African American, I also thought of folks I grew up with, who, when I grew up with them, were known as Jackson Whites. Later these same folks became known as the Ramapo Mountain People. The Ramapo Mountain People look like they have a combination of African and European ancestry. David S. Cohen, a New Jersey historian, says he can support, with genealogical records, that they are descendants of free blacks and Dutch settlers. Many don't want to be African American or Dutch. They want to be Native American. That group changed their name to Ramapough Mountain People. The New Jersey hills they claim as their home are normally spelled "Ramapo." Changing the syllable "po" to the syllable "pough" was meant to be authentically Native American. The Bureau of Indian Affairs refused to identify them as Native American, but the state of New Jersey did extend recognition. I wondered what the NMAI would have to say about the identity of kids I used to play with, the Van Dunks, the De Groats, the De Freeses, and the folklore, controversy, and legal wrangle about their identity.

I went to the NMAI "interactive" room where there was a bank of computers against a row of windows. In the museum's database, I looked up "Jackson Whites" and "Ramapo Mountain People" and found nothing. An Asian woman with a thick accent approached me and offered help. I told her what I was trying to research.

She took the mouse from my hand and clicked on an icon that allowed me to send a museum postcard to a friend. She encouraged me to do so. I explained again what I was trying to do. She kept trying to get me to send a postcard; she assured me that I could cc it to myself. I gave up. I left.

The carefully landscaped area surrounding the museum is beautiful, as is the museum's curvaceous exterior. Four boulders mark compass points. The boulders come from Hawaii, marking the west, Canada, marking the north, Chile, marking the south, and Maryland, marking the east. "Grandfather rocks" were blessed by Native American religious leaders before and after placement on museum grounds.

In my mind, I methodically applied the NMAI's criteria to an imaginary museum. I imagined a taxpayer-funded "National Museum of the European" on the National Mall where only directors and curators who could prove authentic European ancestry could work. I imagined boulders from Norway, Greece, Russia, and Portugal deployed at cardinal compass points in an attempt to lasso all the disparate ethnicities and religions of Europe into one people — *ein volk*. I imagined someone from the "Church of the European" blessing "grandfather rocks" and the taxpayer footing the bill for that religious ceremony. Any such museum could only exist in some crazed nationalist dystopia — the fever dream of a neo-Nazi.

I sat next to the manmade pond, complete with cattails. "Gurgalee!" I was startled by the strident and unmistakable call of a red-winged blackbird, a bird I associate with the swamps and woods of Wanaque. Sure enough, a red-winged blackbird was clinging to a cattail on a busy Washington, DC, street. I shelled and ate a couple of peanuts. A female mallard swam toward me and floated in the pond, staring at me. I watched her orange feet paddle gently beneath the surface of the clear water. I don't know if peanuts are good or bad for mallards, so I did not share. Native American ethnobotanists had planted culturally significant plants around the outside of the museum. These plants included the cattails, corn, beans, squash, and pawpaws. In front of the tobacco, some wag had planted a "No Smoking" sign. It was the most daring political statement at the museum.

I wept. This museum's five-hundred-year backstory of intertwined genocide and infatuation has everything to do with the reasons I went to the monastery to beg God for a job. By writing the dissertation I wrote, by saying that eating at McDonald's is not the same as genocide, I went against the grain. Powerful people decide that you are either a genocidal imperialist or a politically correct liberator. On the identify checkoff list, there is no box for "great-granddaughter of serfs, daughter of coal miner and housecleaner." When the elephants fight, the grass gets trampled. I'm the grass.

People with my degree, if they don't teach, sometimes get jobs in museums like this one. I couldn't get hired here as a janitor. Heck, they've probably got an ideological purity test for that job as well. I wonder if Ishi himself could have passed it.

I realized that I had unwittingly sabotaged my own life. Staying up late, getting up early, spending days in the library. Wasting my prime earning years as a penniless grad student with a chronic illness. I may as well have opened my veins into a sewer. As I sat on the edge of the artificial pond, I didn't care if I never stopped crying.

A man approached me. He was wearing glasses. He had a receding hairline, but otherwise abundant hair. His subtle but warm and genuine smile charmed me. He reminded me that he had stitched his cherished manuscript, his life's work, into the lining of his coat. The coat was taken from him as were his parents, his brother, and his pregnant wife. All were lost. He reminded me that after surviving Theresienstadt, Auschwitz, and Dachau, he went on to write *Man's Search for Meaning*. "Everything can be taken from you but one thing: the last of the human freedoms. To choose your attitude in any given set of circumstances." I nodded. Of course, this man did not approach me in the flesh as did the female mallard or the red-winged blackbird, or the foolish woman at the NMAI. But for Viktor Frankl's sake, I stopped crying, and I got on with my day.

I visited the Washington Monument, the Lincoln Memorial, the World War II Memorial, and then I walked to Nathan's.

◆

Nathan took me out to dinner at a Tibetan restaurant that served Nepali food: rice, lentils, and vegetables. Perfection. I always crave Nepali food after a tough time on the road. I told stories and Nathan looked on: we re-enacted *My Dinner with Andre*. I always tell the tales of my brushes with synchronicity to Nathan. He is very smart, and he believes in nothing other than material reality. I wait for him to show me why I, too, should believe in nothing. I want him to demonstrate, with mathematical formulae, why my meeting a theologian who had written his dissertation on one of my heroes and had once dated a "Danusia" was nothing to be amazed by. Rather, Nathan said, "Of course that's all beyond chance. No gainsaying it. I believe that these odd things happen to you. They always happen to you. They do not happen to me, so I need not attempt to understand or assimilate them."

Nathan gave me a hard time about my having peed in poison ivy. He says he gets it. How would he know? He never mentions doing any outdoor activities. He told me to wash my walking stick. That seemed extreme, but I did.

Before leaving the next morning, I mentioned to Nathan that we'd probably not see each other for another ten years. He didn't use that mention as an excuse to produce any sentiment. I said, "I love you forever," and I do — not I will, but I do, because love interferes with time as a trip to a monastery does. I left.

◆

I walked from Nathan's to the National Cathedral. It's in a neighborhood of embassies and expansive homes. There is a luxury housing development under construction across the street. A massive billboard advertises this development as offering cathedral views. They should have low-cost housing there for the deserving poor. But don't get me started on how we need to resurrect the concept of the deserving poor. But we should.

The National Cathedral is a replica of a gothic cathedral. That it is primarily Episcopal is ironic; I wonder if it is ever mentioned in any of its official literature that Henry VIII, in founding that church, and his successors encouraged desecration and destruction of gothic cathedrals as part of their war against Catholicism. I adore Beowulf. My English prof told me there may have been other Old English literary gems like Beowulf that had been similarly preserved by Catholic monks. We'll never know; Henry's reformation ransacked Catholic monastery libraries. Many ransacked libraries, including Oxford's Bodleian, were left without one single book. Ninety percent of English art was destroyed. In this sense, the National Cathedral is comparable to the NMAI. Man destroys a culture, and then he preserves a denatured remnant in mothballs.

The majority of stained glass windows or stone carvings I paid any attention to bragged of the accomplishments and, often, the generosity of this or that benefactor. I found nothing spiritual or inspirational in these artifacts, no matter their technical qualities. The space window, containing a piece of rock from the Moon, was lovely. Blue and black images are outlined in red; with the sun coming through, the red outline was vivid and beautiful.

Outside, I scanned the gargoyles to find Darth Vader. A docent walked by; I asked her for help. She had a French accent. She said, "You need binoculars to really see him."

I said, "*J'ai mes jumelles avec moi.*"

"You speak better French than I do!" she exclaimed. I get these compliments from the French, and I like it.

The National Cathedral is just perfect. Like a gingerbread house is perfect. It's possible I was so unmoved by it because I had three separate encounters with icebox people.

In the ladies room, a well-dressed, WASPy-looking woman with a snide voice told me that my backpack strap was hitching up my dress. (Have I mentioned how heavy—and poorly designed!—that pack was?) She was correct, but I was still washing my hands; I'd be fixing my hem in a moment. She was too quick to find fault.

Another well-dressed, WASPy-looking woman chased me into the sanctuary and ordered me not to "wander around."

I had been appropriately quiet and reverent. "Do you work here?" I asked.

"No, but you should not be wandering around this church!"

I was wearing a denim dress I bought in a secondhand store and carrying a backpack. This woman was wearing white pantyhose. She turned and began to stride, huffily, away.

"Shame on you," I whispered, but loudly enough for her to hear.

I had to find a computer to buy my Greyhound ticket home. I began to ask people in official garb if they knew of a nearby public library with internet access. I asked a priest. He looked like he had stepped out of a Masterpiece Theater production. He was tall, handsome, and slim; his priestly garb was spiffy and fresh. He said no, he was not local. He was about to drive home to New York. I thought, golly, has God just sent me a ride home? "Do you need a passenger?" I asked, eagerly.

He looked me up and down and laughed at me — out loud — and moved away.

I wish I had said, "Excuse me for mistaking you for a Christian."

I walked toward the Georgetown public library where I bought and printed my Greyhound ticket. A beautiful, young, African American reverence librarian (I like that typo too much to correct it. It's a sign of how retreat lingers even after you reenter profane reality) gave me great directions. She guided me to a metro stop from which I could get a train to my next and final DC tourist destination, America's largest Catholic church: the Basilica of the National Shrine of the Immaculate Conception. Her directions were really good in that they were descriptive and accurate, and when I said I'd as soon walk a bit to get to a good public transportation stop, she directed me to that exactly.

I emerged from the subway and came across a scruffy, skinny young man in cutoff jeans and oversize shoes. He was headed into the subway. I asked him where the basilica was. He spat chewing tobacco on the ground. He then turned around and, without any fuss, escorted me all the way to the basilica, which was a good five-minute walk away. Then he turned around and went back to the subway.

The basilica is kitschy. It opened in 1959, and its aesthetic style is very much from that era. The gigantic mosaic Jesus on the ceiling at the end of the main aisle has blond hair, and he looks like a member of the Beach Boys.

And yet I felt a profound spirituality there that I did not feel at the National Cathedral. Not once did anyone make a crack about my poor clothes or my backpack. (By the way, that backpack was pretty heavy. Not sure if I've mentioned that.) I wasn't the poorest-looking person there. The neighborhood is godawful. You ride through slums to get there, not through expansive ambassadorial mansions.

The center aisle is lined by chapels devoted to Mary as she is revered in various countries. These aren't rich countries, and the people who revere her are often history's losers. There is Our Lady of Czestochowa, Poland; Our Lady of Sorrows from Slovakia; Our Lady of Siluva from Lithuania; Guadalupe from Mexico; Antipolo from the Philippines; and Our Lady of China. There are at least two black Marys, Czestochowa and Antipolo, one Indian Mary, Guadalupe, and Our Lady of China is completely Chinese in appearance. She is surrounded by clouds typical of those found in Chinese art. Her gown appears to be silk, and Jesus is wearing red, the color of vitality and good luck in China where brides wear red. The image is a Chinese artist's realization of a Chinese woman's vision of Mary. I love it when my church is small "c" catholic; catholic means "universal."

There were Filipinos praying there, and black people. The worshipers were nothing like the hordes of undifferentiated WASPs at the National Cathedral. I like that about Catholicism. And I like it that you can always hear babies crying in Catholic churches. We don't hide babies in special soundproof cubicles.

◆

I wanted to stay longer, but I had bought a Greyhound ticket for six, so I did something atypical for me: I bought the souvenir booklet and left. The skinny kid with the chaw was emerging from the subway just as I was entering it. (Really. I do not make any of this stuff up.) I smiled and waved; so did he.

Last minute panic—I had miscalculated space and time (nothing new) and had to run to get to the bus station. Walked beside a Jamaican man in a red fur cap. (In DC? In summer? One must suffer to be beautiful.) He was skinny and young, so he kept me at a quick pace. Got to the station just in time. Hoped I'd have the seat to myself. Did not.

She was blond, and she looked a bit puffy and vulnerable. The kind of person susceptible to skin cancer. She also had a pronounced sadness about her eyes.

She offered to help me put my backpack in the overhead compartment. I said, no, I'll wrestle with it and get it up there. I offered her some of my lemon drops. She said, no, if she eats anything sour, she gets headaches. Uh huh. Vulnerable.

"Heather" is a filmmaker. She had just been at the SilverDocs Film Festival in Silver Spring, Maryland. She pointed out that she is a struggling artist, so she had to take the bus. This means, of course, that she comes from a social class of people who feel that they must offer explanations as to why they are on a bus, not in a private car.

I didn't think that that was why she was sitting next to me. Looking at her, so I could see it when it happened, I asked, "Have you any interest in Poland at all?"

Her eyes lit up, as I expected. "I do, actually, a lot." She is not of Polish descent; she's French and German. But she finds Polish men sexually attractive, and Krzysztof Kieslowski is one of her favorite filmmakers.

Kieslowski lards his films with significant coincidence. His coincidences, though, are never conclusive. God is dyslexic in Kieslowski's world. People living parallel lives have near-encounters, but those encounters don't add up to any concrete payoff. In *Red*, an elderly judge whose heart had been broken years before when he was a law student is befriended by a gorgeous young woman who is involved with a law student experiencing something like what the judge had experienced. But there is no Hollywood ending, just that unlikely brush with parallel worlds. I want the Hollywood ending.

Heather and I talked, without let-up, for the entire four-hour trip.

Heather told me she is an only child from near Toledo, Ohio.

She feels most at home in Manhattan and couldn't stand even a foray into Brooklyn. "I like to be where it is happening."

We talked movies. Douglas Sirk, Rainier Werner Fassbinder, Kieslowski, David Lean, Andrzej Wajda, Roman Polanski, Akira Kurosawa, Zbigniew Zamachowski, whom, *psia krew!* she, too, finds sexually attractive. We talked good movie theaters, like the Paramount in Oakland and the UC theater in Berkeley. I asked question after question, "Who are your influences? Who would you like to emulate? Have you ever seen a movie do something that you wanted to be able to do? What is your ultimate goal?"

After she answered these questions, she turned them on me. I said that when I see something wonderful in a movie, I want to tell others about it. When I read something wonderful in a book, I want to write that way myself.

I talked about *The Haunting*, and *Swept Away*, about how they both have surface stories that can be taken a certain way — horror and S&M — and subsurface stories that are quite different, powerful and provocative, and she asked me not to say anything more about them. Hearing me talk about them, she couldn't wait to see them, she said, and form her own impression.

She told me a story that made me laugh out loud and bend over and slap myself, even in a Greyhound seat. "Roman Polanski has a much younger French wife. She met Roman Polanski's sister, who had been in Auschwitz. She saw the tattoo on Polanski's sister's arm, and she said, 'Oh, we have so much in common. I also write telephone numbers on myself to remind myself of them.'"

"Since you told me that story," I replied, "I have to tell you my one funny Auschwitz story.

"In Poland, you meet people who have somewhat logical reasons for being there. My dad was Polish; that's my excuse, although my other siblings couldn't care less.

"But you meet people like Laura del Sol, and that really makes you, or made me anyway, wonder about fate, wider and invisible forces at work on human destiny.

"Laura was not Polish, not Jewish. And yet she left her life in a bourgeois suburb and gravitated toward Berlin, Poland, the Holocaust.

"She lived in Berlin for a while, not knowing why she was there. Her life was disturbingly amorphous. She had to move to a cheaper place. A friend showed her a dump, trying to talk it up. She saw what looked like a pancake folded at a right angle, stuck against the wall and the floor. She stared at it and said to herself, 'If that's a pancake, I'm leaving Berlin.'

"It was. She did. But where to go? Poland. Auschwitz. Somehow, she was driven to get to the heart of this historical event in which she had no ancestral share.

"She was on the guided tour at Auschwitz. The rote nature of it was not doing it for her. She felt there was a deeper truth there, one she wanted to penetrate. She saw a group of Hasidic Jewish men. She left her tour group and began to follow them. She followed them into a room — and found them all facing urinals! "

Heather and I talked about how Polanski's *Knife in the Water* is a disguised Holocaust film; we talked about how Polanski's *The Pianist* is an overt Holocaust film. She had read his biography and she said that you can see that Polanski had injected a lot of his own experiences into the movie, even though it was based on Wladyslaw Szpilman's memoir. We talked about that scene in *Rosemary's Baby* where Polanski makes the audience crane their necks to see Ruth Gordon behind a bedroom door.

As the sun was setting and casting its final rays into our bus, I mentioned that I don't write anymore and have pretty much given up. She was insistent.

"You can't give up. No matter how many rejection letters you get. That's all part of the process. You have to keep creating."

She showed me a film festival program guide; that's where I saw her name.

"You don't look like a 'Heather,'" I said. "How about 'Stella'?" I asked, pronouncing a name that had been pounding against my eyelids the entire time I chatted with Heather.

She stared for several seconds. "It's interesting that you should say that," she finally said. Stella is her best friend's long-awaited baby. Her friend was in her late thirties and, for many years, was unable to get pregnant. Finally, Stella. "She is the greatest baby on earth. I know everyone says that, but in this case, it's true."

As we got closer to the city, I squirmed, feeling for pen and paper. "I want to give you my email address," I said.

"Isn't it better if we don't know each other's names, as with the drivers who pick you up when you hitchhike?" she said. I was hurt and confused, but I complied. After that I was very quiet and reserved, but she kept talking, in an ever more self-exposing way. I don't understand how one could talk about such intimate matters and then announce that you never want contact with your interlocutor again.

I couldn't help but mention, "We already know each other's names. I saw your name when you showed me the film festival program. You heard my name when I mentioned to you that The Theologian had known a woman with my name."

"You're right, Danusha," she said, and I was amazed. Many people need to hear my name several times before being able to reproduce it even inadequately. She had heard it once, when I spoke it inadvertently as part of a longer narrative, and she had it down. I wonder if she, too, like The Theologian, had had another Danusia in her past.

As we were pulling in to the Port Authority, I turned to say goodbye. "When you are rich and famous someday, I will tell people that I once sat next to you on a Greyhound."

"Same here," she said with a smile. "That Danusha. She was the one who asked good questions."

POSTSCRIPT

Bieganski was considered by three more academic publishers after my 2005 monastery retreat. The editor-in-chief at one highly respected Catholic university press said, "We like it and want to publish it. The problem is you are Polish Catholic. We need to get a Jewish scholar to endorse it."

"A Jewish scholar does endorse it. Antony Polonsky."

"He won't work; his name sounds Polish, not Jewish. We need someone more overtly, visibly Jewish, with a Jewish-sounding name."

In the end, they found they could not publish the book.

Bieganski was finally published in 2010, when it won the PAHA Halecki Award.

The *Shofar Journal of Jewish Studies* called it "Groundbreaking."

American Jewish History said that *Bieganski* points out that the Brute Polak stereotype "gives the illusion of absolving those who failed in their own test of humanity" during the Holocaust.

It was the subject of a cover story in the highly respected *Tygodnik Powszechny.*

John J. Mearsheimer, R. Wendell Harrison Distinguished Service Professor of Political Science at the University of Chicago, said that "*Bieganski* is a truly important book. Goska does a first-rate job. Let's hope that this book is widely read." James P. Leary, folklorist, University of Wisconsin, said that *Bieganski* is "A powerful, provocative, ultimately profound work of scholarship . . . for anyone wishing to fathom the interworkings of class and ethnicity in an America that has all too often fallen short of its promise."

I have been an invited speaker on *Bieganski* at Georgetown, Brandeis, William Paterson University of New Jersey, Indiana University Bloomington, Central Connecticut State University, University of Wisconsin — Madison, Catholic University of Lublin, the Krakow Jewish Culture Festival, and the Markowa Museum, site of the heroic Ulma Family.

A couple of months before *Bieganski* was accepted for publication, I received an out-of-the-blue email from Arno. We hadn't been in touch in years. He proofread the final copy of the book, aiding me greatly. He posted one of the first Amazon reviews, opening with this story:

> The Talmud records edited discussions between rabbinic scholars on legal and literary-interpretive topics. Two particular rabbi-scholars frequently appear in tandem, commenting and responding to each other's opinion. These two are named Rava and Abbaye. One day in Talmud class, my Talmud teacher, a devout Polish Jew, commented that "Rava and Abbaye go together like ham and eggs." I saw the jaw of one of my classmates nearly hit the floor. "But Rabbi," he stuttered, "what do you know of ham and eggs?" My teacher replied "I never tasted them, but I've heard they go together well." So too Poles and Jews. They seem to go together. Poles and Jews. Jews and Poles.

◆

My sister Antoinette succumbed to cancer on April 10, 2015, as I was rubbing the soles of her feet and telling her there were people she could boss around in Heaven. She was my third sibling, after Phil and Mike, to leave this earth well before the completion of her Biblically allotted three score and ten. I undertook to edit and publish this document partly as a project to help me get back into the swing of things after her death. She was my Corsican twin, and now there is no one left who understands me when I say, with mock, wide-eyed alarm, "That's far. That's way far. You cannot walk there from here."

After Antoinette received her diagnosis, I bought an almost twenty-year-old car so I could take care of her. I used that car in December, 2013, to make my first trip to the Edwin B. Forsythe Wildlife Refuge, where I passed within six feet of a peregrine falcon perching—where else—on a refuge sign. I wrote about this unforgettable encounter in this blog post: <http://save-send-delete.blogspot.com/2013/12/owlgasm-snowy-owl-irruption-2013-at.html>

◆

In spring of 2018, my publisher, Christine Cote, and I were doing the joyous work of preparing this manuscript for publication. One evening, through email, I learned that my brother, Joseph Goska, succumbed to cancer on April 27. He was much smarter than I, not to mention tall, slim, and spectacularly handsome. Since I am a Bohunk workaholic, I returned to proofreading the pages Christine had sent me. I couldn't help but notice something I had not at all planned. I write frequently about my own siblings in this book, and about sibling relationships in general. Joe was my only sibling whom I don't mention by name. He was the oldest, the one who never hit me, but who did threaten to sell me into slavery. I was in the car with Antoinette when I became a birdwatcher. To pursue my hobby, I needed binoculars. I pilfered a pair from the bedroom of my brother Joe. He never asked for them back. I birdwatched with those binos on three continents, until they were colonized by a particularly gluttonous subcontinental monsoon fungus. Among the items I inherited from Joe were an Audubon wall calendar, an Eddie Bauer down jacket, several pairs of cargo shorts, excellent for hiking, and a rubber snake. Thank you, Joe, especially for that first pair of binoculars.

◆

Nathan and I have not seen each other since June 2005. He's doing really well and I am proud of him. Whenever I doubt myself as a writer, I remind myself that he used to read my scribblings in Berkeley and saw worth in them before I did. I trust his taste above all others.

◆

Heather is now a wife, mother, and the chair of a university department.

◆

Every few years or so I google The Theologian. His life does not appear to have changed dramatically; it remains superficially enviable. I don't say "superficially" because I have any evidence to the contrary; I do not. I am merely reporting what I see in photographs and online publications. His hair is greyer. On his handsome face, I see that same kindness that comforted and astounded me so very much on that Virginia road — kindness I have never forgotten and still, for want of a better word, miss.

◆

From: Danusha V. Goska
      Wed, May 20, 2015 at 12:39 P.M.

To: Chief of Police, Berryville, VA

Hi, I hitchhiked through Berryville, VA, ten years ago, June

2005, and a police officer named Vic gave me a ride. He was very helpful.

I am curious if Vic is still on the force. If so I'd like to send him a thank you.

From: Travis M. Sumption
       Wed, May 20, 2015 at 1:43 P.M.

To: Danusha V. Goska

Dr. Goska, The deputy you encountered that day was Deputy Victor Sutherland. Deputy Sutherland became very ill in 2008 and died on August 8, 2008. Vic was an awesome person and a true friend. Thanks for asking about him. You brought back some fond memories!

Travis M. Sumption
Chief Deputy
Clarke County Sheriff's Office
Berryville, Virginia 22611

Notes

1. Most Bible quotes in this book are taken from the New International Version. In a couple of places, indicated in the text, I quote the King James Version. The following quotes come from the New American Bible: Jeremiah 12:9, Sirach 13:17, Wisdom 11:24, Genesis 1:27, and 1 Peter 3:15. Isaiah 13:21 is quoted from the NET Bible.

2. While editing this manuscript in 2015, I inserted a handful of anachronisms: [p. 176] I mention using the films *300* and *Apocalypto* in classes. They were both released in 2006. The point I am trying to make in that passage remains the same. Before these films were released, I would attempt to make the same point using different media. [chapter 8] I mention a conversation I had with Crystal about a film clip posted on the web. The film clip is from the September 2014 People's Climate March, and Crystal and I had our conversation then. That conversation is typical of many I had before my 2005 retreat. [pp. 137–38] Wojciech Inglot invented porous nail polish in 2009; Muslims began to adopt it

in 2012. Apart from these and similar anachronisms, I retain the point-of-view of the original account, written in 2005.

3. The entire Bible is available to read here: <http://www. vatican.va/archive/ENG0839/_INDEX.HTM> Protestant translations, including the King James translation, is here: <https://www.biblegateway.com>

4. This site provides one of many online Bible Concordances: <http://biblehub.com/concordance>

5. My sources for geological matters include the following: "The South American Appalachians," by Ken Croswell, published in *Earth*, July 1993, page 13: <http://kencroswell.com/ SouthAmericanAppalachians.html> and *The Geology of Paterson, New Jersey, with a Field Guide*, by Lubov Drashevska, available here: <https://www.discoverpassaiccounty.org/DocumentCenter/ View/116/Geology-of-Paterson-Field-Guide-With-a-Field-Guide-PDF>

Chapter Two — My Backstory, Or Why I Doubt

6. "Save Mount Sutro Forest: Eucalyptus Myths" insists that many species of birds and insects utilize California's eucalyptus for home and food. When I used to hike in Berkeley's eucalyptus, I didn't see or hear other wildlife. A report, supported with convincing research, is here: <https://sutroforest.com/ eucalyptus-myths>

7. There have been many high-profile exposés of the politicization of academia, political correctness, and identity politics, and the concomitant abuse of adjunct professors. These include: "I'm a Liberal Professor, and My Liberal Students Terrify Me," by Edward Schlosser, in *Vox*, June 3, 2015: <http://www.vox.com/2015/6/3/8706323/

college-professor-afraid> and "Professors on Food Stamps: The Shocking True Story of Academia in 2014," by Matt Saccaro, in *Salon*, September 21, 2014: <https://www.salon.com/2014/09/21/professors_on_food_stamps_the_shocking_true_story_of_academia_in_2014>

8.   That recent approaches to diversity in higher education have penalized poor whites is documented in articles such as "How Diversity Punishes Asians, Poor Whites, and Lots of Others," by Russel K. Nieli, who discusses the work of Thomas Espenshade and Alexandria Radford, authors of the award-winning 2009 book *No Longer Separate, Not Yet Equal: Race and Class in Elite College Admission and Campus Life*. Nieli's article is here: <https://www.princeton.edu/~tje/files/Pub_Minding%20the%20campus%20combined%20files.pdf>

9.   [p. 39ff]   Stephen E. Glickman offers a good overview of the hyena's reputation in "The Spotted Hyena from Aristotle to the Lion King: Reputation is Everything," published in *Social Research* 62, no. 3, 1995.

10. [p. 39]   Statistics on hyena neonate mortality are found in "Masculinization Costs in Hyaenas," by Laurence G. Frank, Mary L. Weldele, and Stephen E. Glickman, *Nature* 377, 1995, 584–85.

11. [p. 39]   The account of a hyena attacking its twin while still in the amniotic sac appeared in the *Los Angeles Times* on May 3, 1991, under the headline "Science Animal Behavior: Hyena Study Finds Hormone-Aggression Link": <http://articles.latimes.com/1991-05-03/news/mn-888_1_science-animal-behavior>

12. [p. 40ff]   Regarding matriarchical clans, see "Hyena's Hormone Flow Puts Females in Charge," by Natalie Angier,

New York Times, September 1, 1991: <http://www.nytimes. com/1992/09/01/science/hyenas-hormone-flow-puts-females-in-charge.html?pagewanted=all>

13. [p. 40]   Laurence Frank's theory about female hyena infanticide is discussed by Vicki Croke in "Hyenas Trade One Bad Reputation for Another," *Chicago Tribune,* March 4, 1992: <http://articles.chicagotribune.com/1992-03-04/ features/9201200641_1_hyenas-laurence-g-frank-cubs>

14. [p. 42ff]   Roger Tory Peterson's biography is here: <http:// rtpi.org/roger-tory-peterson/roger-tory-peterson-biography>

15. [p. 45]   Natan Slifkin, "A Close Shave with a Hyena," *Rationalist Judaism* (blog), July 20, 2013: <http://www. rationalistjudaism.com/2013/07/a-close-shave-with-hyena.html>

16. [p. 45ff]   The first site, below, includes discussion of the hadith allowing Muslims to eat hyena meat and the report that Arabs find it delicious. Otther sites declare hyena meat *haram,* or forbidden; one such site is second, below, with a report of how popular hyena meat is among Muslims in East Africa: <http://www.islamweb.net/emainpage/index. php?page=showfatwa&Option=FatwaId&Id=88523> <http:// eshaykh.com/halal_haram/is-hyenas-meat-halal-wahhabi-cleric-causing-storm-in-kenya-and-somalia>

17. [p. 45]   The Talmud offers a magic spell, involving a hyena skin, to cure rabies: <http://www.rationalistjudaism. com/2013/11/mad-dogs-and-rabid-hyenas.html>

18. [p. 46]   Mention of the 1642 "Decree on the Protection of Animals and the Environment" is available on page 814 of *The Encyclopedia of Religion and Nature,* edited by Bron Taylor, published by Continuum in 2005.

19. [pp. 47, 52]   Quotations of C. S. Lewis are from *Surprised by Joy: The Shape of My Early Life*, published by Geoffrey Bles in 1955.

20. [p. 47]   Quotation by George Bentley is available in "World's Only Captive Hyena Colony Shutting Down at UC Berkeley," by Mary Papenfuss, *Reuters*, May 7, 2014: <http://www.reuters.com/article/us-usa-california-hyenas-idUSKBN0DN03R20140507>

21. [p. 47]   Laurence Frank poignantly describes his loving relationship with Tuffie in "Spotted Hyenas: Gender Bending, Enchanting, Formidable," by Vicki Croke. This August 2, 2014, article appears on 90.9's WBUR's *The Wild Life* website: <http://thewildlife.wbur.org/2014/08/01/spotted-hyenas-gender-bending-enchanting-formidable>

22. [p. 47]   The interpretation of Shenzi as wearing eye shadow and lipstick is here: <http://villains.wikia.com/wiki/Shenzi,_Banzai_%26_Ed>

23. [p. 47]   The translation of Shenzi into English is available in the *Swahili-English Dictionary*, by Charles William Rechenbach and Angelica Wanjinu Gesuga, published by Catholic University of America Press, 1967.

24. [p. 48]   Medieval images of hyenas are available here: <http://bestiary.ca/beasts/beastgallery153.htm#>

25. [p. 53]   An account of the discovery of North America's only known hyena and a photo of Oliver Perry Hay are available at these links: <http://www.smithsonianmag.com/science-nature/north-america-once-had-hyena-its-very-own-180960673> and <http://haygenealogy.com/hay/images/ophay1925desk.jpg>

26. [p. 55]   "The Heaven of Animals," by James L. Dickey, may be read in its entirety here: <https://www.poetryfoundation.org/poems/42711/the-heaven-of-animals>

27. [p. 57]   Alan Dundes discusses Lajos Ami's worldview in an introduction to the essay "The World Conception of Lajos Ami, Storyteller," by Sandor Erdesz. This introduction appears on pages 315–16 of the book *Sacred Narratives: Readings in the Theory of Myth*, published by the University of California Press, 1984.

28. [p. 68ff]   Mary McGann discusses the death of her husband, Professor Tim Wiles, here: <http://survivorsofsuicide.weebly.com>

Chapter Three — Washington, DC

29. [p. 76]   Henry David Thoreau, *Walden; or Life in the Woods*, Boston Ticknor and Fields, 1854. The quoted passage appears in chapter five, "Solitude": <https://www.gutenberg.org/files/205/205-h/205-h.htm>

30. [p. 80]   DuPont's history of contaminating soil in northern New Jersey is discussed in the article "Dupont Deal Gave State More Tainted Soil," by James O'Neill, writing in *The Record* on December 10, 2010. The article is archived here: <https://www.northjersey.com/story/news/environment/2010/12/06/dupont-deal-gave-state-more-tainted-soil/94963596/>

Chapter Four — Berryville, VA, Monastery

31. [p. 93ff]   Comments about Rachel Carson's spiritual stance are from "The Secular and Religious Sources of Rachel Carson's Sense of Wonder," in *Rachel Carson: Legacy and*

Challenge, edited by Lisa H. Sideris and Kathleen Dean Moore, SUNY Press, 2008.

32. [p. 93ff]   One account of the impact of Rachel Carson's *Silent Spring* may be read here: <http://www.pbs.org/wgbh/pages/frontline/shows/nature/disrupt/sspring.html>

33. [p. 93]   The quote about Rachel Carson as a high priestess is from *On a Farther Shore: The Life and Legacy of Rachel Carson,* by William Souder, Crown Publishing, 2012, 365.

34. [p. 94]   The estimate of mosquito reproduction is here: <http://worcester.mosquitosquad.com/blog/2016/5/10/mosquitoes-worcester-whats-water-got-do-it>

35. [p. 94ff]   The quote about the nostrils of the peregrine falcon is from an email from Michael Garets of the Peregrine Fund to the author on August 3, 2017. Garets cites *The Falcons of the World,* by Tom J. Cade and R. David Digby, Cornell University Press, 1982; and *Understanding the Bird of Prey,* by Nick Fox, Hancock House Publishing, 1995.

36. [p. 95]   The quote about St. Francis and the falcon is from *The Little Flowers of St. Francis,* translated and edited by Cardinal Henry Edward Manning, published by T. N. Foulis, London, Edinburgh, and Boston, 1915.

37. [p. 103]   The portion of the Rule of Benedict quoted in the text, "On the Reception of Guests," is available here: <http://www.osb.org/rb/text/rbeaad1.html>

Chapter Five — The Contemplative Life

38. [p. 114]   The quote from Sir Charles Napier appears on page 35 of *History of General Sir Charles Napier's*

Administration of Scinde, and Campaign in the Cutchee Hills, by William Francis Patrick Napier, published by Chapman and Hall, London, 1851.

39. [p. 116]   The Metropolitan Museum's grimacing Olmec figurine, Accession Number:1983.424, may be viewed here: <http://www.metmuseum.org/art/collection/search/314609>

40. [p. 117]   Robin Heyworth discusses *caritas sonrientes* statuettes in her May 19, 2014, *Uncovered History* article, "Mesoamerican Caritas Sonrientes": <https://uncoveredhistory.com/mesoamerica/mesoamerican-caritas-sonrientes/>

41. [p. 116]   Authors Lorena M. Havill, Diane M. Warren, Keith P. Jacobi, Karen D. Gettelman, Della Collins Cook, and K. Anne Pyburn discuss Mesoamerican tooth modification in their article, "Late Postclassic Tooth Filing at Chau Hiix and Tipu, Belize," in the 2006 University of Alabama Press book, *Bones of the Maya: Studies of Ancient Skeletons*. An abstract of their article is available here: <https://uthscsa.influuent.utsystem.edu/en/publications/late-postclassic-tooth-filing-at-chau-hiix-and-tipu-belize>

42. [p. 123]   Marianne Williamson's quote on "our deepest fear" is available on her website: <http://marianne.com/a-return-to-love-2>

43. [p. 123ff]   Rabbi Brad Horwitz posted one version of the folktale about the Jew who saves a monastery. His piece is entitled "Folktale Illustrates Core Jewish Value." It appeared on May 2, 2012, at the St. Louis Jewish Light website: <http://www.stljewishlight.com/opinion/dvar_torah/article_1e71b5c2-946c-11e1-9cee-0019bb2963f4.html>

44. [p. 126ff]   St. Alphonsus Liguori's quote about prayer is on page 8 of *Seeking Jesus in Everyday Life: Prayers and Reflections for Getting Closer,* by Julie Davis, Niggle Publishing, 2017.

45. [p. 126]   The Aggadah passage about the creation of Adam is on page 6 in *A Treasury of Jewish Folklore,* by Nathan Ausubel, Crown Publishers, 1961.

46. [p. 127]   Reflections on confession are from *The Medieval Sinner: Characterization and Confession in the Literature of the English Middle Ages,* by Mary Flowers Braswell, Fairleigh Dickinson University Press, 1983; and "Poet and Sinner: Literary Characterization and the Mentality of the Late Middle Ages," by Mary Flowers Braswell, in *Fifteenth Century Studies* 10, 1984.

47. [p. 127]   Root, Jerry. "'Space to Speke': The Wife of Bath and the Discourse of Confession," *Chaucer Review: A Journal of Medieval Studies and Literary Criticism* 28, no. 3, 1994, 252–74.

48. [p. 128]   Dr. Zahi Hawass reports that the builders of Giza were not mummified in "The Discovery of the Tombs of the Pyramid Builders at Giza": <http://www.guardians.net/hawass/buildtomb.htm>

49. [p. 128]   The BBC reports on Egypt's animal mummies in its May 11, 2015, article, "70 Million Animal Mummies: Egypt's Dark Secret": <http://www.bbc.com/news/science-environment-32685945>

50. [p. 129]   The Sobek quote is in James P. Allen's book, *The Ancient Egyptian Pyramid Texts,* Society of Biblical Literature, 2005, 64.

51. [p. 132]   The mummified falcon that died of
forced overfeeding is covered in Hannah Osborne's article in
International Business Times, September 3, 2015: <http://www.
ibtimes.co.uk/ancient-egyptians-bred-force-fed-kestrels-religious-
offerings-gods-1518362>

52. [p. 133]   Rabbi Shaye J. D. Cohen's quote about the
unlikelihood of Christianity's rise is available in transcripts of the
April 7, 1998, PBS *Frontline* broadcast, "From Jesus to Christ":
<http://www.pbs.org/wgbh/pages/frontline/shows/religion/why/
legitimization.html>

53. [p. 134]   The quote from the Venerable Bede is found
in *Ecclesiastical History of the English People*, edited by D. H.
Farmer and Ronald Latham, translated by Leo Sherley-Price,
Penguin Classics, 1991.

54. [p. 136]   The University of Michigan Library
maintains an online concordance to the Koran. The results of
a search of the word "face" in the Koran is here: <http://quod.
lib.umich.edu/cgi/k/koran/koran-idx?type=simple&q1=face&s
ize=First+100>

55. [p. 137]   Al-Islam.org's quotes about monasticism may
be read here: <http://www.al-islam.org/180-questions-about-
islam-vol-2-various-issues-makarim-shirazi/33-how-does-islam-
view-monasticism>

56. [p. 138]   "The Basics of Muslim Prayer" is here: <http://
www.sunna.info/prayer/TheBasicsoftheMuslimsPrayer.php>
More about Muslim prayer is available here: <http://www.
muslimconverts.com/prayer/how_to_pray.htm>

Chapter Seven — That Is He

57. [p. 162]   Our Lady of the Mississippi Abbey explains the Benedictine vow of stability here: <http://www.mississippiabbey.org/Vows>

Chapter Eight — Bird-Watching

58. [p. 204ff]   Quotes about raven attacks are taken from a *Daily Mail* article, "Attack of the Killer Ravens: Flocks Are Suddenly Slaughtering Lambs — What Is Going On?" by Jane Fryer, May 4, 2008: <http://www.dailymail.co.uk/news/article-563931/Attack-killer-ravens-Flocks-suddenly-slaughtering-lambs--going-on.html>

59. [pp. 207, 216] Xavier Le Pichon was interviewed by Krista Tippett for the radio program formerly known as *Speaking of Faith*, now known as *On Being*. The interview is entitled "The Fragility at the Heart of Humanity." That interview is archived here: <https://onbeing.org/programs/xavier-le-pichon-the-fragility-at-the-heart-of-humanity>

60. [p. 211ff]   The Agamemnon quote is from Aeschylus's play *Agamemnon,* translated by E. D. A. Morshead, published by P. F. Collier and Son, as part of *Harvard Classics, 1909-14,* edited by Charles W. Eliot.

61. [p. 239]   You can read more about Judith Neulander and self-identified crypto-Jews in "Mistaken Identity? The Case of New Mexico's 'Hidden Jews'," by Barbara Ferry and Debbie Nathan, in the *Atlantic Monthly*, December 2000: <https://www.theatlantic.com/magazine/archive/2000/12/mistaken-identity-the-case-of-new-mexicos-hidden-jews/378454/>

62. [p. 241]   You can read more about David S. Cohen's work on the Ramapo Mountain people in his paper, "The Name Game: The Ramapough Mountain Indians," available on the internet at this link: <https://www.academia.edu/1225640/The_Name_Game_The_Ramapough_Mountain_Indians>

About the Author

Danusha Goska was born in New Jersey to peasant immigrants from Poland and Slovakia. Her grandfathers were coal miners. Her dad mined coal as a child and fought in the Pacific Theater in World War II. Her mom cleaned houses and worked in a candle factory. Danusha has lived and worked in Africa, Asia, Europe, on both coasts, and in the heartland, of the US. She holds an MA from the University at California, Berkeley, and a PhD from Indiana University, Bloomington. Her writing has been awarded a New Jersey State Council on the Arts Grant, the PAHA Halecki Award, and others. Reviewers have called her work "inspirational" and "groundbreaking." Her book *Save Send Delete* was inspired by her relationship with a prominent atheist. Julie Davis, author of *Happy Catholic,* called *Save Send Delete* one of the ten best books of the year.

SHANTI ARTS

NATURE · ART · SPIRIT

Please visit us on online
to browse our entire book catalog,
including additional poetry collections and fiction,
books on travel, nature, healing, art,
photography, and more.

www.shantiarts.com